RENEWALS 458-4574
DATE DUE

**WITHDRAWN
UTSA Libraries**

China Calling

China Calling

A foot in the global door

Alex Mackinnon
and
Barnaby Powell

© Alex Mackinnon and Barnaby Powell 2008

All rights reserved. No reproduction, copy or transmission of this publication may be made without written permission.

No paragraph of this publication may be reproduced, copied or transmitted save with written permission or in accordance with the provisions of the Copyright, Designs and Patents Act 1988, or under the terms of any licence permitting limited copying issued by the Copyright Licensing Agency, 90 Tottenham Court Road, London W1T 4LP.

Any person who does any unauthorized act in relation to this publication may be liable to criminal prosecution and civil claims for damages.

The authors have asserted their rights to be identified as the authors of this work in accordance with the Copyright, Designs and Patents Act 1988.

First published 2008 by
PALGRAVE MACMILLAN
Houndmills, Basingstoke, Hampshire RG21 6XS and
175 Fifth Avenue, New York, N.Y. 10010
Companies and representatives throughout the world

PALGRAVE MACMILLAN is the global academic imprint of the Palgrave Macmillan division of St. Martin's Press, LLC and of Palgrave Macmillan Ltd. Macmillan® is a registered trademark in the United States, United Kingdom and other countries. Palgrave is a registered trademark in the European Union and other countries.

ISBN-13: 978–0–230–21019–6
ISBN-10: 0–230–21019–8

This book is printed on paper suitable for recycling and made from fully managed and sustained forest sources. Logging, pulping and manufacturing processes are expected to conform to the environmental regulations of the country of origin.

A catalogue record for this book is available from the British Library.

A catalog record for this book is available from the Library of Congress.

10 9 8 7 6 5 4 3 2 1
17 16 15 14 13 12 11 10 09 08

Printed and bound in China

Preface xi
Acknowledgments xv
List of figures and tables xix

Introduction 1

Part I: General perspectives on change
Introduction 5
Executive summary 7

Chapter 1: Convergence and divergence 9
Crossvergence 10

Chapter 2: Decision making and problem solving 13
The nature of the process 14
A shift to the West 16
A dynamic system 18

Chapter 3: Imitation and innovation 20
A sincere form of strategy 21
Imitate to survive 22

Chapter 4: Paradigms and worldviews 23
Living in the past 24
Have faith 24

Chapter 5: Strategic shock 26
Bounded rationality 26
Cusp catastrophe 27
Stamina wins 28
Imitation rules, probably 28

Chapter 6: National strategies 30
Change and control 30
Opportunistic behaviour 31
Approaches to time 32

China moves centre stage	33
Three dimensions	34

Chapter 7: Chinese practice and Western theory — 36
    Strategy from culture — 37
    A base of resources — 37
    Controlling transactions — 38
    Now we know *guanxi* — 38
    Keep your options open — 39
    A common set of laws — 40

Summary and discussion — 42
    Three key functions — 43
    Greed and *guanxi* — 45

Part II: Chinese explanatory perspectives

    Introduction — 47
    Executive summary — 52

Chapter 8: Transvergence — 55
    Measurement is not management – financial transvergence — 56
    Management is not measurement — 58
    Parallel lines converge only at infinity — 61

Chapter 9: Induction or deduction — 64
    The elusive fluency of real dialogue — 66
    A relational redeployment of assets – *renqing* — 66
    Big problems come from lots of little problems – so why not fix the little ones first? — 68
    The truth and nothing but the truth — 70
    A knack by any other name — 70

Chapter 10: Adaptation — 73
    The best in the West may be least in the East — 75
    Surprise, surprise — 76
    Break glass in emergency only — 77
    A nation torn in half — 78
    Holding the centre — 79
    Fiction and fact — 81
    'Proceed feast for orders' — 83
    Meeting halfway — 85
    Totalitarianism or communism — 86

Contents

Chapter 11: Chinese reality	**88**
Democracy for a gerontocracy	90
China rising – peacefully	91
The changing reality	92
The 4 Cs	94
Trust and trustworthiness	95
Now that all the barbarians are within our gates	97
Or how to maintain a well-concealed sense of the ridiculous	98
A silk purse from a sow's ear	99
Opening the little red book	99
Commissioned navvies on the march	100
Uniformly negative limits	101
The wretchedness at the heart of things – disease and pollution	102
The air stinks and the dust settles everywhere in Beijing	104
Culture and society – a home truth	105
Chapter 12: Harmony and people	**106**
An agreement to agree on detail later	107
HRM – one human does not a resource make	108
A philosopher, a sage, not a warlord nor a high priest	108
A modern promise of prosperity, but with a catch	110
A double of the other gender	111
Imported provision for the afterlife	112
Alternative lifestyles	113
How to make work play and play work	113
Keeping the ill-wind away	114
Chinese man's most important commodity	115
Linguistic mountain-crossing demands adverbal tensing	117
Becoming your own alter ego	118
The world's most-spoken secret language – clues to breaking the code	118
The Chinese reckon in millennia	121
San shi liu ji – zou wei shang ji	121
Values are the mainspring	122
Chapter 13: Beyond control	**124**
Western leaders are trained in the West, but Chinese leaders are also trained in the West	124
The transfer of information – a Chinese intranet	125
Open plan problem solving	126
Meaning from form	127
Ringing the changes	127
Guanxi – not a provincial but a global network	128
The relationship matters	130

There are no short cuts, but your reputation will precede you	131
Tenets and beliefs to live and die for	132
MBA (Marketing By Asia)	132

Chapter 14: Chinese strategy — 134
- Opportunism is costly to control — 135
- How much is an investment worth? — 136
- Recommendations — 137
- Spanning the boundaries — 138
- Human obligations or manipulative methods? — 139

Summary and discussion — **140**

Part III: Chinese predictive perspectives
- Introduction — 143
- Out of China — 144
- Tapping into the Asian source — 145
- The surplus – silver mountains of the mind — 146
- The other great Asian giant — 147
- More BRICs in the wall — 149
- Executive summary — 151

Chapter 15: National controls — 153
- The past is the future China — 154
- The future Asian nightmare — 155

Chapter 16: Strategic controls — 159
- Local inroads and responsiveness — 160
- Petulance or power — 162
- Here comes the judge — 163
- Feeling the stones — 163

Chapter 17: Modern Chinese management — 165
- Stakeholders — 167
- Mutation in major national characteristics — 168
- The meeting of the waters — 170
- Ring out the changes — 174
- Implications for organizational structures — 176
- Strategic implementation – political implications — 176
- The individual but collectivist Chinese manager — 177
- International adaptation and interpretation — 179
- The bubble that tries hard not to burst — 180
- Brain gain rather than brain drain — 182

Contents

Chapter 18: ChinaTech — **185**
   The thrust of technology and innovation – overtaking the West or
      replacing the Soviets? — 186
   By their brands ye shall know them — 188

Chapter 19: *Qu xiang he fang*? — **190**
   Westward Ho! — 191

Chapter 20: Unpredictable conclusion — **196**
   Going global – spurred by WTO entry in 2001 — 197
   The Olympic effect – brake or booster? — 199
   In conclusion? — 200

Summary and discussion — **203**
   Superpower? — 204
   A probable conclusion — 205
   Organizational competitive advantage — 205
   A final discussion — 207
   In closing — 211

Postscript — **214**

References — **215**
   Part I — 215
   Part II — 218
   Part III — 221
   Glossary — 223
   General references — 229

Preface

The sleeping dragon of past centuries has awoken, breathing fire, brimstone and retribution on all interlopers who have so affronted China in the past. Or so the myth of Chinese economic power clouds the misunderstood reality.

Lord Macartney, Britain's first official emissary to the Chinese court in 1793, was understandably piqued at being on the receiving end of a smarting Imperial brush-off from Qian Long. After all, it was an awful long way to trek only to be dismissed as the equivalent of a modern day traveling salesman. 'The Empire of China', he wrote, 'is an old, crazy, first rate Man of War.... She may, perhaps, not sink outright; she may drift some time as a wreck and then be dashed to pieces on the shore; but she can never be rebuilt on the old bottom'.

A touch of sour grapes and a strained metaphor here perhaps, but he has a point: just what is this bottom? He was right, but not quite in the way he thought. This hull or bottom he describes is not so much rotten or holed as weighed down with such a ballast of ancient sediment that just staying afloat has been the major national mission of the Chinese. Waterlogged and overloaded, the ship of this enormous state still keeps her prow fiercely erect – in spite of catastrophic flooding (China's sorrow – when the Yangtze River burst its banks every year) and an overwhelming population. Just think what great dams and small diaphragms will do to keep China ship-shape and seaworthy.

But perhaps the Chinese recognized the imperialist attitude of the British? Perhaps they were right to reject a trading nation who forced smoking pipes and cannon on them. A couple of hundred years later, in 1984, the British Prime Minister Margaret Thatcher slipped on the steps of the Great Hall of the People in Beijing. This very human stumble was depicted by the Chinese press as clear evidence of her pangs of conscience for the wounds inflicted on China by the British annexation of Hongkong nearly 150 years earlier. She had indeed caused a wound, but not the one that Beijing thought. The wound she had succeeded in opening up was the yearning of the Hongkong people for the missing fourth dimension of China's modernization – democracy, and its 'running dog', a respect for human rights.

Once the fortunes of Hongkong, political and economic, had been determined, the way was clear for China to open up shop for inward investment, to redevelop Shanghai as a competing national magnet for trade and to show just how non-negotiable was any question of independence for Taiwan. These initiatives have maintained those vital points of friction needed to resolve the conundrum of the shape and sphere of influence of the future Greater China. And how that sphere is expanding!

Within Greater China, individual rights remain subsumed to Chinese values – values with strict deference to hierarchy. Hongkong's administration was to be governed, according to its first Beijing-appointed Chief Executive, by Chinese values: 'trust, love and respect for our family and our elders; integrity, honesty and loyalty to all; commitment to education; a belief in order and stability; a preference for consultation rather than confrontation'. As an optional extra, he also mentioned 'a preference for obligation rather than individual rights'.

That small point Mr Tung mentioned as an aside, that 'preference for obligation rather than individual rights', is the most pivotal point of all. The Chinese live constantly as part of their extended family back and forward over time. They advance into the future facing backwards, honoring their ancestors, exacting obedience from their children. A Chinese 'obligation' means an unquestioning and unflinching devotion to family welfare and interests and by extension to the greater family of the nation. It is almost as if by pulling on one loose thread of individualism the entire relational fabric of society would unravel. In such a context, dare one equate 'individual rights' with 'human rights'?

Rights or no rights, Chinese individuals are now flourishing in China and overseas. In China, the domestic economy is creating rich individuals and entrepreneurs, and hierarchical obligations are definitely decreasing. The old imperial injunction to 'tremble and obey' has already lost all its force. It began to fade with the reforms from 1978 onwards and finally flew up and away from Tiananmen Square in 1989. The individuals capable of accepting the autonomy offered by

Preface

new freedoms and opportunities are certainly different. The modern Chinese manager is one of those individuals, still family orientated but with connections to international China, a global, expansionary China. A China which is moving its hierarchical authority overseas – Africa, South America and the Middle East are being wooed into the family networks.

Global China casts a long shadow. Now that the Europeans, Americans and Russians have packed up almost all their tents and gone home from colonies and protectorates around the world, the remains of Empire are plain to see – either in confidently independent new states or in the shambles of fragmentation and disorder. It is in the diaspora of the Chinese – from the Nanyang (South Seas) of Malaysian tin-mining, island-hopping and trading, to a United States of railroad building and gold-mining – that we can observe the initial seepage of adventurers seeking a better life becoming a licensed overspill. It had been a crime punishable by death to leave the motherland. However brave or desperate they were, it was a one way trip for these early Chinese migrants. Never was such a shadowy Empire acquired with such stealth, such low-vaunted and secretive entrepreneurialism and endeavor.

With outposts in Vancouver and San Francisco, London, Amsterdam and New York, Jakarta and Singapore, Ho Chi Minh City and Manila, these Overseas Chinese clansmen are the humming live wires of vast networks of fixers, godfathers, shock-absorbers, power-brokers and go-betweens with China for finance, trading, sourcing, technology, partnership, agencies and investment. In their host countries they have kept to themselves and quietly made money. The more tedious activity of sovereign government is left to the locals.

Like the early Irish in Boston or the Scots and French in Canada, the Overseas Chinese are the pioneers of the movement to expand their homeland beyond the borders of its Great Wall and to engage fully with the global marketplace. They are the new citizens of the world, pulling the strings of economic exchange in favor of the motherland. A Western educated Chinese knows more about the West than any Westerner does of the East. The Chinese see individual rights sunk in Guantanamo Bay and democratic principles gerrymandered to local big business, but they also see obligations to themselves and to their families of more importance than Western democracy.

Acknowledgments

Our principal aim in writing this book is to meet requests for help from those dealing with Chinese global expansion. For the intrepid venturing into China there is a wealth of information provided by the business and academic communities. For those scenting the gathering storm, nervous of answering their domestic door when China calls, there is fear. Fear caused by a serious lack of familiarity.

To explain and expand on Chinese 'ways of doing things' we have trawled through general and particular texts on international business. We feel that a close examination of Western strategic theory and Chinese actual practice is the best way to bridge the barriers and to predict Chinese global actions. To equip Western watchers of China with sufficient basic knowledge in responding to the impact of expansion from the East is our objective.

Our bibliography is extensive but does not do justice to the accumulated wisdom of others. We most appreciate the works of investigators such as Herbert Simon, Henry Mintzberg, Elisabeth Marx and Richard Lewis. Their insights into problem solving, strategic thinking, cultural dimensions and national characteristics provide a solid Western foundation for understanding the Chinese manager and the Chinese way of doing business. And for those who wish to read and gain Chinese insights, Yadong Luo is an eminent researcher.

Chinese strategy is simple: create opportunities by whatever means but exploit them through a set of relationships based on mutual obligation and reciprocity. Diplomatic, military and economic treaties often create such obligations. Legal enforcement of the resulting exchange is then unnecessary and agreements can be continually amended between signatories. Global expansion is thus between networks, not between countries or organizations, but between those who represent their networks. Investigations by businessmen and academics show the nature and extent of Chinese network controls over Asian strategies.

If we were to pay homage to one more Western author we should choose a shrewd and seminal management primer of the 1970s, *Up the Organization*, by Robert Townsend. His book, although now somewhat outdated and cheerfully politically incorrect, dealt with relationships between people and management in US organizations. Our book deals with people and management in Chinese organizations. In particular, it focuses on a modern Chinese resource, the global manager, this person to whom the world must now relate.

Individual comments gleaned from published academic papers and from newspapers and journals are referenced in supplements to each of the three parts of this book. Experiential and anecdotal evidence also arise from our own backgrounds in trading, shipping, investment and development banking of over thirty years' engagement with the Chinese world. We trust that even those who have read widely will appreciate this sighting of the other side of the global coin. Many have quoted liberally from traditional Chinese sages. We show what the sages' ancient advice has created.

But we also acknowledge that modern sages are commenting on China. There is an increasing number of Western 'war stories' on the bookshelves – all telling how ventures in China can go wrong more often, perhaps, than right. This is not that type of book. We are more interested in telling how the Chinese are getting it right. We wish not only to describe but also to explain and elucidate. In this respect we are indebted to many Chinese colleagues, whose knowledge and advice provide the template for our structure, and whose modesty puts the onus on us to tell their tales clearly. However, Miss Jin Pan, a recent Master's graduate from a British university, deserves a special mention. Her understanding of the bridge between West and East helps put modern China into context, in particular the views of the younger generation, often overlooked when the West focuses on Chinese hierarchy.

To those who have not read *Up the Organization*, please do so. An idea of where the West could have arrived in terms of human relations management is a useful starting point in the understanding of Chinese managers. Managing the dynamics of reciprocity between human beings is the tool most sought after for successful strategies. The Chinese, in their overseas quest for national advantage, wield this implement well – the West's grip is tentative.

We gratefully acknowledge permission from PriceWaterhouseCoopers and Sir John Stuttard to quote from his book *The New Silk Road*

Acknowledgments

and from Professor Luo for permission to use his diagram of Chinese *guanxi* elements which we incorporated into Figure III.1. The excerpt from *Days* from *Collected Poems* by Philip Larkin © 1988, 2003 by the Estate of Philip Larkin is reprinted by permission of Farrar, Straus and Giroux, LLC and Faber and Faber Ltd.

Finally, we must thank Alex Dawe and the staff of Palgrave for their help in the production of this book – in particular, Ian Kingston who cheerfully put up with our constant tinkering during the editing stage. We apologise for any errors and omissions, which ultimately rest, not at a global door, but at ours.

Figures

Figure I.1	15
Figure I.2	44
Figure II.1	142
Figure III.1	172
Figure III.2	207

Tables

Table I.1	32
Table I.2	34
Table I.3	35
Table I.4	40
Table III.1	197

Introduction

Forty years ago, an eminent management researcher, Peter Drucker, argued that profit is the cost of uncertainty with knowledge as its controlling resource. The modern manager knows that knowledge is now no longer a sufficient control over profitability. The modern cost of uncertainty lies with the poor *interpretation* of knowledge.

The 2008 credit crunch and cash write-offs had early warning signs, from the HSBC sub-prime problems in the US to the Shanghai stock market drop in early 2007. Global linkages create perspectives not previously anticipated by North American and European business. The capitalist difficulties in the West allow the Chinese to nod knowingly that the 'foreign moon is not more round'. Rational thinking in the East and West is asymmetric yet because something is foreign we all tend to assume that it is better or worse than our homespun values.

Our book is therefore different from the main categories of comments on China. It is about the *relational* nature of Chinese practice viewed from within Chinese walls. It is, ultimately, about managing economic expansion, control and governance in terms of global problem solving from a Chinese, as well as a Western, perspective. With Chinese funds flowing into the Western economy, there is no doubt that Asia has easily wedged open the door of capitalist opportunity.

To interpret the view from the other side, Part I presents a general, theoretical overview of concepts of change relevant to different managerial characteristics. Part II starts with a question – how did China get to where it is? We then configure theory and practice into a simple futuristic prediction in Part III; and add our own contextual scripts to ease the flow.

Our primary aim in this book is explanatory. We prepare a guide to the changing trends in the management of Chinese organizations.

Information is presented in a straightforward manner. Our secondary aim is predictive. Everyone devises strategies to deal with uncertainty. If our interpretation of how the Chinese are adapting traditional strategies at a global interface is accurate, then we can provide predictive tools to the international manager.

Western lenses tend to focus upon Confucianism, its effect on Chinese thinking and the way things are done in China. Confucianism, it must be remembered, is not so much a religion as a set of moral precepts governing human relationships. Those precepts are designed for Chinese families and imperial subjects. They *do not* provide for dealing with foreigners!

Chinese managers based in, or visiting, the UK (with Chinese organizational subsidiaries or for management education) have kindly provided personal and background research material. We have combined the findings of this Chinese 'expatriate' research with domestic research on organisations in China.

We describe interesting effects at the boundary, the *confluence* of Anglo-Saxon and Chinese ways of doing business. It is the confluence of the different approaches which creates the dynamics of change – the new strategic flow. Success, at the meeting of the waters, requires the foreign manager to practice patience and reciprocity and the Chinese manager to shorten the ladder of hierarchy and 'power distance'. Globalization needs adaptation not confrontation.

We review Chinese values and characteristics using Western strategic thinking to understand this new global hybrid. The personal and relational nature of Chinese reciprocal transactions creates considerable uncertainty when change is managed at an interface. Those who do not believe us may wish to consider the refusal by the Chinese, in late 2007, of a Thanksgiving Day visit by US warships to Hongkong. Mess us about with the Dalai Lama, they cry, and we'll mess you about as well! We therefore make a series of contentious points to create a mindset not normally associated with Western beliefs and values.

Our ultimate intention is to enable the global practitioner to avoid only taking leads from global standardization, especially of regulatory and legal environments. We provide a background to Chinese practices and language to create an understanding of where China is meeting Western ways of doing business. The pace of change is swift, with modern Chinese management reacting quickly to globalization. The Chinese are adapting Western styles of doing business to create their own competitive advantage. It is this strategic adaptation in Chinese ways that we aim to explain.

We cannot, of course, provide a totally global interface; rather we have drawn our predictions from a focus upon a Chinese and an Anglo-Saxon (British) interface. North American readers will have to adjust that focus for themselves. European readers already well understand and interpret the cultural nuances of cross-border management. Chinese readers, of an inquisitive bent, will have the opportunity now to view themselves through British lenses.

We are all witnessing a change in the strategic locomotion of world power. The present credit crunch and stock market collapse are rapidly writing down Chinese investments in the West, yet paradoxically are strengthening Chinese economic buying power across the world. We present an understanding and interpretation of that paradox. We do not dwell on the effect of the Chinese culture and Confucianism on global expansion, nor on the resumption of Chinese business and traditional trading after socialist subjugation – nor even on economic analyses of Chinese organizations and their difficulties with Western ways. Rather we map the mentality of Chinese investors, State and entrepreneurial, as they emerge into a dynamic global presence. We get behind the inscrutability.

PART I

General perspectives on change

Tou shi wen lu – throw a stone to find a way out of the darkness (*Chinese proverb*)

Introduction

In providing some insight for those wishing to understand Chinese expansionary strategy, we avoid jumping from observations on China to predictions on China. We wish to substitute new thinking for old, to both explain and interpret the past and the present. A solid foundation can then be used to build and create explanations, interpretations and predictions for the future.

To underpin our arguments, we have sectioned Part I into seven partially overlapping categories. Each category creates a perspective which, it is hoped, is global in its application. However, from our Celtic-Anglo-Saxon standpoint, we know that we are bound to bring our own personal and national baggage into the theoretical train of thought. Please bear with us as we unpack our material.

Each category is designed to stand alone but with an information track leading into the second part of our book. This allows our contribution to create your interpretation of Chinese ways of doing things. Our interpretation takes something we can all understand, the national and managerial values controlling general behavior, and shows how adjustments in these values affect expansionary strategies.

Management is a general category. Although we research the more accessible business manager, change in national characteristics also allows us to comment on potential political, societal and military strategic behavior. Not all Chinese behave the same. We examine the modern Chinese internationalist. He or she may as yet be atypical, but our intention is to give you an advance description of the human shape of Chinese things to come.

Arriving at some understanding of the Chinese mindset and value system will involve a brief excursion into abstract ideas – or rather a brief departure from matter and practice into the realm of thought and theory. Regard this as a partial code-breaking exercise, much like beginning to learn the Chinese language. It will build blood and muscle tissue onto the bare bones of existing knowledge and perceptions. This enigmatic code will prime the imagination and stretch the cognitive faculties.

Bear with us on this slightly strenuous, outward journey – the effort will enhance the view from the other side developed in Parts II and III.

China calling

Executive summary

This part provides an insight into, and basis for, the shaping of both Chinese and Western mindsets in approaches to general strategic thinking.

1. *Convergence and divergence* deals with the extent to which the Chinese are being drawn to adapt their practices *strategically* to secure and maintain competitive advantage at the global interface, outside China.

2. *Decision making and problem solving* covers the fundamental differences in approach between East and West to strategic solutions for a pluralistic world.

3. *Imitation and innovation* examines the nature of control structures and hierarchies, their relative flexibility and readiness to imitate or innovate.

4. *Paradigms and worldviews* looks at the differing sets of assumptions and standpoints coloring the strategic views and perspectives of Eastern and Western practices.

5. *Strategic shock* addresses the problem of rational incongruities in Eastern and Western behavior.

6. *National strategies* highlights national characteristics, as deeply embedded controls, and their impact on the formulation of strategy.

7. *Chinese practice and Western theory* provides a synthesis of perspectives and the extent to which they may be applied to Chinese institutions and organizational activities.

Summary and discussion – A theoretical background to Western and Chinese thinking is provided. Western and Chinese thinking arrive at improving competitiveness and gaining an edge from quite different vantage points.

CHAPTER 1

Convergence and divergence

> To compare and contrast
> (*a precursor to interpretation*)

In his book *Bloody Foreigners* the need for a means of comparison is argued by Robert Winder as essential to see the outline of another's national character. Those without the means must adapt their views on the world. Yet, whether business entrepreneur or military general, we are often averse to dealing with change. Although its unpredictability means that particular expertise is highly sought after, with foresight, knowledge, luck and judgement amply rewarded, maintaining the cutting edge of that expertise can, paradoxically, also prevent change.

Intense political and economic lobbying by Western politicians and businessmen has forced the Chinese to build their doors facing outwards, altering the outline of the Chinese national character. A convergent change away from traditional Chinese practices to those of Europe and America gives the West an advantage in China. But open doors also let old Chinese practices enter the West. Are we adaptable enough to discern that changing character?

The Western perception of any Chinese 'westernization' is more self-serving than real. The arts and sciences of Chinese and Western thinking may indeed converge, but only towards a centre of action quite unlike present practices. The idea of the Chinese merely imitating Western practices is not really convergence. This section argues that the Chinese are accepting the benefits of adopting and adapting certain techniques and practices of the West, but by putting a Chinese slant on the outcome.

Change implies that there is some standard of comparison available to gauge size and direction. When two management styles meet there may, in fact, be a total failure to compromise. Those involved in mergers and acquisitions recognize that you get no change from failures. Yet in a global arena there are consistent claims that compromise between national managements must happen; that there is only one way to achieve this fusion – the Western way – and the Asian will follow. This is an enormous error.

Managers in government, in business and in the military are there to solve strategic problems, and change should be measured in terms of problem solving. Variety in terms of acceptable solutions creates a higher chance of gain. Laying off one's bets lowers the likelihood of a loss. There is, therefore, considerable debate about the rate of change in adaptive suppleness when comparing national and global ways. The debate centres on the potential convergence or divergence of strategic decision making when contacts are increased on a global scale.

It is, of course, possible to argue that any distance between Asia and the West is closing, but that some key differences will remain, in particular institutional and personal controls determined by the family, government, regulatory environments, religion, sex and age. Western thinkers cannot see this. In February 2008, several Nobel prizewinners linked the Beijing Olympics to Darfur and the power of Chinese influence over the Sudanese government. China complained 'You don't understand us'. Given the West's poor record of intervention in sovereign affairs, the Chinese should have said 'We don't understand you'. There remain many differences in comprehension between East and West; and they are not born of perversity.

Crossvergence

To get round this problem, a hybrid term, 'crossvergence', has also been argued to produce a unique type of behavior. The concept has gained in popularity. Crossvergence depends upon both economic ideology and individual values being taken into account. A move from Chinese communism to Western capitalism is supposed to result in a hybrid style of management, free from historical values of national culture or economic ideology. Hybrids are also multi-directional. For example, if the USA maintains its capitalist ideology but embraces the principles of Chinese relational networking, then US managers are crossverging their strategies.

And relational management (a key Chinese feature) is creeping into Western business. 'Silos', the closed networks of managerial expertise, are creating Chinese walls and lowering economic value generation between networks. Within networks, trust may be high and relational information easily transmitted, but not outside them. What's causing such a change in Western management and governance practice? We believe it is a natural reaction to excessive external control. Defenses are raised when a manager, perhaps more susceptible to basic economic influences, reacts to forces outside his or her network of influence.

Our contention is therefore simple. It is economic exchange, the driver of trade over millennia, which is forcing change. This change is affecting basic individual values, the values derived from past national and family struggles for survival. When survival strategy squeezes the purse, hearts and minds will follow. (A Scotsman applying for a job at a Jewish company was once told 'We'd like you to join but we do not pay top dollar. But you're Scottish and we're sure you'll understand that!')

National traits will remain recognizable but some convergence in behavior will be caused by external influences (for example, Chinese in Western environments). It is unlikely, though, that any convergence can prevent Chinese organizations and networks from maintaining their singular stance in reacting to global forces. Such uniqueness is sharpened by transnational strategies which 'are *simultaneously* locally responsive and globally integrative'. A unique set of strategic values evolves.

This unique set is evolving rapidly in the Chinese who venture overseas. They are retaining their personal practices of developing relations rather than contracts. They are adept at letting lawyers have their say to suit local legal requirements, but whether they then accept ultimate penalties for any failure to perform is doubtful. The Chinese prefer to renegotiate and a contract is just that – a relational agreement to renegotiate.

It is these personal values which are best conditioned to create competitive advantages and to develop greater problem solving expertise. Knowing the relational attributes of Chinese managers can help explain their strategic processes and managerial capabilities. Better the devil you are about to know than the devil long gone.

CHAPTER 2

Decision making and problem solving

> *Shi yi chang ji yi zhi yi* – To control the foreigner, first learn his ways (*Chinese saying attributed to Wei Yuan, of the first Opium War*)

The prospect of a sea of problems needing containment will be familiar to the time-pressed in many walks of life. Most of us take the easiest route to a solution. The quickest route is the route taken before – the problem is thus adapted to one already solved. To improve decision making and problem solving, management gurus and training courses are the first (and easiest) recourse, find a new teacher and go back to school. For the militarist, staff college beckons. This chapter queries that apparent route to improved problem solving.

The major problem is one of accepting the need for change in *how* things are done. Lateral thinking is a good example of trying to change mindsets. So is cross-cultural negotiation. Change, convergent or otherwise, will then occur in the way we make decisions and solve problems. Some call this change 'restless capitalism', arguing that it is a complex, self-correcting dynamic system, evolutionary in nature. We believe it is complex and dynamic, but argue that the evolution is primarily imitative: we copy success to survive better. But things go wrong in the attempt to imitate others – some type of mutation always occurs, either through excessive caricature or through immature copying.

Feedback in the imitation becomes very important. The dynamic depends upon the feeding back of successful solutions. The dynamics are non-linear: not chaotically so, but with continuous and imprecise adjustment to decisions and solutions. Within an abstract environment, bounded by national culture and economics, problem solving systems are part of the national and corporate way of thinking. Abstract or precise rules are established which influence the course of strategic decision making. The demand for the Chinese to accept Western legal and accounting principles is one way of setting the rules of the system. The demand by the Chinese for the West to accept Chinese military expansion is no different; let's all play by the same rules.

This only partly solves the problem. Managers are certainly involved in problem solving, and decisions are part of the process, but decision making, within any institution or organization, also extends into the area of implementation. Intuitively, a strategic problem cannot be resolved until decisive steps, such as implementation, are successful. Decisions unrelated to problem resolution are trivial in the process. Decision making mainly emphasizes choice, whereas problem solving emphasizes successful implementation of the chosen solution.

The nature of the process

The nature of highly reasoned decision making appears to have ten elements, ranging from:

- *Recognizing* and *Clarifying* the problem, *Framing* the question, *Ascertaining* the situation and data, then

- *Developing*, *Evaluating* and *Choosing* alternative solutions, leading to

- *Implementing* a solution, and finally *Evaluating* and *Re-evaluating* the outcome of all decisions.

This is, essentially, the decision making process structured in Figure I.1. It is also, clearly, a problem solving process.

The solid arrows indicate the initial flows in the process, with feedback loops, via the dotted lines, allowing the circled elements to be reassessed. Two consecutive loops, primary and secondary, are indicated in the problem solving process – separated by the action of choice.

Decision making and problem solving

System functions

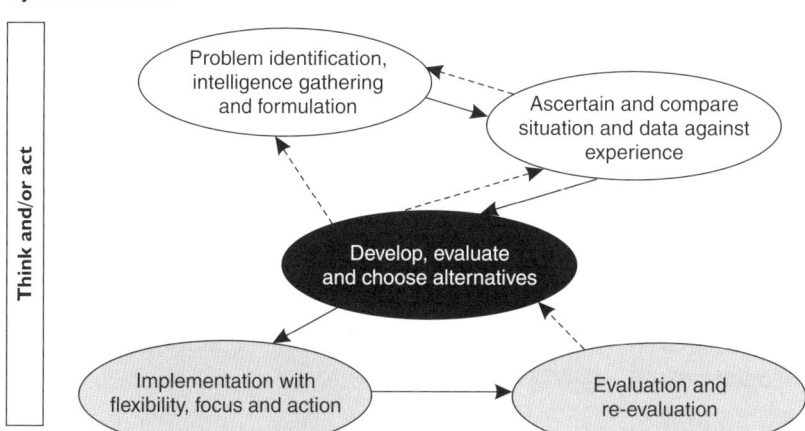

Figure I.1 Strategic problem solving.

The primary loop is a 'paralysis by analysis' loop and best suited to publicly paid Brussels bureaucrats. A continuous repetition of problem clarification and the development and evaluation of alternatives then allows choice to be postponed indefinitely. Those retaining sufficient interest in the democratic process are not subsequently offended when it comes to voting time. Those wishing to see some action merely become increasingly apathetic. Military staff officers may recognize the primary loop, and field officers the secondary.

Business does not have the luxury of taxpayers' income streams (although public–private partnerships are coming close) and often commences problem solving in the secondary loop. Unlike the game of Monopoly, there are no rules on where to start. The 'seat of the pants', intuitive or action-orientated secondary loop, is a trial and error process. Insufficient analysis and evaluation may lead to considerable errors and, as several CEOs of large public companies have discovered, punitive trials.

The differences between East and West can now be understood. The following characteristics are common to experience-based Asian (particularly overseas Chinese) management:

- *Hands-on experience* – with a high level of senior management involvement
- *Transfer of knowledge* – by conceptualizing rather than analytical skills
- *Qualitative information* – externally sourced, sometimes subjective and often networked
- *Holistic information processing* – more intuitive and less sequential
- *Action-driven decision making* – reflecting an authoritative management

The implication arising from Asian problem solving styles is that the formal process in the primary loop in Figure I.1 is not normally part of the Chinese way of doing business.

The overseas Chinese, as the main economic actors at the interface with global business, have been part of a turbulent colonial diaspora in the wake of departure from their mainland. They have demonstrated particular skills in short-term wheeling and dealing. Their trading is hands-on and action-driven. If we consider the differences between the elements and flows in Figure I.1, it is the secondary loop which appears to be geared to Chinese problem solving.

A shift to the West

Any decrease in the relative importance of traditional Chinese practices should cause a shift towards the primary loop in Figure I.1. There would then be an increase in more formal, Western problem solving techniques when the Chinese operate overseas. Such a change is now happening but it is *in addition* to traditionally intuitive ways – not instead of them. In other words, those in the field are also learning how to think globally.

The Chinese can now commence problem solving either formally or intuitively. Recognizing when to choose which route makes a manager truly expert. Western expatriates in China know this. Chinese expatriates in the West know this. It is time for westerners in the

Decision making and problem solving

West to recognize when to choose. But why do different nationalities start at different points in the cycle? If different national strategists produce different solutions to one problem, then is it because the respective processes commence differently?

Those with basic mathematics will recognize a simple analogy. One may solve the problem of finding the square root of 4 by starting near 2. Another may start near -2. The same iterative, trial and error, process shows that both are right and that both have different answers. The impact of experience on how we solve problems can depend on where we start the process, with a guess based on past practice to develop future solutions. An inevitable return to known and tried solutions is the simplest option but can fail when past experience is different. The Chinese experience is considerably different from the Western.

For example, the popularity of *Freakonomics*, a book extolling the virtues of looking at the world differently, would indicate that many are interested in querying, or having someone else query for them, accepted perceptions. Unfortunately, as we have shown, the decision making process creates feedback loops which ensure a preference for past solutions. Throwing out the preferences, but not all the solutions, is the answer.

It is hardly surprising, therefore, that the elementary steps in decision making are subject to national, structural differences. Past practice ultimately affects behavior through values and attitudes, creating new patterns of behavior from any change in basic beliefs. An infinite regress is prevented by earlier 'postulates' or previous beliefs and past behavior patterns. Neither the chicken nor the egg came first, but the dinosaur.

What this means for international managers, unfettered by domestic tradition, is that creativity in strategy is feasible. Preference in decision choice is ultimately governed by core values. If present decision making behavior does not succeed under present value structures, then our beliefs must be altered to achieve future success. A dynamic system will give feedback and adapt basic thinking. Future ways of doing things will depend on changing present attitudes and behavior. The cultural feedback loop depends on *time*.

A dynamic system

The principles of a dynamic system have three elements. There is a *space* in which the dynamic system operates. This could be, for example, strategic management, operations management, financial management, whether to build a nuclear submarine, or whether to buy a new car or not. There are *rules* for deciding how to move from one point in the *space* to another. Buying a new car, for example, might require considerable problem solving practice if the *rules* are laid down by your spouse!

While we may differ in our sense of *time* and in the rationale for our *rules*, we share *space* as the incontrovertibly human place we inhabit. We all actually live, as Philip Larkin queries in more metaphysical vein, in days:

Where can we live but days?

Ah, solving that question
Brings the priest and the doctor
In their long coats
Running over the fields

And night then follows day! The *rules* are always – but not always seen to be – *time*-dependent. To change the *rules* within the *space*, then the controls over the *rules* must be altered or adapted. And that is our problem: what is happening to dinosauric ways of doing things? What is changing when Chinese ways start to join with Western ways and how long will change take? What do those conjunctions say about China as it tramps around the globe, a dragon on the loose?

We say that it gives the Chinese a great national advantage – Chinese *relational* rules are joining with Western *contractual* rules to increase their chance of success. The West relies heavily on its lawyers, the Chinese on their relationships. Both require reciprocity – the former with a hefty fee and the latter with a future deal – and, as global complexity increases, neither one is completely effective on its own. The Chinese will reciprocate but are not, therefore, merely copying all Western methods, they are deliberately avoiding the difficult ones. Their basic strategy, their theoretical solution to future uncertainty, is to innovate through adaptive imitation, a 'pick and mix' strategy. Just as the West might feel it can ignore UN resolutions if it feels like it, the Chinese will also turn their blind eye to legal precedents. Rules are to be chosen, not imposed.

CHAPTER 3

Imitation and innovation

Imitate to survive
(*from Darwin to Deng*)

The simplest way to bring about change is through imitation. If a problem solution is successful in one dynamic system then copying it in another can produce a quick fix. The style of organization, for example, often indicates industrial imitation. Manufacturing companies tend to structure themselves along process or divisional lines, conglomerates by product, banks by function. As evolutionary theory puts it, the controls over organizations tend to resist mutations, even when presented as desirable innovations.

Many Western companies possess an adaptable, flexible flat structure. Asian institutions, by contrast, are more hierarchical. In the global arena, imitation of structure is changing the international Chinese companies into flatter, pro-active structures whilst domestic organizations mainly retain hierarchical decision making. This section shows how Asians are adapting and are increasingly fleet of foot.

Chinese global managers are recognizing modern styles of international contract and the nature of enforcement. The Western position on contract law, we must remember, developed over the past five hundred years. In Europe, up to the Middle Ages, contracts were enforced by relational means. Any failure in a valuable relationship risked one's reputation and resulted in the threat of economic ostracism, a highly effective sanction, prevalent still in China. Yet opportunistic behavior in the legalistic West has not been eliminated. Organizations and their activities have at once become more legally restricted and more opaque.

The Western penal code could not and did not prevent the leaders of organizations such as Enron, Tyco International, WorldCom, Par-

Imitation and innovation

malat and Refco from taking opportunistic advantage of shareholders and investors. Nor are the bankers, brokers and advisors guilt-free. Opportunism is not confined to the lower orders in mercantile trade. 'Sub-prime' describes financiers as well as mortgagees.

Complexity in the West creates chances for the sharp operator. Opportunistic Chinese are not, therefore, likely to feel intimidated by complex arrangements. Indeed, the more complex a deal the better the opportunity to imitate Western failures to enforce its terms. Hedge funds and their opacity could prove to be imitative gold mines for the Chinese financial entrepreneur.

A sincere form of strategy

Initial resistance to change is common. Evolutionary thinking argues that large organizations and Chinese networks, across the national spectrum, will avoid decisions which are truly innovative. The state enterprises in China are in a period of uncertainty and partially resistant to change. To retain stability at an interface, it is adaptive imitation, not innovation, which is the sincerest form of strategy.

The Chinese will therefore look for opportunities overseas where the *rules* are clear. The capitalist system is very good at laying down rules and the Chinese are seizing their chance. It is preferable, cash in hand, to purchase a company than to start as a competitor. Private equity firms such as Kohlberg Kravis Roberts use extensive gearing to raise the cash. The Chinese will just raise the cash.

Innovation is unlikely to occur (from a purely economic perspective) if the use of others' acceptable solutions is preferable to hazarding new solutions. The Chinese have recognized that when is 'now', but also that how is 'whatever works'. Imitation is self-correcting through trial and error. The benefit to the Chinese organization is that the trial and error outcome is likely to be more acceptable over the longer term if they imitate the private equity companies. And the benefit to the Chinese government and military is no less. By copying Western styles of government, when subverting individual rights to economic development or to the war against terror, the Chinese are simply imitating a 'democratic' process.

Imitate to survive

Innovate or die is easily amended to imitate and survive. It is much simpler to copy the controls already endemic to an institution or industry than to actually change them in a creative fashion. Partial innovation is a result of change caused by old solutions not matching new problems. It is this process which can be called a gradual 'paradigm shift' and it depends upon accepting that change is needed. The true revolution for paradigm change occurs when a totally new perspective resolves more problems better. Deng Xiao Peng recognized this when he started the Age of Reform in the late 1970s.

For the Chinese their paradigm shift is more likely to be towards the purchase of Western organizations than the innovation needed to expand their own institutions overseas. Economic expansion is allowed, military control is not, but then what is one without the protection of the other?

Paradigms and worldviews

> A paradigm is simply an acceptable worldview
> (*a modern method of understanding*)

The term 'paradigm' is commonly used as a conceptual framework or set of parameters accepted by many as defining how the world is viewed or 'sized up'. It is bandied about to explain stock market peaks and why the direction is always upwards. It is not, however, merely a new example of another economic environment that is being described, but more a distinct way of thinking. It is a perspective on how we interpret and solve problems. For example, 'Cold War' is a neat paradigm term to describe the historic nuclear stand-off.

It is hardly surprising, therefore, that the historian and science philosopher Thomas Kuhn was not always clear and consistent in his development of the term 'paradigm' when he published his groundbreaking work over forty years ago. A paradigm is normally accepted as the communal sharing of linked assumptions. The set of assumptions, our balance sheet of the world's phenomena, constitutes our view of reality. The anthropologist sees this as cultural values and beliefs, the businessman as a strategic perspective. They are both right.

Knowledge is subject to linked assumptions of the world. And here lies the rub – the West and East do not have the same set of linked assumptions. The real world, and how we understand and acquire knowledge of that reality, is subject to our personal, communal and national faiths and beliefs.

A paradigm, or perspective on the world, makes it impossible to alter the view of the world from within. This is called 'incommensurability' of paradigms and any choice or acceptance of a particular worldview, or paradigm, can only 'be made on faith'. A faith in formal thinking or subjective argument is, therefore, no less legitimate than a faith in intuitive thinking or objective analysis. Where you start and end your problem solving cycle is up to your own faiths and beliefs, your own paradigm.

Living in the past

But it does not lead to innovation – whilst young pups may yearn for new tricks, old dogs do not teach them. It is those who live in the past who are condemned to rely on their blistered, weathered experience. Understanding one worldview from within the other is not possible. They create their own different rationalities.

'My wife does not understand me' is thus a quite legitimate complaint – provided she has a different worldview. However, it may be that she understands her husband very well; could she have multi-tasked from two separate paradigmatic viewpoints? Can paradigms be switched at will? Much modern strategic training is designed to do just that.

Advances in science (and human endeavor) occur when a framework of beliefs, for example, a strategic paradigm, is altered for the better – when greater understanding overthrows past theoretical structures. There is no suggestion that different paradigms *necessarily* provide different levels of explanatory or predictive power; comparison depends on interpretations of outcomes.

Have faith

Concentrating on the term 'strategic paradigm', not only as a single worldview, but as a faith-driven belief in preferred action, highlights the differences between institutions and organizations, Western and Eastern. The faiths and beliefs of the national individual allow different strategies to become acceptable to different organizations.

A simple example would be that of competing in an economic transaction. The Chinese global strategy needs to create a relationship and then form the transaction around the relationship. The Western domestic strategy needs to create a transaction based on a contract. The techniques are similar: meet, negotiate, agree terms. Both strategies are different. A global strategy cannot always be domestic. Neither the Chinese nor Western strategy is necessarily better than the other. An integrated paradigm must be adopted. This common boundary for transactions is called compromise.

From an alternative viewpoint, what can the West do to adapt Chinese techniques? The Western reliance on contract law and its enforcement (lawyers remain in demand but are not necessarily popular) must alter towards a greater reliance on relational enforcement, increasing trust and taking personal responsibility for actions. As any religious fanatic or convert will attest, faiths and beliefs are strong and directive. They dictate rational behavior within their own paradigm.

It is on the satisfaction of relational obligations, controlled by mutuality and the giving or exchange of personal respect (known as *face*), that the Chinese paradigm is based. Their way of doing things deals nicely with contractual complexities. Now they can add Western legal niceties. Indeed, they can even use the legal wording to thwart foreign companies who do not have the right contacts. After all, protracted litigation in the West is not unusual. Nearly twenty years on from the worst oil spill in Alaskan history – the *Exxon Valdez* – the local residents are still fighting in US courts for compensation.

The Western demand for increased legal enforcement over contracts and agreements with China is really a demand for a Western paradigm. Yet the Western paradigm has failed – complex contractual governance is *not* resolved in court. Courts are for the simple man in the street, for the parking fine or fraud or murder; but to resolve complexity? Seldom.

It is therefore difficult to use one's own paradigm to alter a worldview from within. We all need to get out a bit more.

CHAPTER 5

Strategic shock

> Rationality is dependent on your worldview
> (*and so is your irrationality*)

Rationality is intertwined with values, faiths and beliefs. It is nationally specific. We can consider rationality to arise from differences in the way 'in which a group of people solves problems and reconciles dilemmas'. The 'way' is deemed to be rational by one group of people but can be irrational to another. Defining Chinese business methods as irrational and chaotic is a blinkered definition from within one's own paradigm – truth is paradigm-specific.

The individual in the problem solving process, however, is also affected by cognitive limitations. Strategy is culturally controlled and its outcome can be just as surprising. Two basic elements are involved in every decision – fact and value. Uncertainty and the limits of human analysis create conflict. Decisions, and even the educated guess, in tackling uncertainty or ambiguity can be neither fully informed nor fully rational. Management researcher Herbert Simon argues that it is not possible for any single isolated individual to reach high degrees of rationality.

Bounded rationality

We all therefore pursue 'bounded rationality' – behavior that is meant to be rational, but suffers from limitations caused by factors such as lack of knowledge, foresight, skill and time. Looking for the sharpest needle in the sewing box is less likely to produce a timely solution than finding any needle sharp enough to sew with.

Strategic shock

The timely solution is 'satisficed'. When confronted with a number of variables, 'satisficing' can therefore be a rational act.

Recent research identifies three factors to be major controls over decision making. Firstly, uncertainty, and its impact on bounded rationality, remains a prime factor. Secondly, personal emotion, stemming from the individual, affects the decision. Thirdly, the social context in which the individual acts is also an inescapable control. In particular, personal experience and the social context will both control behavior and inhibit deviation from the group norm.

The response to uncertainty is to formulate a strategy. Strategy is, therefore, embedded in the distinctive problem solving process of the national character. Social contexts may, when problems have several distinct solutions, create alternatives that converge to a decision appropriate to only one social context. An American context or a German one? – choose Ford or Volkswagen; is it Japanese or Danish? – choose Kirin or Carlsberg; brand names and national identity create specific products and strategies, especially when managers operate within their own corporate constraints of bounded rationality and satisficing.

Cusp catastrophe

Increased uncertainty, however, starts to play havoc with emotional and social dynamics. When subjected to conflicting strategies over the same uncertainty, the system goes into strategic shock. People panic. We have all seen it. When in trouble or in doubt, run in circles, scream and shout! A 'cusp catastrophe' is the simple dynamic term.

In global business, two simple control variables compete in the same space – the domestic way of doing business can clash with the international way. The *space* in the control system – the state variable – is not therefore the cause of the cusp catastrophe. The criteria governing conflicting *rules*, different ways of doing things, cause the dynamic system to break down. Nations and civilizations can crash catastrophically (systemically as well as alliteratively speaking, that is). A strategic choice between *rules*, within the same *space*, is needed.

If we consider what happens when two different organizations meet, within the same industry, there is little difference in the *space* variable.

It is the distinct strategic *rules* set up by each which separates the competitors. Acquisitions perform better than mergers for that reason – one clear and distinct strategy is dominant from the outset. Allowing different *rules* to merge, before cusp catastrophe occurs, depends upon true compatibility beforehand, and how often is that the case? There is certainly little to no compatibility between Western and Chinese strategic *rules* in the respective domestic paradigms. A clash or even a cusp catastrophe could occur at the global boundary. Political and military clashes are inevitable when *rules* conflict.

Stamina wins

Greater standardization in global economic exchange, such as that within the World Trade Organization (WTO), is thus the simplest way for global *rules* to merge. The benefits to Chinese organizations, once they adapt from domestic *rules* to global ones, will rest with international mergers and acquisitions. Chinese organizations will, systemically, seek compatible mergers, cash-led acquisitions, and political and strategic alliances for global integration. A playing field, the *space* for the game, is there and only the *rules* of the game need learning. Moving the goalposts, or even playing uphill, will make little difference in the long term. The competitive advantage will depend upon stamina.

Stamina is not short term. The *time* element in a dynamic system enables the *rules* to be adapted quickly, but the adaptation is longer term, a mutation. To explain this further, consider the imitation of insurance practices. The dynamics of that industry involve front end placement of risk and back end sharing of risk. Given its experience and expertise, Lloyd's of London can closely calculate the premium needed to accept risk. The Chinese have little experience here – the *rules* are difficult to imitate. Lloyd's has a front end competitive advantage.

Imitation rules, probably

The back end, the reinsurance of risk, has simpler *rules* in splitting the bet of an experienced risk assessor. Here the *rules* lend themselves to speedy imitation: the risk has been calculated and capital for a proportion of potential losses is all that is required. The Chinese now have an increasingly large reinsurance capability (with China Re growing faster than Swiss Re) and their insurance companies are on the global prowl for investments. Ping An Insurance is, for example, buying Asian assets from Fortis Bank.

The Chinese imitate quickly where the *rules* are simple. Where imitation by the Chinese is a threat, the Western strategic solution must be to accelerate consolidation through mergers or acquisitions, using size as the defensive resource. The problem is that, unlike American football, switching from large defensive teams to swift attack teams is *time*-consuming.

An alternative Western defensive strategy for competitive advantage is to retain complicated *rules*, making imitation difficult. Herein lies the Chinese advantage. The Western capital markets make, in the main, consolidation of resources relatively straightforward. Cross-border purchases are in the nature of globalization, but the Asian relational markets make consolidation in China more difficult. Unlike stocks and shares, it is difficult to buy and sell relationships.

CHAPTER 6

National strategies

> Strategy is a communally common theory for advantage
> (*and is nationally common*)

Values dictate cultural behavior, which dictates strategic decision making. That nationally specific concept means that it is time for the business practitioner to set aside the consultants' handbooks and the business school training. Strategy and national ways of doing business are part of the same problem solving dynamic system.

Strategy provides a theoretical argument when dealing with uncertainty. It might be vague, it may result in a plan, but it remains theoretical. Past practice, often subject to singular national regulations and institutional impacts, shows the way in which thinking is done in the face of past uncertainty – the outcome of successful past strategies. In this chapter we accentuate the formal nature of our argument, at greater length and with more intensity than in the previous chapters.

At any level, problem solving and decision making provide control systems for effecting strategies. Narrow, bureaucratic controls provide strict corporate guidelines. A work hard, play hard management style creates risky strategies – both in business and social relationships. In explaining how national characteristics feed into institutional and organizational strategies, we now provide an understanding of the overall dynamics.

Change and control

Change in the governing controls affects strategic decision making. The manager is looking for more alternatives to provide different so-

National strategies

lutions. Systemically, therefore, adaptation in strategy will depend upon increasing the variety of problem solving techniques – adding to, rather than rejecting, past solutions. Western economic theory also argues that increased variation in resources improves strategies for competitive advantage. Western economic theory, however, is focused on the organization.

The Chinese organization is quite different. It is composed of collectivist (allocentric), group-dominated individuals representing their own networks. Interpreting the Chinese manager using Western strategic concepts requires an initial warning that we must compare a Chinese *network* with a Western *firm*.

We have already laid down a marker arguing for a dynamic, system framework rather than a linear, logical, Western framework when thinking globally. Describing the strategic system in terms of *space*, *rules* and *time* across paradigms provides a useful way of interpreting the changing and adaptive nature of global controls.

The Chinese control system can, at this point, be best illustrated by invoking Sun Tzu and his *Art of War*, a popular handbook on Wall Street. His strategic advice on generalship and the waging of battle is primarily opportunistic, excellent for winning skirmishes and temporary advantage, but not for sustaining the effort needed to maintain a real, long-term presence in alien territory.

Opportunistic behaviour

Opportunism is at the periphery of strategy, almost a tactic. A long-term core strategy should be both flexible and sustainable, with the retention of competitive advantage being more important than the immediate gain. Modern Chinese strategy aims to colonize by creating and taking opportunities, with Western techniques used for the colonization and Chinese tactics deployed for the battles. The *space* has different but compatible *rules* for the short- (battle) and long-term (colonization) *time* requirements.

This would be common sense: horses for courses. Strategy then tends to become an adjective – strategic thinking, planning, implementation, management, control, and more. Alternatively, strategy is preceded by an adjective – emergent, prescriptive, descriptive, evolutionary, classical, and more. Strategy is abstract, figurative, more difficult of definition. It is as though we are supposed to have an *a priori* grasp of strategy, its meaning and its purpose, but then require immediate categorization before we can use it. Strategy is *not* a plan, but may be formalized or modeled into one.

But if strategy is common sense in dealing with the future, then ways of doing things must be communally common. Business concentrates on the way in which economic things are done by a particular community at a particular time. Descriptions of different ways of doing business create nouns to strategy's adjectives. There are all-encompassing names for the observable, verifiable ways of living and thinking and doing of a particular people. These ways program behavior and are communally specific. In fact, we know that managers of different nationalities tend to solve problems differently but that their solutions cluster according to their national identity.

Approaches to time

One of the more useful breakdowns of national ways of solving problems describes the characteristics of a nation in a category associated with *time*. Those who think that time is a smooth monochronic flow and those who believe time is fragmented, or polychronic, are treated to an insightful set of perspectives by a business professional, Richard Lewis. He categorizes different national ways into the two polar opposites of linear and non-linear approaches to *time* in the global *space*. We highlight the approaches in Table I.1.

Table I.1 A linear to non-linear demographic scale.

Linear	Straddle and reactive	Non-linear
Germans, Swiss, Austrians Americans (White Anglo-Saxon Protestant) Scandinavians, Finns British, Canadians and New Zealanders Australians, (white) South Africans Japanese Dutch, Flemish Belgians	Other American cultures French, Walloon Belgians Koreans, Taiwanese, Singaporeans Czechs, Slovaks, Slovenians, Croats, Hungarians **Chinese** Northern Italians Chileans	Other Slavs Portuguese Spanish, Southern Italians, Mediterranean peoples Indians, and other Indian sub-continent Polynesians Latin Americans, Arabs, Africans

National strategies

The linear approach, exemplified by Swiss and Germanic efficiency (with methodical planning, punctuality, job orientation, competent delegation and focused communication) is challenged by the polychronic people of the world. The non-linear, talkative, people orientated individuals who juggle facts, do several things at once, pull strings and seek favors, delegate to relations and are very flexible in their commitments, will drive the monochronic managers absolutely spare. An Austrian dealing with a Brazilian will need a Chinese intermediary.

The nature of the groupings indicates a clear split between the national characteristics of the world. It is, nevertheless, a judgement call on how the individual strategist within each nation will behave. (The term 'ecological fallacy' applies to the belief that any one member of a population will conform to the description of that population.) Averages are what count and the odds favor organizational behavior to breakdown in patterns similar to Table I.1, subject to their national composition.

And here lies China's strength. From a specific national perspective, the tabulation of national cultures provides an interesting contrast between West, East and Africa. The point to ponder is the positioning of China. The Middle Kingdom is central to the developed and developing nations, it appears better placed to straddle global business than the West alone. Indeed, China's advances in Africa are aided and abetted by the West's focus on post-colonial, interest-bearing aid – but with conditions! Chinese assistance is not more altruistic, but it is less confrontational. China looks to trade resources at the lowest transaction cost whilst keeping future options open and unspecified – basically an Asian hire purchase scheme.

China moves centre stage

China is moving into its preferred central role. To see this change, four nationally derived dimensions are often used to describe national cultures: whether they act collectively or individually; whether they *kowtow* or argue with superiors (their power distance); whether they have aggressive behavior and are high in masculinity (women managers can also be aggressive); and whether they prefer long- or

Table I.2 Strategic adaptation.

Strategic implication	Global Chinese direction
Individualism – Reflects contractual governance	Increased individualism creates greater task commitment and increased use of contracts over relationships
Power distance – Reflects hierarchical structure	Lower power distance implies decreased autocratic behaviour and greater lower level managerial involvement
Masculinity – Reflects aims of goal achievement	Increased masculinity results in the pursuit of assertive, rather than harmonious, managerial relationships
Confucian dynamics – Reflects time orientation	A decrease in long-term orientation and increase in short-term orientation results in lower levels of traditional strategies with increased focus on rapid outcomes

short-term time spans in decision making. The changing Chinese manager, taking strategic decisions in accord with nationality, can be categorized along the four dimensions of Table I.2.

The strategic implications in Table I.2 show a theoretical global direction and explanatory structure for those Chinese with global ambitions. The strategic boundaries are a mixture of national and managerial characteristics.

The dimension clearly related to strategic adaptation is the power distance dimension – flatter structures are more flexible and can incorporate other changing individual characteristics. The converse is not, however, quite so clear. Can a hierarchical structure allow increased individualism, masculinity and short-term behavior? Probably not. An individual Chinese manager with Western characteristics is more likely to leave a traditional, hierarchical organization and seek pastures new – with a joint venture company in China, or overseas.

Three dimensions

Another picture of the nature of managerial adjustment can be studied by looking at behavioral patterns from yet a further perspective. (Different worldviews need several perspectives.) Three basic managerial dimensions have been argued to indicate global differences and can be tabulated with their strategic positioning (Table I.3).

Table I.3 Managerial dimensions.

Dimensions	Global problems
Orientation	Switching between bureaucratic and relationship approaches – task or people. Individualism versus collectivism. Specifics versus context.
Task approach	Tolerance of ambiguity. Structured versus fluid. Time is sequential or synchronized. Long versus short term.
Communication and presentation style	Switching between a factual based approach and an expressive style. Formal to informal style of individuals. Neutral versus affective cultures.

The implications for Chinese adjustment at a Western interface are simple. There should be a decrease in collectivism with an increase in orientation towards specifics. A more structured task approach should result in a decrease in long-termism. Communication should be less high context (face-to-face) with an increase in formal presentation and factual analysis skills.

The idea of the Chinese changing their problem solving methods is now seen to imply a direct effect on how they do business. The Chinese overseas will imitate Western ways, but not before testing and adapting them into a preferred hybrid version – imitative yet innovative. The corollary also holds: the Anglo-Saxon should be more aware of high context behavior, relationship approaches and fluidity in task demands. Certainly, any alignment with the Middle East and Africa, indeed with any non-linear nations, is a minor adjustment for the Chinese but a major adjustment for the West.

The Westerner is meeting Chinese opportunism on the Western front, at home and globally. Remember Newton: for every action there is an equal and opposite reaction; push the open market door and out will pop a Chinese open marketeer. To recognize the dragon in panda disguise the West needs to focus on the differences in characteristics but then use the similarities to gain a clearer strategic insight.

Is this perhaps too much to ask from a strategic paradigm? We do not believe so.

CHAPTER 7

Chinese practice and Western theory

> The theories of the West versus the practices of the East
> (*understanding one with the other*)

The phrase 'on the other hand' is often credited to economists and provides a useful array of unconsidered theoretical alternatives. Certainly strategic theory has more than two limbs. A slowly protruding extra limb is emerging in China as a suitable appendage to allow 'on the third hand', the Chinese middle way. We will examine contrasting interpretations, showing how even eccentric strategic paradigms can be assessed on their implications for Chinese strategy. We will also provide a direct link with Western thinking and Chinese practice.

We know that Chinese managers presently in very senior roles do not have wide exposure to Western managerial practices. But that position is now changing rapidly with many younger managers obtaining senior positions in the entrepreneurial sectors, especially IT. It is Chinese middle managers, upwardly mobile and experiencing Western practices (with many managers trained in the US) who are more likely to spark strategic change than older Chinese chief executives. Western organizations are no different – the pressure for improvement may be downwards, but the push for change is more often upwards.

The change in Chinese strategic characteristics has not received the studied Western theoretical attention it merits. Some strategies, for example, may allow remnants of communist planning to survive, but recent experience indicates that there has been considerable trial and error reform. Evolutionary strategies require Chinese market systems to be efficient, yet this is not the case, with, for example, currency and quota restrictions on trade. Legal systems are slow to change and arbitration provides a handy midway point for the Chinese. Why should the world go West when, as George Orwell pointed out, *'it's an eccentricity to be white'*?

Strategy from culture

Strategic thinking emphasizes an alignment with national cultural characteristics. Culture has one overriding feature – controlling adjustment to behavior and emotion *through* the social context. Strategy also has one overriding feature – controlling adjustment to uncertainty and complexity *within* a social context. Two factors in problem solving, uncertainty and the social context, are thus combined. Add in an emotional leader of an organization and you have the 'wild card' third factor.

The leader may set a general direction, but we often forget that it is the manager who seeks the advantage, who arranges the loans and negotiates the contracts, who conducts the economic exchange. Can we extend Western economic ideas to explain and predict how a Chinese manager will behave under the changing rules of a global game?

A base of resources

If we accept that organizational resources are formed from and by national and social managerial groups, those resources can be considered as intrinsic values and not just tangible assets. Resource base theory therefore assumes *that an organization is composed of resources which are difficult to imitate yet which provide an economic advantage over others*. This concept, however, does appear to be rather static. Existing values and assets need an interaction with a dynamic system to adapt for future uncertainty.

Chinese resources are generated and interact through relational networking, a well-known but not fully understood practice called *guanxi*. This term will be explained in more detail throughout this book. It is an important concept to grasp as it is often misunderstood. Basically *guanxi* is a network of resources which are traded under implicit rules. As *guanxi* also governs transactions, economic theory should be applicable to Chinese strategy.

Controlling transactions

Transaction cost theory, which then *identifies the least expensive control over economic exchange*, has a potential 'fit' with *guanxi* and a 'fit' with decision making and with change over specific social contexts. Transaction cost theory deals mainly with controls and governance, lest contracts be subject to opportunistic behavior. Chinese *guanxi* deals with controls and governance lest relationships and reciprocity suffer from opportunism. Opportunism, in the sense used here, refers to self-interest seeking with guile. Negotiating in bad faith is an example, when one party suffers loss to another's gain. In China this would result in a severe loss of face (*mianzi*). A loss of face in Chinese transactions is not only embarrassing but serves to lower an individual's transactional worth. It is not dissimilar to losing one's credit rating – life gets difficult thereafter.

A Chinese network therefore resolves opportunistic behavior internally without legal costs. It is self-auditing and defends against coercive enforcement by the state. Undercover networked trade, black or white market but involving mutual obligation, remains a redeployment of assets, a trade in resources. The redeployment is not necessarily optimized or 'satisficed' but grows more complex until incomplete. An incomplete contract is one which may best be governed by the relationship between the parties. Western courts *may* look to the intentions of the parties when reviewing contractual problems. The Chinese *always* look to relational obligations and reciprocity (known as *bao*). Reciprocity, as we will see in Part II, is absolutely imperative to successful Chinese transactions.

Now we know *guanxi*

There are sufficient grounds, therefore, for identifying *guanxi* not merely as an organization of individuals bound together through trust, mutual obligation, and communal understanding, but as a strategic control system. Chinese leadership considers 'dredging *guanxi* and making it better for achieving the decided strategic intention' to be important in controlling strategic implementation. The problem solving process is a *guanxi* control subject to internal trust. Trust is warranted when the gain outweighs the risk. This concurs with ancient and modern *guanxi* decision making.

There are Western theoretical and practical analogies with *guanxi*. Transaction cost theory notes that trust is dependent upon cooperation and reputation. Trust is a less expensive method of governance and is certainly cheaper than a load of New York lawyers. But it is expensive to gain and maintain trust in China. Entering and furnishing the network with trustworthy actions is not cheap, but it is a needed dynamic. Western strategic theory, and the Chinese practice of trading in resources such as reciprocity and face, affirms the concept of *guanxi* as a dynamic system – linking directly with an integrated set of Western ideas.

Keep your options open

To integrate resource base theory with transaction cost economics (incorporating basic opportunism) would support the concept of using a conflationary approach to strategy. But one more theory has to be built in to our foundations. Real option theory requires that managers effecting economic exchange do not forgo *the chance of creating claims on future opportunities resulting from their present transactions*. Such claims on future options are implicit claims in terms of human obligations (known as *renqing*) within *guanxi*. In other words, the Chinese have a practical dynamic system which includes resources, transactions, and the ability to create and maintain future options through *renqing* obligations.

The three Western legs of the strategic milking stool are resource base, transaction cost and real option theories. The Chinese cow can be milked using networked resources, transactional *guanxi*, with face (*mianzi*) as an important resource, and the future but possibly expensive obligations of *renqing*. This is all well-tried and eminently sensible and the Chinese (yet again) have been putting it into practice for several millennia.

A common set of laws

Agreements on Chinese transactions correspond, in primary content and obligatory nature, with the governance provided by Western contract law. Table I.4 shows the correspondence.

From a Chinese perspective, however, any assumption that a Chinese calculation on future transactional returns is based on the same formulae as in the West must be treated with caution. Rational arguments behind Western decision making can easily conflict with traditional Chinese ways of decision making. Rationality is nationally (and organizationally) specific. The real option analysis by Chinese managers will be different from the Western analysis.

The *renqing* principles, that the options are real and have future value, are acknowledged under the nature of their obligations in China. There is, nevertheless, a manipulative element. The uncertain, implicit nature of *renqing* future obligations is not necessarily identifiable from the initial investment in the *guanxi* transaction. There is the potential for an increase, not decrease, in the uncertainty of the exchange system. The more problematic outcome is related directly

Table I.4 *Guanxi* interpretation.

Western business exchange	*Guanxi* network exchange
Predetermined and/or voluntary	
Transactional and informative	
Reciprocity and consideration	
Private law over opportunism	Internal governance over opportunism
Individual (idiocentric) self	Collective (allocentric) self
Formal audit	Internal audit
Contractual	Trusting
Task orientation	Relationship orientation
Short term	Long term
Statutory 'face'	Transacted 'face'
Entry barriers vary	Entry barriers high

Chinese practice and Western theory

to unspecified, relational future options generated by *renqing* obligations. Knowing you have an obligation but not knowing its size or timing is pretty scary. High levels of trust ease the fear. In a more complex, global environment any strategy to limit uncertainty must focus on decreasing the relative importance of future *renqing* options.

Western strategic theory thus dictates Western actions across economic and cultural borders. The Westerner should enter a *guanxi* network to control opportunistic behavior, should ensure that *mianzi* (face) is given to Chinese partners, but should be very wary of creating *renqing* obligations of an unspecified nature. It is a bit like being married. When a wife presents her husband with a bill for a new Mercedes Benz it is likely to be accompanied by the reminder that 'you promised to love, honor and cherish'. The new car is the manipulated outcome of an unspecified obligation. High trust levels are essential to avoid surprises.

We have used the concepts in Part I to create a solid trustful base for our explanation of Chinese behavior. It is a base that strategic practitioners will certainly be aware of (and may even be experts in) but a base that can also be universally applied to any national entity and expansion strategy. The theoretical arguments presented so far and derived from Western principles create a predictive format capable of interpreting Chinese organizational and managerial behavior. We will look at the present behavior in practical detail in Part II.

Summary and discussion

In Part I, we have concentrated on the theoretical background to Western and Chinese thinking. The way in which we consider problems is different across nations; the way we acquire and treat knowledge is different; and a joint approach to global problems is feasible but differences in upbringing, education, religion and our respective senses of belonging to separate racial communities imply incompatible problem solving approaches. Indeed, the nature of our problem solving is dynamic: we follow basic *time*-dependent *rules* according to the perceived contextual *space*.

We highlight, therefore, decision making differences and where those may converge or diverge as globalization increases. In this respect we focus on uncertainty within the realm of economic exchange. Organizations exist to exchange resources and managers control that exchange. Exchanging knowledge does not require an understanding of how a transfer in knowledge as a resource occurs (that is called teaching) but does require an interpretation of the resource itself. The value of knowledge is in its understanding.

Western economic theory seeks to explain and to predict economic trends and behavior. Economists also provide explanations for global investment decisions by modern multinational firms. Answers vary; multinationals are mere organisms mutating to global evolutionary trends, firms are the tools and toys of strong leaders, organizations are cultures (even Australian organizations), firms invest to generate short-term, quarterly performance. But we often forget that it is the manager who seeks the advantage, who arranges the loans and negotiates the contracts, who conducts economic exchange – and Asian managers are different from Western managers. Can we extend Western economic concepts to explain and predict how the Chinese will behave under the changing rules of a global game?

Understanding relational networks is essential in explaining Chinese practices. In the West, unfortunately, the network concept has become confused with social connections. Chinese economic networks are systems, systems capable of effecting economic exchange without wastage but with maximum future gain. Social connections help. The Chinese call these connections *guanxi*. They also call their transactional and information system *guanxi*. There is a transaction cost associated with *guanxi*. Try uttering the word whilst rubbing your forefinger and thumb together – it helps emphasize the cost of connections. Better still, think mobile phone networks: there is a cost of using and a cost of entering another network. A Chinese network is a system designed for economic, and telephonic, exchange.

Three key functions

Three functions drive the network system. Western transaction cost theory explains the benefits, trust is high and costs are low within a network. Connections create and expand resources, explained by resource base theory. Within *guanxi*, there is a future investment return or obligation (*renqing*), explicable by real option theory. The problem for the West is that managers are often taught to consider transaction cost, resource base and real option theories as separate economic explicators of investment decisions. Only recently has there been a Western realization that ambiguities arise when the theories are not integrated. The Chinese have practised a combination of all three for many centuries. The communist blinker on the Confucian eye of the Chinese trader has not dimmed an ability to spot a deal in the making. Do not let that word communism fool you – Mao maintained a traditional, imperialist hierarchy. Figure I.2 provides a simple mapping.

When doing deals, Western theory argues for a control over opportunism – self-interest seeking with guile – through contract law, but also notes that as a contract grows more complex, governance decreases (exemplified by Enron, Parmelat, *et al.*). The Chinese welcome complex deals. Governance then becomes relational, a traditional network control based on ostracism and the threat of 'losing face'. A simple contract, evidenced for example by bills of exchange or lading, is not a problem. Chinese global expansion would then result in acceptance of international law for basic control systems

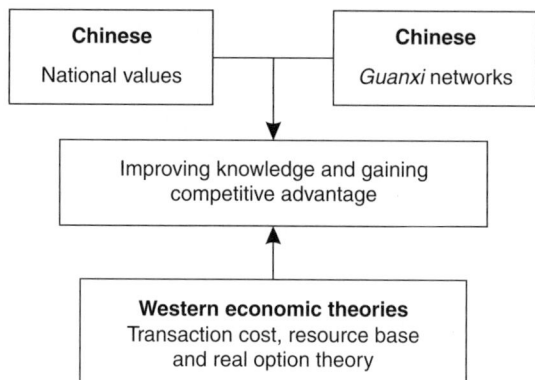

Figure I.2 A global strategic interpretation.

but with relational controls governing opportunistic behavior for complex arrangements. *Caveat regulator*.

Resource base theory also partly explains Chinese practices. Networked investments generate economic exchange under a strategy of seeking competitive advantage. If there is a weakness in resource base theory it is in the dynamics of how the resources interact when transactions take place. A combination with transaction cost theory helps explain how to best regenerate resources when conducting economic exchange. Chinese *guanxi* uses the transaction activity globally to expand the relational resources when larger deals are essential. Legal advice often follows, rather than precedes, the deal. The Chinese will thus rely on arbitration procedures rather than confrontation in courts of law, but will prefer arbitration after, rather than before, action.

Finally, real option theory must be considered and integrated if Chinese networks are to be understood. Real option theory argues that a manager when writing a contract should also maximize any potential options for future business. The *guanxi* system does this through the creation of *renqing* (reciprocal obligations). There is, nevertheless, a manipulative element. The uncertain, implicit nature of Chinese reciprocity is not always identifiable from the initial investment in the *guanxi* transaction. There is, therefore, the potential for an *increase*, not decrease, in the uncertainty of the *guanxi* system, related directly to unspecified, future options generated by *renqing* reciprocity. Knowing you have granted an option but not knowing its size or timing can be stressful. High levels of internal network trust ease the fear.

Greed and *guanxi*

It is, therefore, not a question of greed overcoming fear when the Chinese invest in a risky deal, but of greed overcoming *guanxi*. Where there is a lack of networked connections, as in the case of peasants rising up against prefectural authorities, distrustful confrontation will follow. Chinese economic exchange is integrating on a global basis, but the system of networks is fragile. Clear contractual consideration, with an unequivocal trust in international legal enforcement, is required to ease tensions. Relational trust depends upon acceptance as partners within a network. The potential for confrontation can be lessened with mutual respect. Do Brussels and Washington treat even each other in a trusting, mutually respectful fashion? Western ways are hardly harmonious.

What implications for international expansion arise from our brief interpretation of Chinese economic behavior? Two important directions for investment and trade arise. Firstly, any reliance on legal controls over a contract implies that the contractual terms should be as simple as possible (law schools please note). Secondly, a long-term contract is not a short one gone wrong but a short one kept open. Any future investment returns on complex resource exchange are uncertain unless a trusting relationship of mutual reciprocity exists. In global terms, therefore, the guardians of the cultural and mineral resources of Africa and the Middle East should prefer a reciprocal Chinese relationship to a complex North American contract. Western economic theory helps explain why – Chinese practices show how.

The need to look at Chinese practices and their network dynamics together, in a holistic fashion, implies a parallel need for integrating Western theory. Unfortunately, there is not yet a 'unified' economic theory acceptable to Western scholars. This is unsurprising, given the many alternatives open to challenge in their problem solving systems. The Chinese, on the other hand, are practical people and seek action, not alternatives. The expansionary nature of China's political, economic and military governance can be explained by transacting simply for what you want, by increasing your overall resources and by keeping options open. Integrated theory and unified action are the foci of Part II.

PART II

Chinese explanatory perspectives

> One of the world's oldest civilizations also has much to teach the foreigner: the skills of listening and understanding different points of view, the arts of strategy and negotiation, the power of reconciliation and compromise, and unique perspectives on recognizing and developing competitive advantage. (John Stuttard in *The New Silk Road* – Introduction)

Introduction

The central part of our book brings together a kaleidoscope of past and present observations on China, the Chinese manager and the Chinese organization. It is designed to show how the general perspectives in Part I can be used to understand Chinese strategic behavior, how theory can be applied to practice, how China got to where it is and what makes it tick. John Stuttard, a Lord Mayor of the City of London, gives a warning to those who ignore the Chinese perspective – you may lose the advantage.

To assist the reader, there are also seven chapters in Part II, but they are less formally structured than Part I, to create a sense of the Chinese intuitive feel for knowledge. The overlap between sections is designed to provide a holistic overview of a rapidly changing strategic style. The overview creates a particularly Chinese perspective on management, but also allows a Western interpretation across what can best be described as a gradually narrowing gap in mutual knowledge and understanding.

The hapless Lord Macartney, on his arrival as the first British emissary to the Chinese court, was not dismissed by Qian Long simply because the Emperor rejected his petition to set up an embassy in Beijing in 1793. At the time, it was understood that he was sent packing with all the precious mechanical marvels of Western invention he had brought as gifts because he failed to *kowtow* to Qian Long, who felt his mandate threatened by surly foreigners at court.

What is much more likely is that the Emperor had heard from his spies in India that the British had used trade to open the way to control and administer much of the territory there. The Chinese had no interest in nor need for trade with foreigners. They believed themselves quite justifiably to be self-sufficient. Their real concern was then – and is now – territorial integrity, the security of the Chinese Empire. Thus, the impetus which such a permanent mission would have given to Chinese commerce was lost and the process of industrialization set back almost a hundred years.

Faced with having to deal with each other, the Chinese and Westerners viewed one another with bemusement and dismay. Each must have struck the other as absurd. To the Chinese, Westerners were simply rude and hairy interlopers who had strayed in from the nether regions of the earth with nasty habits – an impression quickly reinforced by the odious opium trade. The Chinese called them 'raw', while those who had bothered to immerse themselves in a little local custom were called 'cooked'. The West found China caught in a curious kind of time warp; apparently hidebound by ritual, elaborate dress and highly formalized manners.

From the vantage point of hindsight, it is easier to see how totally out of sympathetic phase China and the West must have seemed to each other. Macartney came from an England and a Europe in the tumultuous throes following the French and the American Revolutions. The Age of Reason had dictated Tom Paine's *Rights of Man*. The divine right of kings was shaken to its foundation. The supreme individualist and common man, Paine, had decreed that no barriers like monarchies should be interposed between man and his Creator. He had no obligation to an earthly lord. The temper of his times could not have been more distinct.

An other-worldly deity, whether Creator or Lord of Heaven, would have been anathema to the Chinese, for whom divinity resided firmly in their midst and at their head with the Emperor in fearsome and absolute authority over them all.

Hindsight also permits us to acknowledge that Western and Chinese societies have evolved at markedly different rates. Much of this has to do with technology and the very belated arrival of an industrial revolution in China. After the fiasco of 1793, a further century of mutual incomprehension passed, while various intrepid missionaries, traders and diplomats dimly perceived the extraordinary nature of this vastest of countries, apparently sunk in stasis and immiseration. Traveling scholars and scientists from the West discovered to their immense surprise that China had invented and developed several ingenious and labor-saving devices long before these devices had appeared in Europe. This prompted the inevitable question as to why the country had then remained so underdeveloped.

A useful trigger to this debate on the whys and wherefores of China's apparent backwardness or arrested development is 'Needham's Puzzle'. Joseph Needham was a Cambridge University biochemist who became a devotee of China through his research. He worried this enigma into several volumes of exhaustive enquiry. Plainly stated, his grand question, his Puzzle, was this: given that China had the biggest economy in the world in the 18th century and an evident capacity for technological invention and bureaucratic control, why had the country not become a major power? Or, put another way, why did science and capitalism evolve in the West and not in China?

Interestingly enough, the classic and traditional Chinese answer to this question is disarmingly unexpected. It is two-fold:

1. Science had never been on the syllabus of the eight-legged examination for recruitment to the ranks of the civil administration. The scholar-official class thus remained ignorant or simply unaware of its potential;

and

2. The Chinese revere nature and viewed science as tampering with nature and therefore harmful.

What is significant about these answers is that they probably would not have occurred to Western thinkers or scientists, since they represent that peculiar cast of Chinese mind which sustained an effective and stable civil administration for over two thousand years.

The West routinely ascribes China's apparent stasis to several perfectly plausible root causes, such as:

- Confucianism – and the static ordering of society and relationships.
- Demographics – the sheer number and density of people living off such limited natural resources.
- Education system – based on rote learning of classical texts rather than the nurturing of an enquiring mind.
- Natural disasters – earthquakes, famines, flooding, typhoons and epidemics.
- Male supremacy – the principle of favoring male over female.
- Subject status of all Chinese – with very tight limits on individual autonomy.
- Social mobility – severely restricted to those successful in the Civil Examination for entry into the scholar-official class.
- Face/public esteem – held in higher regard as a mark of social standing/status than mere money and wealth acquired through commerce.

However, the real reason is most probably the precise inverse of this last factor:

- Low esteem for, and hostility to, the merchant class.

This meant that China did not harness until the late 19th century the locomotive power of free international trade and investment, since it lacked and is still largely deficient in the institutional infrastructure for economic exchange, ownership and accountability which we take for granted in a pluralist society.

A major inference from this missed opportunity is that Western capitalism did not arise as a driving force in society – even before the 'socialist parenthesis' of over sixty years of imported Marxist-Leninism – simply because money was taken to be a part of the spoils and entitlement of office. Capital is passively rather than actively acquired through corruption and 'clipping the ticket' rather than personal endeavor and industry. At the same time, it may also be deduced that institutional rigidities have impeded and continue to impede the development of a market economy. It is not communism that holds China back, it is the remnants of imperial bureaucracy fixed in the mind of the individual and in the centralized governing controls of the Party hierarchy.

Executive summary

Part II reflects on the nature of the current Chinese reality. It shows how the past illuminates the present of an ancient civilization and how it so powerfully prompts the heart and mind of Chinese in their quest for overseas expansion.

8. *Transvergence* is the term we use to describe how the Chinese modify their traditional value systems when dealing with foreigners.

9. *Induction and deduction* highlights the difficulties arising when the Chinese, who are inductive in their reasoning, meet the apparently equivocating, deductive Westerner.

10. *Adaptation* addresses the art and practice of change and the differing routes and processes by which strategies are created by Western and Chinese organizations.

11. *Chinese reality* deals with some of the more common, but extraordinary, phenomena and major enigmas of Chinese life and ways of doing things – particularly the notion and practice of *guanxi*. The reality of the Chinese environment is such that it is 'exportable' with extensive overseas networking.

12. *Harmony and people* highlights the primacy of relational governance in China versus the contractual enforcement of the West. Language structure and word usage ensure that harmony, especially at a network's business boundaries, is not so much conformity to foreign ways but more a desire to avoid confrontation.

13. *Beyond control* examines how individual Chinese behavior is adjusted by the group to implement strategy within a closed circle of trust, while Western freedom of expression and individual initiative may be cautiously imitated. Caution is less strictly observed overseas where the learning process is accelerated.

14. *Chinese strategy* is traditionally socially based but is slowly adapting, in a trial and error fashion, to external market forces. China's sphere of influence extends globally and their political, economic and military strategies are increasingly competitive.

Summary and discussion – Chinese values are adapting to accommodate business relationships alongside a reliance on traditional *guanxi* networking. A preference for arbitration as a contractual enforcement tool would be a global Chinese compromise. There is no indication that the Chinese will adopt the practices of the highly regulated West either at home or overseas.

CHAPTER 8

Transvergence

> Same bed, different dreams
> (*Chinese proverb*)

If the Chinese ways of doing things are not converging to Western ways, what are they doing? The argument for a term like 'crossvergence', suggesting that change in economic ideology creates a unique value system, has no clear empirical findings. Imperial remnants and Stalinist communism have not caused any lasting ideological damage. Chinese central planning is more imperialist than communist. The Chinese have retained their traditional value systems, but will adapt them for dealing with capitalist foreigners. The argument thus changes to focus on what it is that is adapting, now that old economic models are found seriously wanting.

National values and appropriate strategic changes must ensure a domestic control but also allow for global adjustment. This process we call *transvergence*. Transvergence occurs when a networked strategist accepts both national and non-national influences. A unique value and belief system is formed. Such a system is a domestically responsive but globally integrative means of controlling strategic expansion.

The most appropriate control allows flexibility. Modern Chinese organizations have considerably reduced their previous vertical hierarchical structures to provide lower levels of management with greater autonomy. It is the younger, junior and middle management who are adapting the Western techniques and tools for use in domestic and global strategies. We show, in this chapter, the new assumptions.

Socially embedded strategies, such as those valuing the group context, maintain the traditional domestic response, the old ways. The new global configuration is a trial and error process. It is based on strategies adjusting to the international situation. At a global interface, strategies can be copied and crafted. Necessity is the mother of imitation.

The imitation can be seen in the Chinese hybrid of contractual *and* relational governance over deals done in the international arena. There are legally binding contracts with Europeans and relational mutual obligations with Africans – a choice of control. Resistance to change at a senior management level is slowly eroding. Organizations (and *guanxi* networks) still tend to avoid innovative decisions, but the balance between adapting and innovating is a fine one.

Any confusion about convergence to the West can be interpreted as stemming from the imitation of strategic processes. The Chinese are, above all, practical people. Where it works it will be used. Successful contractual governance, for example, is now being copied for simple transactions, such as product purchases and contracts of carriage, with Chinese transvergence subsequently following.

Measurement is not management – financial transvergence

The natural sciences know the limits of uncertainty. The more we try to measure an electron's position, the less we can know of its momentum. Chinese managers understand the uncertainty concept. Try to measure a company's present position to any great extent and the magnitude and direction of growth will fade. Concentrate on measuring growth and the present position becomes the past.

There are several sets of accounts in a Chinese organization. An entrepreneur will hold the cashflow and growth estimates. The immediate family will be privy to the color of these numbers – be they black, red or blue sky. Senior management will have a profit and loss account highlighting poor performance. The financial department will be sworn to secrecy and any accounts for the taxman will be just shy of bankruptcy. The network defines the accounts.

The West also has levels of financial production: a summary for the board, management accounts, statutory detail for investors etc. But the West is regulated by generally accepted accounting principles and the figures correlate. The Chinese system is an internal, networked audit. The network itself is based on a need-to-know principle and is very subjective in its production of financials. Networks act like paradigms of interpretation. It is difficult to understand another set of figures from observation of one's own.

As more Chinese organizations move into public listings and operations, a groundswell of demand for change in financial practices is now becoming louder. But Chinese managers domestically provide for the network's needs. The balance sheet will show the best forward position for the investor, but the worst present position for the taxman. Figures must be treated with great caution. The Chinese demand some leeway in their financial standards.

If growth is the key, then forget the present position. Growth prospects are a mixture of information and transactional network strength and network merger possibilities. Mobile phone companies again provide a useful analogy, the difference being that mobile phone networks are objective. Chinese networks are not.

Newspaper articles discussed an investment by the Royal Bank of Scotland (RBS) in the Bank of China. One argued that RBS may have negotiated compensation terms if the Bank of China should end up with financial problems not discernible from its published numbers. It further argues that nobody in the West can claim to put an accurate value on a stock percentage of a Chinese state-owned bank without fooling themselves. Whilst we do not dispute the basic journalistic argument, we would further argue that there is no clearly negotiated compensation at any stage in a Chinese deal. The Chinese never want an established relationship to end. RBS is married and a network divorce will be costly to both parties. Rising prices initially made the deal look good but recent falls have dropped the RBS investment to below the IPO pricing. The assets on the RBS balance sheet are illiquid and long term.

The value of a relationship in China is in its network potential. At an interface, when negotiating or analyzing investment strategies, the businessman must establish the information network level in advance. How much information is passed between the two parties is dependent upon the levels of trust. At the network periphery, low levels of trust imply low levels of information. The West must realize that trust cannot be bought, it must be earned. Becoming trustworthy is the challenge. An investment into a network (*guanxi* connections) is one of time and of relational development.

There are estimates which put the cost of cultivating and maintaining a *guanxi* network at 3–5 per cent of business operating costs. In a land where legal and auditing enforcement is minimal, it is equivalent to the line denoting professional expenses in a Western profit and loss account. Western financial scrutiny must accept that as the norm.

What must also be accepted as the norm is that, although Chinese companies listed on stock exchanges are now attempting to conform to international financial reporting standards, transactions between businesses under common ownership will not have to be reported if they involve state-owned enterprises. The potential for massaging of figures is manifest.

As with parallel imports, China operates a widespread parallel banking system for overseas transactions and cash remittances by individuals: overseas Chinese earnings are typically paid to an agent in London who then authorizes disbursement of funds in Beijing – a mirror payment. While no money laundering can be proven to take place in London, it indubitably does in Beijing, whence counter-funds are routinely disbursed all over the world, as any rigorous audit trail will ultimately show.

Management is not measurement

To give some measure to types and degree of adaptation in mentality, we summarize anonymous comments from a senior Chinese manager in a UK subsidiary of a large Chinese state-owned organization. He paints a picture of frustration in problem solving and a desire for change in the Chinese way of doing things:

> I mean of our whole company, at that stage we had over 100,000 employees country-wide and we had less than 100 expatriates [selected from] basically the business knowledge and your English....

> Individual firms in China keep doing new things... new kind of management style... definitely changing... rapid change in many ways....

> We have an older generation and a young generation. Before the young generation move to important positions taken by the older generation, you yourself are going to be changed. If you are not changing yourself you are never going to end up being in that [senior] position....

The return of the expatriate seeking promotion requires the resuming of traditional ways of doing things to conform to the selection procedure for senior management. Traditional values will change but by osmosis in corporate procedures. Reduced hierarchical structures will catalyze the process.

It is apparent that new ideas and new techniques will not be immediately acceptable to senior managers in China:

> I don't think, I mean, the Chinese managers are kind of liking some of the ideas. They know what is good and what is bad – I mean management-wise. But we need tools. I often use the method that of, how to say this, that is, like, I mean digging a tunnel. When I was digging a tunnel back in China I am using kind of very simple tools....

> The kind of culture of this management (Chinese in UK) is quite different, but to some extent it's appealing. I mean there's two sides of this creation, like – let me give you an example – like the culture of the power. The power distance in this company is much shorter than that in the head office in China....

> ... a lot of things are happening in China as I mentioned. There are large potential markets, a lot of opportunities to make quick money, big money. Like IT areas, like management consultancy, like broking areas – insurance broking, security broking, all that sort of thing. It could be successful overnight....

The managerial comments above would not be unusual from an experienced Western manager. It is the opportunistic nature of the comments that strike a decisive tone. The relevant interpretation, however, is more difficult. This particular manager has two hats to wear – a domestically responsive one and an international, globally integrated one. Once the two hats are on the one head, after his return to China, we should expect to see an internationally adept and extremely capable modern Chinese manager.

However, the only clear indication of value preference is for a lower hierarchical Chinese structure with the autonomy of managing with the right 'tools'. And this is from a senior manager – imagine how the middle managers must be champing at the bit.

Nevertheless, there is a fear in China of the drift to the West being too fast. In contrast to the 'expat' Chinese manager, another senior manager – based in China but on a UK management course – is much less aggressive in any desire to change:

> ... not only light industry... in the past steel industry controlled by the government, but nowadays gradually open, gradually open.... Well, in the short period the government policy will play an important role, in most industries. But I think as time passes well we shall be what's market oriented. So that's why, well, China is a socialist country but we are now falling in the way of Chinese of socialist society with Chinese future, with Chinese characteristics. We are now crossing a river by touching the stones under the water, because nobody before us has... we are now exploring a new road....
>
> We are now learning management from developed countries. But we shall not take them directly because we are not feeling the stones, and we just extract some good things. We shall not follow the westerners to make the same mistakes, just like meat-processing. Well many years ago western people found that the pork was very fat so they changed some genes... and developed lean style, lean eat pork. But after many years of running, well, they've found now that not so tasty... so a lot of western people, they complaining, the new lean style of pork, it's not so tasty... so they have to turn back trying to avoid the mistakes....

Here is a clear example of why Western ways are not necessarily the best for China and the Chinese people. Instead of a convergence to the West, there is a divergence from recent practices back to Chinese ways of doing things. There will be other traditional industries with similar poor experience of adopting Western ways direct without any adaptation to suit Chinese practices. Perhaps China's recent stance against importing American pork products is as much cultural protection as trade protection.

There is a clear distinction between respondents, overseas and domestic. For the moment, we simply show two extremes of globally aware Chinese management. The modern manager lies between the two. The Western analyst, relying only on the westernised Chinese manager for information, can easily overestimate the domestic rate of change. Conversely, the overseas rate of change is much more easily underestimated.

Parallel lines converge only at infinity

We do not believe that Chinese ways of doing things will converge to the West. There is cultural and strategic adjustment occurring in China, but it is primarily an adaptation of Western ways, a transvergence. The problem with transvergence is that it indicates convergence in some areas, such as management techniques, but also divergence away from any immediate adoption of Western paradigms.

Rather than belaboring the issue at this point, let us put this in longer term perspective. Just imagine what would happen if convergence were to take place within the ideologically and geographically closer Asia-Pacific region. Perhaps we should see: a disarming informality in the Japanese; a reflective calm in the Filipino; an old world courtesy in the Cantonese; financial propriety in the Malay; contractual clarity in the Indonesian; absolute discretion in the Thai; the refreshing breath of a united Korea exuding the democratic freedoms of Singapore; an inhibited, parochial China attended by Taiwan as a client state; and a cultural awareness in the Australian backed by the industrial clout of New Zealand. Convergence to the West? The Chinese? Once Asia converges then we'll think about the West.

Our point is that Asia is tribal. Within China there are also different management values. A Chinese respondent, an academic with a PhD in the field of economics, argues that:

> another difference is, in the South, when people fight they use language. In the North when people fight they really

fight, using their hands... but afterwards they become friends again... in the South after fighting they probably never talk to each other...'.

Northern Chinese may come to blows but then everything is forgotten and friendships are refreshed. The Cantonese, on the other hand, remember any slight and can wait a long, long time to get even. The Northern Chinese sound more Irish than their Southern cousins. Rugby would be their sport, with the Cantonese perhaps preferring a few rounds of Russian roulette. Over 5,000 years, Chinese history still retains quite marked geographical differences.

Indeed, the Chinese have their own perspective on their vast country and multiple dialects. When a wife finds that her husband is having an affair then, if she is Cantonese, she would wait, keep quiet and concentrate on the family until the husband returns home. For a Shanghai wife, the beauty salon, make-up and the latest fashions would all be deployed to win back the husband – then she drops him and zooms off with her latest boyfriend using the funds from the family firm. If from Shandong, she gets her brothers to beat up her husband and then divorces him knowing that it was worth a few broken legs and lost fingers. But a Shanxi wife would complain and complain whilst eating stacks of comfort food until the husband dumps her for being so fat. And so the city tales of communal personalities are told.

China itself is not therefore truly convergent. The traditional prefectural control, residing some distance from Beijing, is not an example of distance creating freedom of action but a confirmation of different tribal networks and 'ways of doing things' within China. Where managers are born, brought up and educated explains their behavior and their strategic thinking. The internal adjustments in China are tribal and national.

The disruptions often reported in the domestic and foreign press are geographic and cultural clashes, not of law or failures in due process, but of the divergence between tribes. The farmers know their local land ownership, the building developers know local political power. It is the clash of networks, not of civilizations, that defines friction in China. The domestic transvergence to a new way of doing things is presently painful. The foreigner is not part of the adaptation but may be the catalyst. Whether the foreigner will escape the crucible of fomentation unchanged and intact is yet to be seen; he certainly forms the reaction.

The disturbances in Tibet certainly foment fear and anger – on both sides. In mid-March 2008 the foreign news services, such as the BBC and CNN, were jammed and pictures prevented from reaching residents in China. Paradoxically, in preventing insurrection against the state, China is following international precedents and international law. Tibet is accepted as internal to China (as is Taiwan when the USA finally acknowledged Beijing in 1978) and it is how, not why, the disturbances are quelled that is the issue.

China's actions are often seen as vitriolic. Drop acid into water, however, and it disperses without trouble. Drop water into acid and you'd better stand back – or don safety glasses. It is the external drip into China that fires the Chinese mind, the 'do not meddle in my affairs' attitude. The Dalai Lama recognizes this and exhorts the world to engage with China. It is the fear of China on the tribal doorstep that is catalytic in the extreme.

CHAPTER 9

Induction or deduction

> To know the road ahead, ask those coming back
> (*Chinese proverb*)

Western theory is based on logic. Our reasoning is analytical and follows a strict process of deduction within a defined structure of cognition and categorization by name, type and recognizable phenomenon or happening. The Chinese take a broader view of why and how things happen and do not ascribe effects to causes in quite the same way as we do in the West. They are, in short, much less abstract and arrive at their own understanding through experience and direct perception, which enables them to square and accept apparent contradictions.

The inductive process of moving from a particular event to a general prediction is common in human experience. Taking certain observations, interpreting a pattern and using the pattern as a basic theory for predicting a future observation is not unreasonable. The old warning, that once is happenstance, twice is coincidence and the third time is enemy action, is borne out. It does not necessarily explain, but it certainly allows a course of action.

Deduction is primarily the process of moving from general events to the particular. Western techniques, however, allow deduction to flow only from the rejection of a 'null hypothesis'. The West relies on showing that the 'non-truth' is highly improbable. In other words, if we believe two events or phenomena are different then we test the hypothesis that they are the same. When the hypothesis fails, admittedly at a subjective probability, then we accept that there is a difference. The testing of drugs using a placebo works in this fashion. Once it is shown that the effects of the drug and the placebo are *not* the same, only then do we move on to establishing the efficacy of the drug.

Induction or deduction

The Chinese way of doing things, however, is traditionally derived from practice. In discussing the philosophical history of the Chinese, the primary demarcation of the Chinese mind is in 'terms of its greater *emphasis* upon, and consequent *development* of, the practical as against the theoretical mind'. A theoretical set of general events makes it difficult for Chinese management to establish the particular related event. Testing a 'null hypothesis' is a resultant of Western logic systems.

The Chinese operate in an inductive fashion, having no history of thinking comparable to Aristotelian logic or Wittgenstein's truth tables. The problem with induction, which has worried modern Western philosophers from Hume to Popper, is not seen by the Chinese to be a problem. Chinese managers accept that particular events are likely to form a pattern for future events. This should be borne in mind when discussing business propositions. Western practice is deductive, Chinese practice is inductive.

For those who rely on logic, the Chinese can reply with the raven paradox. This paradox accepts each part of a logical argument. Simply put, we can start with the proposition that all ravens are black. Either it is not a raven or it is black. If it is not black it is not a raven. Under formal logic each statement about ravens is equivalent to the other (the equivalence condition). Logically, we can then argue that lots of black shoes (not ravens but black) and lots of white gloves (not black and not ravens) will help confirm the proposition, through equivalence, that all ravens are black. Isn't logic wonderful!

Western managers may believe that solid logic will see them through any meeting with their Chinese counterparts. Not so – a compromise of cultural thought is needed. Joint discussion should respect inductive, qualitatively sourced arguments as well as quantitative, deductive presentations. Shake hands on the compromise but be careful of conspiracies. Inductive arguments tend to lead to unusual conclusions, many of them dependent on high levels of intrigue. Deductive arguments tend to reject useful but ambiguous situations. Cold logic or heated rhetoric can win a battle but not a strategic war.

The elusive fluency of real dialogue

The Chinese manager moves quickly but is hampered by local practice at home in China. Square wheels do not spin; they grind exceeding slow. The machinery of government controls the pace of commercial life and slows it down to involve several layers of decision makers. This is quite understandable when you realize that the main inductive desire of officials is to keep out of trouble and to avoid accepting responsibility. They have, after all, no incentive and nothing to gain by showing anything other than passive resistance to innovative (i.e. non-established patterns, especially foreign) requests and petitions. What a parallel with Western ways – it sounds like the European Union.

Chinese government has a major 'Brussels' problem to the nth degree: it is not joined up. Different ministries have different networks and do not accept cross-ministerial responsibilities. The Chinese are used to this. Authority levels are still slow to descend from on high, as most officials are insecure about deciding anything. So the *guanxi* network comes into play and is used to discover the true source of power, not just the powerful title.

However, if patience is shown, and understanding and some appreciation of the time and trouble being taken can be combined, good manners are rewarded. Foreign business is not an insincere supplicant for a granting of favors, but a potential partner for Chinese expansion. Bad manners with no patterns of harmony invite sullen and resentful silence in response. Any confrontational behavior is smacked down smartly.

A relational redeployment of assets – *renqing*

The collective rather than the individualist nature of social interaction in China means that understanding is reached much more intuitively through direct perception and impression.

Philosophers like John Locke and John Stuart Mill, whose work most influenced the 18th and 19th centuries and the American Revolution, assumed that the processes of cognition were common to all mankind; that there was indeed some kind of 'universal truth'.

Induction or deduction

In fact, Chinese thought processes are much more in tune with the observations of David Hume, the great 18th-century Scottish moral philosopher, whose writing even now seems to distil the more commonsensical notions of the Enlightenment, particularly his description of 'impressions' as the basis for reasoned action and behavior.

Chinese behavior involves the cultural practice of mutual obligation (*renqing*) – less a scratching of bilateral backs and more a relational need to achieve a dependency upon one another. A dependency to prevent untoward opportunism from arising is deemed not only useful but also necessary. In a domestic environment where economic exchange is now neither state-assisted nor yet contractually enforced in its outcome, the creation of natural reciprocity is the practical result of dealings with one another.

A problem then lies with the extent to which such interdependency can be manipulated. When an obligation, a future option, is created through a relatively inexpensive gesture, then the reciprocal future obligation may still be called in an expensive manner. The benefits of preventing opportunistic behavior by meeting mutual needs and obligations are ensured by the governance control of paying one's debts when due immediately. Reciprocal arrangements are not normally specified from the outset. The size of debt and future timing of its collection could be punitive. It cannot be deduced.

For meeting simple obligations, there is considerable benefit in creating contractual terms. Within China, rather than risk local standing, a potentially dubious economic exchange will be conducted with a stranger (or better still, a foreigner). At the interface between West and East, simple contractual terms with immediate payment of 'consideration' are preferable and acceptable to both parties. Future options of unspecified size and timing need not be granted.

In China, obligations result from the acceptance of an initial benefit or gesture. Whilst refusal of any offering will offend, the best response is an *immediate* gift of similar or equivalent value. Honor is satisfied. Continue to work on the basis of past events creating the relational pattern for future events – Western ways are too testing.

Accepting important Chinese values as worthy of Western adaptation will allow the Westerner to gain access to Chinese organizations. If, after several visits to China, a Westerner is introduced to others as *Lao Pengyou* (Old Friend), he will know that he has earned this noble honorific. However, it does not confer any particular status in itself, or imply a familiarity, much less intimacy, but it is a mark of respect more of the fact that it is the persistent, steadfast individual, and not some faceless title-holder, with whom they have the reciprocal business relationship. Friendship is honorary, no more.

A known body who is trusted and can be relied upon to be straightforward, even companionable, is part of a network. *Lao Pengyou* denotes a level of harmony and comfort in business dealings – a degree of professional parity and trustworthiness, the achievement of fairness and reciprocity. It is a mild term of endearment. For in the trials and tribulations of the workaday world, is it not, as the Master said, a pleasure to have friends come from afar? But friendship may be abused. The Chinese have a blunt saying (*sha qin*) which basically implies that you should take advantage of those with whom you are familiar. Those who are blinded by trust and friendship can be manipulated. The Chinese will try to avoid dealing with friends and relatives (unless honor or obligation call) lest they fall into this trap. Even trust must maintain its armour against manipulation.

Big problems come from lots of little problems – so why not fix the little ones first?

Research in the West indicates that problem solving by the individual depends upon three primary factors: emotion, social context and uncertainty. Emotion is best controlled in a group situation – by the stiff upper lip of the English army regiment, the shrug of the French shoulders, the phlegm of the Flemish. Conflict within the group, in the social context, creates a dilemma, the solution to which can be dangerous to others. The Bahasa Malay term 'to run amok' describes the disastrous effects of individual emotion overrunning the confines of the social kampong.

Will the Chinese break ranks? The social world of their childhood traditionally inculcates a certain collective responsibility, an instinctual inter-dependency. The more individualist West encourages a person towards a freedom of choice, mobility and action constrained only by relative loyalty, affection or dislike, and the law. But China has a pressing problem of individuals in a collectivist society. The single child policy from the 1980s is now a reality for single adults. Where is the socialization of the family in modern China? The Chinese youth are less constrained and more spoilt than any generation. Will they see Western ways as the answer to a lack of brothers and sisters, to a void in traditional behavioral controls? Will they understand that Western individualism is both societal and familial – or will they see it as a panacea to their loss of Chinese tradition?

You have only to look at Chinese paintings to understand how the Chinese used to see themselves, depicted as they always are as figures in a landscape, a man or woman in the midst of nature, merely a part of a much bigger picture. The wider context is everything, the whole field of plans and dreams and people likely to be affected has to be taken into account – not just the possible outcomes and worst case scenarios as imagined in the fevered speculation of Western individualist hypotheses, based as it so often is on contemplation of the thing itself, the issue, the event, the one sole focus of their concern and anxiety.

This is the fundamental difference between West and East in their processes of ratiocination, this difference between focus (on the all-absorbing point of concentration) and background (consideration of the whole) across the greater field of actual and abstract vision. It is a contrast which leads to confusion and mutates into misunderstanding. It is a contrast which may lead to imitation by the individual Chinese as they gain education and experience in the West – a contrast which hopefully will fade over time as the *guanxi* network adapts.

The Chinese may act collectively by nature but overseas their individuality will surprise you. Their emotions are presently more easily controlled by a group and its social context than in the individualistic West. The inscrutable Oriental exists only in legend. The group provides ample scope to express humour, sadness and joy. Those external to the networked group are, until proven otherwise, considered untrustworthy individuals. Emotions are thus repressed until trust allows their expression. This is not inscrutability – lack of trust is obvious to the informed observer.

An astute observer sees cultural patterns as parallel worlds in which problems are ambiguous and solutions may be different. To avoid complete misunderstanding, to prevent small differences in perceived rationality creating confusion, it must be acknowledged that social contexts are rarely equivalent. Why then be surprised when the solution to future uncertainty is different? The social context, the group and individual needs can take priority over the dictates of the market. The solution to the problem is germane to the context. Thus, any apparent failure in logic points to a failure in the interpretation of the context.

If problems arise, long-term solutions will invariably be preferred over the shorter term. Short-term opportunities will not be missed (they are less uncertain with more specific contexts), but the discounting back of a potentially large future problem cuts it right down to size. And small problems are easily resolved: we have, after all, probably seen them before. But the small problem of the single-child policy has not been seen before in China. The context is now one of uncertainty.

The truth and nothing but the truth

The use of Western logic and its attendant 'true' or 'not true' propositions prevents acceptance of mutually exclusive positions at the same time. Chinese arguments, by contrast, in seeking harmony and keeping the network secure, can accept mutual exclusivity. If there are, in any case, two worldly Chinese dimensions – *yin* and *yang* – then a male position is not equivalent to a female position. Yet an event combining both can occur at the same time and place. Without going into further detail it is best to accept that true and not true are possible at the same time. Once again, no room for the null hypothesis.

A knack by any other name

The Westerner will encounter cases of apparent manifest illogicality when dealing with Chinese organizations, situations which will exasperate even the most equable. These arise from interpreting from the wrong paradigm, the wrong contextual frame of reference. Do

Induction or deduction

not attempt to change the circumstances of the situation, for the Chinese will tend to accept conditions as ordered by fate. The Chinese primary concern is to find a solution with the minimum possible loss of personal dignity or 'face'. This is where an uncomfortable fault line occurs between very broadly differing cultures and value systems.

A simple example would be at the network interface between the poor and the rich in China. The man on his creaking bicycle with sacks for saddle bags and a pannier piled high with scavengings from construction sites pedals past a Buick. Inside the luxury car, the businessman in the back seat is on his mobile. The two worlds, the two dynamic systems, are kept apart apparently by mutual distrust. So long as the scavenger on the cycle does not collide with the car, both are safe. Violence is just below the surface – harmony is maintained by separating, in an almost Dickensian fashion, the new nobility from the peasants. No dignity is lost. The solution to preserving mutual face requires mutually disregarding the other's existence. No single-finger LA salute in this encounter.

And yet there is a dual, almost complementary, network of harmony. The Chinese would say that happiness comes to only those that are easily satisfied (*zhi zu chang le*). If you are always on the lookout for the next deal then there is no peace, no happy repose. Perhaps the true value of a network is not one of mutual distrust but of mutual pity. The man on the bike may have attained a level of happiness through scavenging and thus have more in common with the fat cat financier and arbitrageur than first appearances would suggest.

A more complex business example of apparent illogical behavior would be the case of the joint venture with foreigners. A foreign partner may suddenly be allowed, without precedent, to push aside all the normal taboos and boundaries preserving local control in a Chinese district. He is even permitted a majority holding in the new venture. The sector is typically one where resources are crucial to survival, let alone success, such as the petrochemical industry. Here, pragmatism is seen to prevail over all previous logic to secure vital technology, raw materials and markets. The context is different, the *space* of the dynamic system has changed and the old *rules* are no longer applicable. Reciprocity, however, will be expected – especially in overseas acquisitions. Reciprocity is context universal.

Western attempts at being principled, consistent and basing a case on precedent, are countered by the Chinese search for pragmatism, expedience, and, above all, extreme patience in arriving at an acceptable resolution or agreement. The network must benefit from any transaction. They are, however, perfectly amenable to persuasion – a well-prepared case, even if it sets a new precedent and breaks new bounds, will always be considered, particularly if there is a clear mutual benefit in accepting challenging new proposals.

CHAPTER 10

Adaptation

A life of problem solving
(*a perspective on Karl Popper, Professor at the LSE*)

The arch deductivist, the late Sir Karl Popper, is held in high regard in Western philosophical circles but is little known in China. Popper argued that we devise theories for explanatory and predictive purposes and then see if they hold – or are overturned by events. He also argued that advancement is primarily evolutionary and produces a trial and error model to demonstrate his argument. His model is relatively simple. Start with a problem, attempt solutions – theoretical solutions, trials or conjectures – and then set about eliminating our mistakes, the failed solutions.

This Popperian three-stage model is basically a short-form of Figure I.1. An adaptation in strategy flows from the process of continuous correction. A strategy is a theoretical solution for problems of uncertainty and is subject to constant adjustment during the process of trial and error.

Popper's point of entry to his model is anywhere. He argues that the process is not linear but iterative. Chinese management is, from a Western perspective, not refuting Popper's argument for his trial and error process. The Chinese, however, often enter at the trial or implementation stage, happy to eliminate mistakes as they go. One difference between West and East is that the West assumes that the problem comes first. 'If it ain't broke, don't fix it' is a lazy exhortation compared to 'If it ain't broke, but could be better, adapt it'.

The Chinese approach to problem solving is essentially practical. We now know that Chinese society reached a kind of evolutionary plateau by the 17th century. Its civilization had advanced beyond that attained by the Greeks and by the 18th century it had indisputably stolen a march on Europe and the West in technology, administration and probably also in the arts. The Chinese had by then invented:

- Gunpowder
- The magnetic compass
- Moveable type
- Ink
- The wheelbarrow
- Stirrups
- Watertight compartments
- Deep drilling
- Pound canals
- Fore-and-aft sailing
- The sternpost rudder
- Cartography
- Immunization
- Astronomical observation
- Seismography
- Acoustics
- The string telephone
- Fireworks
- Iron suspension bridges
- Porcelain
- Silk
- Book printing
- Printed newspapers
- Encyclopaedias

The progress of this advancement in the practical application of ingenious ideas seems by the 18th century to have levelled out with stability and a sufficiently sustainable pace of development for the Chinese in their supremely well-ordered world. Initial incursions by foreigners from the Far West came as a rude awakening and forced China into a premature and unwelcome engagement with a new breed of exotic beings more extraterrestrial than celestial.

The best in the West may be least in the East

Management at an interface will not automatically involve bringing Western best practice into play. The solution must fit the problem. A practical example can illustrate this point. In the management of a container terminal in Taiwan, general labor was supplemented by local farmers. When harvest time coincided with peak evening cargo handling times, the farmers failed to perform. They were tired. Additional financial incentives achieved little. Sleep was the main aim. Bunk beds were therefore provided but arguments arose over time spent sleeping versus time spent earning. An acceptable compromise involved sleep and piecework, payment for actual work performed rather than time performing it, thus allowing management and farmers to burn the candle at both ends. But at least a common rate of burning was agreed. Piecework is not best Western practice (as the Western unions will testify), but can provide an optimum solution in Chinese society.

Trial and error will provide a greater opportunity for a solution that fits a local business problem than a mere migration of overseas practice. Domestic solutions are open to discussion. The need for flexibility, in a land where labor laws are not always respected (the European Union is no different) means that local solutions are essential. In Asia, the advances from an agrarian, collectivist society to an industrialised and commercialised society have been swift. In spite of this, business practices can remain rooted in the past. Adjustments to change may be generational in their time span. Imitation of foreign practices is not the same as acceptance of these practices. A compromise beats a search for convergence.

Perhaps the most telling example of compromise rests with international trade and quota agreements. Late in 2005, the USA and China were at loggerheads over Chinese import quotas to the US. American negotiators were initially drawing lines in the sand – an American term reputedly from the Battle of the Alamo, referring to a clear divide of principles. The Chinese were open. A compromise was agreed and the Chinese negotiators complimented the Americans on their flexibility during discussions. The US negotiators had seen what European quota inflexibility had caused a few months earlier – and adapted their tactics to ensure a positive response. If only the military can be as compromising.

Surprise, surprise

Core business should always be clearly specified. If it is not, you may have a joint venture in warehousing one day and be in golf courses the next. A core business deemed to be in land usage has merely adapted from one form of land investment and its satisfactory return to another. A foreigner may win, or may lose out from apparent alteration in joint activities with Chinese companies, but must be willing to adapt. Chinese organizational expansion overseas will, therefore, not be in core activities alone but in those support activities related by technique or network.

A great part of the problem arises from the limited and secretive flow of information, best suited to conglomerate internal networks. Chinese walls allow qualitatively sourced 'knowledge' to spread quickly. The prime mover instinct within Chinese management is high. Their expertise in short-term trading and their instinct to see opportunities around every corner make Chinese management believe 'intuitively' that now is the time and now is the hour. Failures result not so much from actions as from prevarications.

Chinese companies also contain core emotional categories of business. A large city company with petrol stations, taxicabs, celebrity limousines and garage repairs is basically in the transportation business, but with backup facilities. The Chinese owner loves the celebrity limousine business (emotionally) and the accountants love the petrol stations and taxis (financially). The mechanics in the garages keep the cars on the road. Problems arise when each profitable divisional business is cannibalised to protect the limousines. A Western owner would take a business view based on the divisional profit and loss or cash account. The Chinese owner takes a preferential view – his business, his happiness, his emotional choice.

Crossing the emotional divide is not recommended to foreign investors, but recognizing the emotional difficulties in any Chinese joint venture is essential. The *tai-tai* (wife) involvement is a similar caveat. Shares in businesses are often held by wives – they may have their own non-profitable shops to keep them occupied whilst the husband keeps his mistresses and money-making separate. Where there is a conflict of interest with a foreigner, the wife holds the conflicting business, under instruction and management of the husband. Knowing who owns what and who controls what is difficult. But then concepts of 'held in trust' or 'offshore company' are not unknown in the West – nor is the attendant smokescreen surprising. Try looking at Mr Murdoch's News Corporation and you will get an idea of how intricate corporate affairs can become.

Break glass in emergency only

Lawyers attending to business with the Chinese are used to pointing out the weaknesses, not the strengths, in legal enforcement. They do not expect any discussion to result in a beautifully drafted legal document. An agreement to agree is a useful device when China calls, as it serves to formulate a relationship. It is also the basis for further negotiation. A contract limits the bounds of further negotiation but does not end future options. Why spend a lot of cash on legally sound, but unenforceable, contracts when investment is better spent on the relationship – developing, maintaining and repairing it. Lawyers are best kept behind glass until really needed – their advice may then be adapted to the situation.

In an overseas environment, the Chinese can become frustrated by the continuous quibbling of the legal profession. In such instances the legal experts should be introduced at the end of the negotiations. A competent manager writing deals for his organization should understand basic legal principles. The lawyers may then tidy up any loose ends. Remember that the Chinese – and so should all negotiators – look closely at the penalties in the contractual terms. As Shylock found out, agreed damages may not be enforceable.

An object lesson: an Indonesian oil producer was looking for a storage tanker to load and store oil, but specified that the owners were responsible for cleaning the ship if it were taken out of storage for actual trading by the producer. The cost of cleaning after several years of oil storage would have been high and many Western shipowners balked at the terms. A Chinese owner picked up the contract, reasoning that any future demand for operational tankers meant that business was much better and that a renegotiation of the cleaning costs, when the time came, would be feasible. The storage contract with specific penalties was merely a route towards a future deal for 'negotiable' damages. Contracts are designed to be renegotiated when the time comes.

A nation torn in half

The nationalist government and its attendant political party were formed in the early part of the 20th century. The Second World War provided an opportunity for communism in the form of Maoist totalitarianism and warlord imperialism to gain a disguised foothold. Subsequent fighting resulted in the flight of Chiang Kai Shek and nationalist leaders to Taiwan, where they took many of the treasures of China with them.

General Chiang and his national party, *pour encourager les autres*, commenced Kuomintang (KMT) rule in Taiwan by shooting several thousand locals in the southern port town of Kaohsiung. If anyone wonders why there is indigenous distrust of the KMT party in the Taiwanese elections, it is because it is as historical as Irish distrust of English rule. The Kaohsiung 'tea party' was bloodily put down.

For the People's Republic of China, however, the potential for reunification with the Republic of China on Taiwan is probably more likely to be secured through the KMT politicians. Both the mainland People's Party and the Taiwanese KMT believe in one China. The problem is that neither rules all of China. Reconciliation through economic and political means is obviously preferable to military action. But strategies are forever opportunistic and options are never closed. The military build up by China is one of resource heterogeneity – submarines to sink Taiwan? Or to avoid US pressure on shipping lanes through the Malacca Straits? Western actions in the Middle East are being imitated and adapted by China in Asia.

Basically, overseas democracy is getting in the way of Asian harmony. In parts of China – especially round the old nationalist strongholds of Kungming – nationalist sympathizers retain some allegiance. The opportunity for any future democracy in China could well result in a KMT opposition. The tolerance of such an opposition would be enhanced if the KMT could bring Taiwan into the fold. Taiwanese calls for independence are primarily calls for recognition, heard but unheeded by the rest of the world.

Economic exchange is, however, allowing the Taiwanese to invade the mainland. During the Tiananmen demonstrations and subsequent dystopian response, American Nike representatives who had fled China to Hongkong were asked, on the CNN news channel, what was happening to their factories. Their reply was simply that they were presently being run by their Taiwanese managers.

Twenty years later, considerable individual Taiwanese investment and expertise are an intrinsic part of modern entrepreneurial wealth in China, thus weakening past levels of mutual suspicion. Economic activity is part of the Chinese character and will prove to be a large part of the answer to the problem of reconciliation. If a broker is required in negotiations, the greater understanding of Western ways is currently found in the Taiwanese.

Holding the centre

What therefore matters to the Chinese is the integrity of their Empire, the control of their boundaries from the Russian rivers of the North to the high mountain passes of the Himalayas in the South. North Korea and Vietnam remain virtual buffer states. Any slackness at the soft end of the border with Central Asia is tautened with oil deals and technology and the bracing presence of the PLA and the blue water Chinese Navy.

The fall of the Imperial Qing Dynasty with the October revolution of 1911 did away with the Emperor but also with the Mandarins, the Scholar-Official class of administrators and magistrates who ruled China in his name. With the cutting off of their pigtails, ordinary Chinese men symbolically dropped their deference to this highly centralized authority and its command to 'tremble and obey' in the face of the Emperor's representative. The new Republic let chaos loose in the land.

Acknowledged as the founder of modern China, Dr Sun Yat Sen did not trust his fellows and set up a government system allowing a cross-check of performance at a ministerial level. Such a cross-check can and does prevent normal administrative action from taking place when it cows officials into avoiding potential challenge and subsequent penalties. Chinese government officials still keep their heads down lest the cross-check turn into a cross-fire. It is ministerial protection at the highest level.

Yet the father of the Canton putsch and first President of the Republic, Dr Sun, great visionary thinker and inspiration that he was, could not hold the centre. The Empire fell prey to competing warlords and finally to Mao Ze Dong and the Soviet system. Generalissimo Chiang Kai Shek (unkindly known to Americans as General Cash My Cheque) was Sun's heir apparent, yet received not the mantle and mandate of power, but the push from the mass of the Chinese people.

Nevertheless, Sun is firmly acknowledged as the godfather of both the Communist and the Nationalist Revolutions, each still competing for moral supremacy in China. His name is revered, as the revisionism of the post-Mao era makes plain. He was the living embodiment of Chinese hopes of redress from the West for all the indignities and wrongs inflicted under the corrupt Mandarins. But he was shouldered ruthlessly aside in the immense power vacuum which followed their fall. He was never allowed to attempt that greatest feat of all: to align China (the Middle Kingdom) in equal partnership with other sovereign peoples of the Earth – an alignment that is now economic and soon to be military in its motion.

The Chinese have suffered the repeated ministrations of meddlesome officials controlling their work, their movement, and even the size of their family. Modernization at a government level is tough and must be recognized as slow and cumbersome. Unlike the European Commission, where the audit service merely notes that the books cannot be balanced, the Chinese system seeks to resolve issues in a modern, focused but flexible fashion. Business continues to push the pedals of reform and the handlebars are now slowly being steered along a Chinese Route 66 – the way to the West. But it is a route first surveyed by Dr Sun.

The Grand Narrative of China, that of the final resurgence of the sleeping giant, so long awaited by figures as various as Napoleon and Nostradamus, was reignited through the agency of this one individual – a Christian, son of émigré sugar planters from Hawaii, sent to study medicine in Hongkong, who dared to foment debate in Guangdong, who had the vision and the outsider's brazen objectivity to aspire to reach up and prod the heavy lids and paint in the eye of the dragon, a very adaptive dragon.

Fiction and fact

The work of fiction that perhaps best evinces the indomitable spirit of Chinese values in action is Andre Malraux's *La Condition Humaine*, about the maelstrom of revolutionary unrest in Shanghai in the 1920s. It is possibly the greatest novel set in China of the 20th century. It provides the reader with a context, a descriptive narrative, into which post-Imperialist China, including Mao and the Cultural Revolution, can be understood without recourse to complicated explanations of power struggles.

Our present work is one of interpreted observation. It deals with a closing reality rather than one of madcap insurrection and the existential meaning of life. It reflects on the Chinese past and present to picture a future and a new generation of Chinese individuals who will be collectively standing up and setting in motion a far-reaching strategy of global outreach, influence and control. Not just standing up in the sense that Chairman Mao bid their parents to do after he had exiled Chiang Kai Shek's Nationalists, but venturing out worldwide to secure the commodities markets and territories which will ensure China's position as a great power to counter the overweening tendencies of Russia and the United States.

The Chinese already have the monetary and military clout to order a goodly portion of the world's affairs. What they do not yet have is sufficient affiliation to, and interface with, the councils of the world and their norms of governance to be a stable element in international relations. Facts are all encumbered with myth and legend and apocryphal stories. What we do know now is the nature of this race. We know its historic habitat, its heroic suffering and its defense of its own ground. Caged and corralled in their own particular sphere for millennia, the Chinese are now coming out of the opened door. They are coming out not as single spies or lone travelers destined to keep their own counsel, like early colonists, but as battalions under a chain of command as swift and secure as that of the Catholic Church.

The question, of course, remains whether their leadership will retain the same levels of faith. If it does not hold firm, China may founder as its leadership falters and loyalty and patriotism begin to hollow out in the face of overwhelming disease or corruption. This is where the West comes in. A wild-eyed Italian visionary, a modern Marco Polo, once told us in Brussels, with a great sweep of his arm, that the EU should extend from Lisbon to Vladivostok.

This is not what we mean at all. The EU has a phrase it uses to justify getting involved in other countries' business – the Rationale for Intervention. Through programs for funding development and technical and educational exchange, designed to hasten the process of familiarization between Europe and the world, China is supposed to be drawn into the loop. China is in fact imitating and adapting the Rationale, for its own intervention in Africa and anywhere that infrastructure projects are of benefit to China.

The Chinese remain bewildered and dismayed that European bankers did not finance the Three Gorges Dam, a tremendous opportunity for cooperation. The Chinese feel that they must go it alone in terms of developing their country beyond its global manufacturing status. We urgently need to draw closer, if fantasy is to have a fighting chance of becoming fact and propagandized fact is to be lain bare as fantasy. There is no doubt that the old diplomatic bargain of recognizing a sovereign state is fast becoming an agreement to turn blind eyes to lawlessness and rapacity to disease and wars of trade. Market economics? Why not social justice! Western and Eastern ideas about the nature and purpose of life on our frangible planet must be reconciled jointly not singly. Why not start with Burma?

'Proceed feast for orders'

Brief and to the lucrative point, this was the typical wireless telegraph command that British owners sent their ships from the first days of Marconi. The result would be the loading of profitable cargoes from the rapidly expanding Far East (feast) trade, oriental commodities for Western consumers. Little has changed in the trading direction since the days of the tall ships, steam and Marconi, yet the advances in Chinese management and organizational practices may end the feast for today's financiers.

The Economist magazine gave its own storm warning in November 1997, arguing that it is impossible to predict any political reaction to a financial crash. As crashes make a substantial redistribution of income inevitable, to or from workers and owners, nasty reactions from entrenched and influential politicians and businessmen are causes for concern. The problem rests with the cursory glances given to financial basics – not the stock price but the investment risk.

Purely financial reviews of commercial situations may well leave unpredictable politics ignored. We've all 'conferred' at morning meetings when fancy numbers, flash figures produced by planning departments, have tricked the eye into looking only at net profitability. Yet the cause and effect are seldom clear – after all, nobody deliberately causes poor results; they are always influenced by extraneous circumstances. Even Barings Bank would have survived but for the 1996 Kobe earthquake.

Managers' own objectives and those of the firm must, magical though it may seem, move in tandem when solutions to problems are being sought. What's more, when different objectives can be melded together and partners' objectives aligned, then joint ventures prosper and contractual difficulties diminish. Discontinuities in the curve of prosperity can be caused by Acts of God, but are more often caused by Failures to Act by Humans.

One of the common failures is not gathering sufficient useful information to improve our understanding of people's attitudes and objectives. To succeed, it is necessary to check and recheck the alignments of a plan, not only with its financial elements, but also with its implementers, operators and processors. The political alignments can be skewed and survival threatened if people fail to communicate, misunderstand each other or, simply, don't get on together. Human relations, not resources, dictate Chinese organizational success.

The success of Hongkong in its early years was its trade: silver for opium. The objectives of the trade were similar (happiness could be bought or smoked) but that did not mean everything was plain sailing. Chinese objections to the drug trafficking were met by gunfire in the Opium Wars. Not smoking, the Chinese quickly discovered, could seriously damage your health.

Needless to say the trade was lopsided and unable to continue under such Western bias. An equitable balance had to be found and profitable results were essential for both sides of the equation. Stability became possible only when the cultures of West and East began to recognize each other's objectives. The merchants and traders from the West could amass considerable wealth much faster than they could at home – thus returning to lives of luxury. The Oriental was in demand for his product: tea, rice, oils and spices could all be sold to the greater gain of the landowner, with the feudal, peasant society supplying any labor needed to meet the demand. The Wealth of Nations was being increased – concentrating in the hands of the few!

To ensure that those prosperous hands were not unduly sullied, intermediaries were relied upon. Today, translating abilities are often mistaken for compradorial skills and cultural misunderstandings arise. The fast-moving financial markets have enabled the automatic intermediary to reply robotically. The computer interface, devoid of negotiating skills or cultural awareness, completes the trade.

To make matters worse, techniques quite acceptable in the West are viewed with great suspicion in the East. Prime Minister Mahathir of Malaysia's spat with the financier George Soros in 1997 was a minor manifestation of the genuine fear that there is no longer local control over internal affairs. But Mahathir was mocked in the West for daring to challenge market forces.

That fear, though, has now spread to the USA. Fears that China will control American debt continue to grow unabated. US debt, from an American perspective, has raced past the Chinese to become a global issue. There is an increasingly unstable equilibrium in the global economy. And with fear comes emotional decision making. Protectionism in the West is increasing – the open door is now deemed to be too one-way. Market forces, the West now proclaims, are fine but only when it suits us. The Chinese note, imitate and adapt, and will shortly turn the West on its hypocritical head.

Meeting halfway

Political management is rapidly advancing in a region which is still shaking off past colonial shackles and post-war communist ideals, a region which is undergoing shocks to its domestic systems as it adjusts to global ways of doing things. The major regional force to be reckoned with is that of China and Chinese values. The traders of Malaysia and Indonesia are predominantly of Chinese origin. The growth of Singapore and Taiwan has benefited from both British and American influences respectively in lawmaking and business attitudes, but is Chinese-inspired.

The only past Western ally in Asia is Japan. A nation which dined to excess in the 1980s continues to grapple with issues which have no identifiable pattern. The character is insular and agricultural in nature and belief – the people wait for the drought to pass whilst conserving resources, trusting that a pattern, a known sequence, will then repeat itself. But the old guard in Japan is now going. A restructuring towards youth, to global values, is occurring at a growing pace. It will take time, however, for Japan's present vacillation, and its indecisive commitments to the region, to change. Meanwhile, it is China which will most probably assert its hegemony over East Asia.

Yet it was always Imperial Japan, not Imperial China, that received most Western encouragement. From the original US naval threats of Commodore Perry in his Black Ship, through lessons learnt from the British in putting down the Boxer Rebellion and the Royal Navy's assistance in fighting Russian expansion in the Far East, to the 'drop first and ask questions later' deployment by the US of the nuclear bomb, the Japanese learned from the West that military might is right. The Chinese know this as well. Any Western *kowtow* to Chinese might is now seen as a weakness in the East. Roosevelt has the historical excuse of being gravely ill when Poland was given to Stalin. Taiwan may become another Poland.

The northern borders are coming down, however, with Japan commencing 'ice-breaking' trips to China and China reciprocating with 'ice-thawing' return visits. The North Korean nuclear crisis has improved China's power base and weakened that of its neighbors and of the USA. China's political demands presently consist of a strategic play aimed at restructuring its external borders. Now Hongkong and Macau, next Taiwan, then the Koreas followed by non-muslim South-East Asia.

For the West to leave the Far East to tidy up its own affairs is an abdication of responsibility for the past. To play political games and then depart leaves the remaining players to adapt the global *rules* as they see fit. The 'Far East' as we have known it is over. The West must now properly understand modern China and play its part in a co-opting that prepares for compromise and prevents future conflict.

Totalitarianism or communism

East Asia is at least not the nightmarish area of darkness predicted by George Orwell in the bleak futurology of his *1984* – a region dedicated to death worship and the obliteration of the self. Quite the reverse: it is presently the area of greatest enlightenment, regeneration, resilience and youth in the history of the planet. Winston Smith and the ever-present TV screen of Big Brother were actually the dystopian, visionary background all along, never a truly inductive focus on the future. Fascism, not communism, was Orwell's nightmare.

Our nightmare, however, is one of the West (probably the US) in conflict with China – a conflict caused by *misinterpreting* China. The Middle East did serve notice on the West, but only after the event. North East Asia is serving us notice now, after a financial event, during a trading one but ahead of a military one. A solution to North Korea needs South Korea, China and Japan – and does not need Western confrontational styles. Did the reunification of Germany need Asian assistance or was it neighborly *glasnost* that aided the breakthrough?

China, its changing values and changing relationships, is a global force with considerable mass and increasing acceleration. Only its direction can be channelled, preferably by its own close neighbors, with the West providing help not hindrance. Hindrance is interference in their 'internal affairs'. The Chinese National Congress emphasizes harmony as a communist ideal and a necessary societal influence – somewhat stronger than that brought to bear by Capitol Hill's lobbyists or Brussels' bureaucrats. Harmony is not a Western outcome, or even by-product, of political objectivity. Harmony is, rather, an Asian outcome of subjective problem solving accompanied by a keen desire to adapt reality and truth.

CHAPTER 11

Chinese reality

> When you drink the water, remember the spring
> (*Chinese proverb*)

Centre of the universe, long known as China to the West and to the Taiwanese as mainland China, the country – its Chinese characters translate as the Middle Kingdom – is geographically central to Asia. The middle (*zhong*) is seized on by Confucius as a protective philosophy; do not stand out as the best or the worst but hide in the middle. The Great Wall of China, a relic of a military defensive system, can be viewed as an iconic shield enclosing and preserving Chinese culture. Within Chinese defenses, however, ancient warlord feuding created an internal, personal and familial system (that term *guanxi* again) – an information network as a protection against the 'tremble and obey' threats from totalitarian power. Protection lay within the family.

The true significance of *guanxi* can probably best be understood in terms of the protection it affords the individual from the arbitrary depredations of the State. In the West, national constitutions protect the individual. The Magna Carta in 1215 ensured that the English King was no longer above the law. It set legal precedents for fundamental human rights, the rule of law and titles and deeds to land, etc. It has been a symbol of liberty for over 700 years. China has no such charter of laws and customs as a bulwark against tyranny.

Family is stability and security in a hostile world. The extended family spanning several generations gives individual Chinese their greatest single sense of self and their true place in the scheme of things. Elder family members are respected and often cherished as a major source of wisdom and worldly wiles. Families are defined by their activities together – these are, largely, festive Sunday lunches and other feast day celebrations, such as Tomb Sweeping Day, the mid-summer Dragon Boat festival and the great recess of Chinese New Year – when they all congregate to gossip and chide and squabble and put each other's lives straight with a sharp word or two and some cash in a red envelope (*hong bao*) for the children.

The Chinese language binds the country from top to bottom in spite of the vastness of its terrain and the extreme differences in local dialects, languages and usage. This is achieved through its common written form. A northerner and a southerner will often try in vain to communicate in speech and, when all else fails, will resort to finger-tracing the character or pictograph of a troublesome word in the palm of the other hand. This brings immediate fusion of minds. The philosopher, Bertrand Russell, called this written language the greatest self-inflicted handicap of any of the world's peoples. (There are 50,000 plus characters to learn – a foreigner would need approximately three lifetimes to master these – although 2,000 should allow you to read a newspaper.)

The Qin Emperor, who built the first section of the Great Wall, is even better remembered for unifying this written language. 'Are there really nineteen variations of one character?' he asked. 'No wonder people cannot communicate!' The handicap, if indeed it is one, has now been largely overcome with the introduction of *pinyin* (spell sound), the Romanised version of the language which is now also taught in Chinese schools. Another highly significant difference in children's capacity to absorb patterns of social action and behavior with their mother's milk is the fact that, while Western infants quickly learn the naming of parts as nouns or words for things, Chinese young more quickly grasp their verbs, how nouns are linked in relationships.

Individual Chinese are thus recognized not so much by their jobs as by their family and their obligations to networked members. Fear of *luan* (chaos) leads the Chinese to create their own stability within the confines of the family. First loyalty is to family members and not the state, which is viewed with suspicion. They will not put their trust in officials, whose job it is to impose authority rather than to look after their civil interests and entitlements. Why do you think peasants take up arms against corrupt officials and land developers? They have no other option.

Family nurtures the young in self-reliance and supports the old in infirmity in China. Welfare has been a family matter – no business of the state until the late 20th century. But the state still dictates that a single child married to another single child may have to look after four parents. A son sending his parents to an old folks' home is *'bu xiao'* or failing in his duty. Should Western corporate activities or affairs of state require the same submersion of the family as that common in Japan, then beware – wrong country! Family duty and filial piety will dictate the deal-making prowess. And that prowess is subject to retaining personal trustworthiness, fired in the kiln of continued relational interaction, reciprocity and obligation.

Democracy for a gerontocracy

Churchill claimed that democracy was the least bad of all forms of government known to man. But he was a western Conservative. Is democracy just possibly a mental space which China's Reform and Opening movement might allow it cautiously at some point to inhabit – as a relief from the strait-jacket and narrowness of a market economy with socialist characteristics? The answer – in a very guarded and qualified way from official sources off the record – is an unequivocal 'yes'. It is certainly not a panacea and could well be a disaster, if not carefully managed. There are several immovable, non-negotiable issues which stand as roadblocks to more democratic freedoms. These are, in order of intractability: recognition of human rights; Taiwan; Tibet; and Xinjiang autonomy.

At village level, elections are trumpeted by the Government: China embarks on the path to democratic reform. At present it is very difficult to foresee any serious political systemic change for twenty to thirty years, effectively a generation. The management of this change is based upon a fairly straightforward social pact between Party and citizen: if you don't support the Party, you can say goodbye to economic prosperity. Both the Party and the people are most scared of a *Da Luan*, a great chaos that could result from economic collapse and the subsequent revolt and vengeance of the masses. Thus it is that the Government justifies its human rights abuses, its harsh treatment of dissidents and its military expansion as protective measures.

Chinese reality

If you want to see how conditions are down on the farm, you can make your way to the Ming Hideaway of Cuandixia, an ancient hive of dwellings as close as the bees that swarm around it on the underside of a mountain some sixty miles north-west of the capital. The little settlement is the extended living space of the local Han family over many generations. The villagers scrape a very modest living from offering overnight stays to visitors from Beijing. The sleeping quarters are cool interiors with rolls of foam rubber laid out over trestle tables. The food they offer is their own supper: tasty herb omelettes, savoury pancakes, tofu and ground corn-cob soup.

With the collapse of the commune system and the closing of most of the State-Owned Enterprises, these peasant farmers and farmhands are thrown back on their own resources and now have to fend for themselves. This is clearly difficult with little or no recourse to other sources of income. They can just about scratch a living from the land they inhabit, but without other activity – sale of handicrafts, local crops and fruits – life is extremely hard, often quite desperate.

As a result, farm workers all over China can often only meet land taxes by further reducing their ancestral holdings. Even voting for better representation is constrained by intimidatory advice on the consequences of marking any but the official candidate's box. Fear is overcoming traditional *guanxi* protection. Not a good democratic omen.

China rising – peacefully

A UK diplomat in Beijing summarizes the evolving British view that China is to be welcomed into the world and to play a bigger role in assisting with international conflict resolution. He alludes to the Iranian situation and also, by implication, to Africa and Darfur, which is a wake-up call to China to get involved in areas where they have tended to turn a blind eye to local turmoil. The outside world, he says, feels less threatened by China as the country extends its influence. As for a longer-term strategy, he believes the West must increase its level of engagement. Yet he forgets the Chinese reality of reciprocity. China will never actively seek involvement in the 'internal affairs' of others because, put simply, China does not want any interference within its own borders. To be asked to help with North Korea, Iran and Burma is different – the 'asker' owes the next favor!

Two main areas may help China ease its entry into world affairs – education and science and technology. The more Europe and China understand each other, the better it will be for both economic growth and for environmental protection. Policy dilemmas in these areas are faced most starkly in China, where it is often assumed that the former can only be achieved at the expense of the latter. Because we need both, there is no real contradiction. Rather, we need to promote with China energy-saving methods which will ensure efficient growth and to incentivise the use of energy-saving transport, in particular. In short, the golden mean of balanced growth. The diplomat's final message is succinctly well put: the West does not fear China; it only fears its failure.

The changing reality

However, the values within the network structures are now changing:

> ... when I was back in China, before I was sent over here, and the major kind of the contacts are from international communities...

> ... in dealing with both your boss and your subordinates you need to be much, much more diplomatic... (in China)...

> ... on the surface like you have been with the company for 30 years, oh you are very loyal. But when the opportunity turned up you are going to go...

We can go further than the personal comments of the respondent. If we adopt an overall statistical perspective over a much larger sample, the changes in Chinese managerial attitudes and behavior can be traced to a decline in certain values and an increase in others – a realignment of *guanxi* practices.

We can argue that a transvergence, a conflation of domestic and global practices, indicates the following changes:

Chinese reality

- Governing behavioral controls are adapting to accept rising heterogeneity in decision making, although the practice of a full range of techniques is acknowledged as difficult until senior managers 'fade away'.

- A mix of relational and contractual governance over economic exchange is increasing, concurrent with greater negotiating adaptability. Strategies remain holistic and group-focused.

- Personal desires are increasing, inferring a change in orientation to tasks rather than purely to relationships – resulting in less harmonious, shorter term strategies which are likely to materialise in business and military expansion.

- Acceptance of Western legal and audit procedures is difficult to foresee in the short term – relational, internal resolution and networked auditing methods will continue.

- Trustworthiness of individuals remains paramount within *guanxi* structures and the need for harmony continues to govern relationships within the network. Short-term transactions outside the *guanxi* network result from an increase in peripheral trust, probably in external legal systems and accompanied exchange enforcement, either through simple legal resolution or more complex arbitration.

- Traditional long-term orientation is accompanied by the continuing importance of shorter term transactional reciprocity. The decrease in hierarchical obligations means lower 'power distance' and less senior level involvement in decision making.

- The importance of 'face' as a transacted consideration within *guanxi* is falling as a national value, but less so at the senior level, suggesting a retention of internal control within the political, economic and military hierarchies. There is likely to be a lapse in anticipated *renqing* obligations, not, however, as a weakening in human obligations, but as a reduction in manipulative relational exchange.

Relationships, the literal translation of *guanxi*, are the personal connections which need to be forged to further any development plans. What this implies in practice is the approaching of people, and their networks, in order to get access to services, favors, permits, approvals or even goods which are proving very difficult, if not impossible, to obtain. An office is either open or closed to an individual, depending on his or her *guanxi*. No money need change hands. The implications of *guanxi* are not cash or gifts (there is no element of corruption here), but a trading of favors. A plastic bag with cartons of cigarettes will get past the secretary's gatekeeping, but best leave it on the way out as a forgotten item.

The timely facilitation by an official of a hard-to-come-by permit or import licence, for example, may be acknowledged by helping him to obtain a particular piece of foreign electro-domestic equipment. When stuck, it often pays to go by the back door (*hou men*) route to achieve what is needed. This is sometimes the only way. It will not cost cash – only a return of the favor received, although the gift of a red envelope (*hong bao*) containing some money may sometimes prove to be a judicious sweetener. This is a small price indeed for such a saving in time, energy and temper. But times change and greed can overcome *guanxi*.

It is the drive, not for a classless society, but for a less unfair split of the market spoils in Chinese society which will help diminish greed and preserve the Chinese network. Modern Chinese political strategy under President Hu is aiming to create a middle class (that word 'middle' again) by pulling people out of poverty, by education, by entrepreneurial expertise, by social and market tinkering. It is the West which is trying to rush things and throwing spanners in the works of political engineering. A middle class is at least a generation away but will happen with patience and perseverance.

The 4 Cs

The Chinese will even offer their own rather glib mnemonic in English for the vital ingredients in the recipe for success in business dealings with them. This is a neat conceit framed in response to the Car – Cooler – Cooker – Console (TV) refrain used to describe Asian aspirations by 1970s Western journalists. It is the new Four Cs: Cash – Clout – Connections – Culture. A shrewd Westerner will appreciate that no single one of these elements is more important than any of the others.

Unsurprisingly, the one that needs more attention paid to it, however, is the last: the need to understand why certain ways of doing things are important to the Chinese, particularly reciprocity and the giving of face. We may find aspects of their behavior either baffling, impenetrable, plain silly or simply hilarious; but the fact remains that once we have entered their dynamic *space* (their heads, not their territory) and wish to engage in a commercial venture with them, then things will proceed as ordered by the twin prerequisites of reciprocity and job creation. The other common benefits expected, profit (or the cost of staying in business) and the technological shunt provided by rapidly accelerated innovation, will remain secondary considerations until pragmatism brings them to the forefront of consciousness.

If culture is 'the way we do things around here', then a possible French variation on this theme might be 'the way we *think* around here'. A French colleague, freed from lackeydom to a defunct philosopher, has bravely admitted that in France, in problem solving, 'the elegance of the deduction is often more important than the observation of the facts'. So it is in Asia: mutual recognition of a spirit of free enquiry and debate allows French baguettes to line the waysides of old Indo-China. There was no point in throwing out culinary style with the foreign occupiers.

Trust and trustworthiness

This section is not about the high moral ground that might be described in a novel by Jane Austen, but about confusion over China in the minds of foreigners. China is an extremely low trust country. There are, as in the West, high levels of internal trust within any familial network. The need for trust at the network boundary in China is transformed into a demand for trustworthiness. Is the transactional partner good for his obligation? Trust in social ostracism or legal governance to ensure that the obligation is met is a separate issue. The trustworthiness and dependability of the peripheral partner is all-important. Some form of mutual identification will help.

For example, a customer, when questioned at a Chinese airline, could argue that a trusting relationship is created only after the individual has bought a ticket. An enquiry as to times of flights is met with suspicion. Is knowledge to be transferred free or does the enquirer actually want a ticket? If the enquiry is only for information then why waste my time, thinks the busy salesgirl! Even after a ticket has been bought further exchanges can be tortuous – polite requests for information are often turned brusquely aside. The importance of trust within the network is offset by total lack of trust outside it. Internal network trustworthiness is accompanied by several other values, notably reciprocity and mutuality. Only then is information freely traded and used.

The Chinese initially identify with certain Western habits and practices more readily and easily than do the Japanese. While the Japanese often appear watchful and inexpressive (looking for a model of behavior as a basis of comparison), the Chinese display altogether livelier spirits – they are naturally friendly, earnest (rather than serious), somewhat conservative and buoyantly cheerful communicators. It assists enormously for a Westerner to have some language facility (however limited) and some acquaintance with Chinese history and culture – they will certainly know a fair amount about the West.

It is the lack of trust shown by the West to China that creates a major problem. Quality control in China is low and Western buyers know that. Their greed forces Chinese short cuts on pricing, sometimes met by outsourcing (another imitation of Western practices) to even lower quality suppliers. Metallic lead in toys sourced by Mattel and breaking plastic bottle caps sourced by WalMart are merely a couple of instances – but it is the fear of Western legislation that is increasing the number of recalls at a rate of more than 20% per annum. With China supplying a good 40% of global products there is an increasing focus on China as the bad guy. Political democratic tricks in the West are decreasing the trust levels. A Chinese factory manager commits suicide and the West still shakes its fist. How many Western CEOs would fall on their sword for their errors?

The Chinese have a pronounced talent for figuring and ready reckoning with numbers. They seem to be hard-wired with a built-in mental abacus for computing. However, there is no need to imagine that their diamond-hard eyes drilling into you with gimlet gaze perceive everything you imagine they do. Your mind may be as impenetrable to them as their impassive demeanour is to you. They are just as often affected by tunnel vision as Westerners are. They even have a phrase for it themselves. They say someone is 'like a frog in a well' in that he sees nothing but the circle of sky above him. In other words, he cannot see the wood for the trees. Quality control is not the problem; trust in a fair price for a fair job is the issue.

Now that all the barbarians are within our gates

Although the Chinese have opted overwhelmingly for Western style dress, this does not mean that they have taken on Western habits of mind or behavior – except perhaps smoking (which will die hardest of all in China). Western attitudes remain an enigma. Chinese inner feelings of superiority lead them to tolerate the West with amused irritation and wonder. This evinces a kind of cordial contempt for inexplicably strange Western ways and the West's unshakeable stubbornness.

The epithet 'foreign devils' has been conferred upon Westerners. It is not really a malign description, meaning in effect little more than 'strange being'; but somehow this slight has become less enigmatically insulting as we slowly become familiars. There is a common Chinese perception of Western traits of character: straightforward, principled at the expense of pragmatism, proud of academic credentials (but often somewhat incapable), morally casual, opinionated without inclining to listen, trouble making, naive and privileged.

It is the Chinese who point out that it was Jesus Christ who enjoined the Christian 'to be as cautious as snakes and as gentle as doves'. The words of the great story-teller, Lu Xun, still resonate: 'The Chinese have either looked down on foreigners as brutes or up to them as saints, but have never actually been able to call them friends or speak of them as equals.' Perhaps Lu Xun, not Thomas Kuhn, first appreciated the subtleties of paradigm incommensurability?

We are not being facile. The fact that the Westerner is never seen to be equal means that there is no way that trust can be the same for a Westerner as for a networked Chinese. Trust, in terms of business, is useful. The higher levels of trust in the West are professional.

Just as friendship is honorary, so trust is utilitarian. The principles guiding friendship and trust are the pursuit of harmony. Harmony is achieved with personal virtues of steadiness and persistence. The foreign devil used to arrive and leave by night – as do saints and sinners, but not equals.

Or how to maintain a well-concealed sense of the ridiculous

The philosopher Bertrand Russell admitted to a fondness for the 'humorous and hairless' Chinese, as if only the hirsute were susceptible to having their wits tickled. While the British shun seriousness, the Chinese shun levity – in business. Where ribbing, joshing or 'poking Charlie' at people and problems are a great emollient in British negotiations, the Chinese prefer the poker face of gravitas. That spontaneous snort of laughter you may suddenly hear will have burst out of deep cover for extreme embarrassment or confusion, never on account of a cunning pun or the wicked enjoyment of another's misfortune. For what is laughter but the dislocation of a mind suddenly ambushed by surprise? The Chinese language does not permit such dissolution in serious discourse.

It was the writer, Lin Yu Tang, who, almost single-handedly, introduced unadulterated humour into public consumption like some delicious contraband. He had studied in the United States and Germany between the wars and seen the light of levity at an early age. In his popular newspaper columns he pursued many of the more absurd anomalies and pretensions of Chinese life in a spirit of gentle, rational enquiry. From his perspective, the Cultural Revolution may be seen to have been an enormous, almost genocidal, sense of humour failure.

Yet from the wreckage of that absurd enterprise, the Chinese have still managed to salvage a penultimate chuckle or two. What really makes the Chinese chortle with glee is the mountainous arrogance of Western deprecation. Human rights pale when Western justice still leaves such a lot to be desired – but what are human rights when Nike can make cheaper footwear in China? It is a source of truly spectacular amusement and mirth to them. It is mad, bad and barbarian and laughed out of court.

A silk purse from a sow's ear

The industrial world in China has been until recently one of meticulous production planning for quotas and massive overmanning. The State Enterprises have provided employment for millions of Chinese who have enjoyed the security of an 'iron rice bowl', that is, guaranteed square meals every day. Now they are being dismantled or made over piecemeal to private and even foreign interests, much as the former East German plants and factories were under the Treuhand. This means a large-scale recycling of personnel into new activities and occupations where they are suddenly expected to learn new skills and be measurably productive to earn their bowl of daily rice.

The dynamics at the global interface are, however, forcing change in response to the opportunity for advancing China. As the Master might have said, the Superior Man will only act when he sees the need to do so – and certainly not at the behest of foreigners. The Chinese individual in a West/East negotiation is now different from the past. More adaptable, more aware of Western ways and more flexible in the acceptance of opportunities, the modern Chinese are quite likely to see the Westerner as mired in past practices suitable only for one-night stopovers.

Arrogance stems from corporate cultures grown from international money centre moulds. The barbarian at the gates now wields an armour of briefcase and Blackberry – an armour that the modern Chinese manager can see straight through. It is the human relationships, the bare bones of trustworthy individuals that count – not the cash.

Opening the little red book

There has been little recent praise for Mao, but there is no reason for a business man or woman to revile him and his followers. It is more important to understand the possible reasons behind his actions.

Firstly, the Confucian principle of hierarchical leadership, the ruler/subject precept, permits a leader – and China has a history of cruel warlords as well as wise ones – to be followed relatively unquestioned. Secondly, the family protects itself and its members through *guanxi*. Having gained power, Mao set about breaking down the *guanxi* (of the landlord class, in particular) as a necessary step to ensure a divide-and-control governing structure. In Russia, Stalin terrorised first the peasants and then everyone whom he saw as a threat to his authority. Mao targeted the family, breaking it up by forced deportation from the cities and by turning son against father and brother against brother.

We acknowledge that deliberate breaking of familial, protective networks is not peculiar to China (the Hitler Youth operated in a similar fashion), but the nature of the *guanxi* networks in China is very strong and fundamental to the collectivist society. The continual use of *guanxi* for economic survival is unsurprising in Chinese society. It is seen as a necessary and continuing prophylactic against any domestic turmoil and global economic malaise.

Commissioned navvies on the march

Armies are more often than not civilians in uniform at a time of national emergency. Members of a standing, regular army normally number far fewer. A legacy from Maoist rule, the PLA in China is something else. It is the nation's task force, combat-ready in the event of war, but otherwise extremely peaceably engaged in the pursuit of commerce – man's most common means of survival.

In a country where private capital is still scarce, the PLA have become entrepreneurs. In short, they are the very model of modern privateers and partners in many foreign-invested ventures. They have become the great make-weight and help-meet in many major projects, from space flights to running discos.

So it has always been in China. A peacetime army is put to work in great enterprises of national reconstruction – not just highways and harbours, but in gargantuan undertakings like the Three Gorges dam on the Yangtze River. The scale is awesome and the payback and time-frame something of a mirage. The PLA and friends labor antlike over the terrain. The army liberates the people! China unlocks its chains! Foreign bankers may have declined the proffered loan mandates, but the Mandate of Heaven has been taken up by the heirs of the Han Dynasty.

Mandates, however, may be illusory. The vast majority of Chinese may be in the economic pyramid but they inhabit its base. Their aspirations and expectations are being heightened by the color television in every family corner. Pyramids are inherently stable if the base is undisturbed. The apex may hold the power but the view of the mandate from the bottom is less and less distinct. Increased overseas focus, tighter controls over pollution, taxing corruption where penalties are difficult, harmony rather than horse trading, and many other less black and white stances on the domestic front all serve to ease the likelihood that the people will call the mandate to account. Yet global greed creates domestic envy and advances corruption.

Uniformly negative limits

There are standard ways of dressing and standard problems to address. Communist doctrine is essentially about mobilising the proletariat, and Confucianism is about their relationship to each other as individuals. Relational problems take precedence over all others – by all means be tough but be fair and above all just in any dealings with others.

But power corrupts and uniformed power corrupts uniformly. Little quarter is given in China. The uniformed police, along the Shanghai riverfront promenade, brusquely drive their electric 'peacekeeping' vehicle in amongst a pleasant field group of Chinese students. The students, regaling each other with anecdotes through little yellow plastic megaphones whilst their lecturers take note of their historical knowledge, move politely aside. There is room for the police to go round the group but no, the assertion of the uniform maintains not the *status quo* but the increasing distance between the people and the party's representatives.

The uniform standard in China is a negative one – do not treat others as you would not wish to be treated yourself. There is no positive direction but a demand to avoid taking the wrong one. Future options are therefore greater in potential variety and the desire for harmony infinite in its potential application – provided that application is within your own network. Treat others as you would be treated yourself, the Christian cultural control, tends towards standardization. Future options are thus limited but allow networks to converge.

Chinese relationships are thus much more varied in their approaches to problems and will adjust to the context, the particular situation defining the problem. Where contexts alter then manipulation through a series of increasing obligations is not at all unusual. The potential, therefore, for negative settlement is high. The answer is to settle obligations as quickly as possible. Never, ever, assume that obligations will go away over time – they will only become more expensive.

The wretchedness at the heart of things – disease and pollution

No matter how purposefully China may move towards a true comity of nations, if the country cannot bring under control and rid itself of its two most crippling scourges – both man-made and both rampantly expanding – it will not prevail. First it must address the internal, private pollution of TB, HIV/AIDS, syphilis and other STDs which have become a serious affliction for its migrant, floating populations. Second, the full extent of its external, public despoiling of the environment must be tackled. There can be no other course, else its population fails.

The other major blight on progress is the widespread counterfeiting, faking and 'knocking off' of other countries' proprietary branded products, euphemistically, if elegantly, known as infringement of intellectual property rights. This makes the Chinese entrepreneur more Raffles, the jewel thief, than the dishonest merchants they really are. Whilst imitation is always flattering, it is only ingenious innovation which will carry China forward into strategic product marketing and placement in the future. Yet many poor workers in China find the West's pricing of intellect an unfair burden set well above the cost of manufacture. The patent protection afforded to life-saving drugs may be seen by many of the world's poor as a trick to kill them off whilst manufacturers get richer.

The SARS crisis highlighted how gravely at risk China was from suffering a major pandemic. Up to that point, Government policy had been not to admit or simply to cover up such outbreaks of infectious diseases and to treat them as a state secret. The bird flu outbreaks also showed a reluctance to share crucial information on the spread of the infection to a wider world. The Government failed to provide the requested avian samples to the WHO and the international community and insisted on developing its own vaccines. The ingrained sense of secrecy and shame over the issue is pervasive.

In the matter of HIV and AIDS, the authorities do realize the full extent of the problem and are tackling it on a broad front. However, a major part of these measures involve simply jailing infected drug addicts and sex workers. The epidemic has not yet reached African levels and the infected do receive free anti-retroviral treatment, but medical monitoring remains haphazard and is at best based on guesswork. Blood donation has been a major source of the disease through infected needles. The likely infected are not routinely tested for HIV, yet xenophobia dictates that those returning from overseas will be! Blood plasma has been pooled and then used for random transfusions with inevitable dire consequences. Another corruption scandal has involved the supply of fake blood plasma as well as fake milk powder for infants.

The Party is aware of the extreme difficulty many Chinese encounter in obtaining medical treatment. There is no effective medical insurance system in place to enable people to meet the expense of any treatment or operation beyond routine clinic visits. Life-threatening illnesses and accidents can only be treated if patients and victims can borrow the money to meet the costs – this often brings crippling indebtedness. By far the most common affliction is hepatitis B, which has become almost endemic to the Chinese. Infants are generally vaccinated against the most common diseases, but there are still large gaps in the provision and availability of treatment, due in most cases to the sheer distance from medical care and lack of money.

The air stinks and the dust settles everywhere in Beijing

Air pollution is now life-threatening in Beijing, and in all the major and minor cities and towns in the country. There are two major root causes of the problem, our foreign correspondent friend claims. Firstly, the old Chinese refrain that 'the mountains are high and the Emperor is far away' portrays a ground level lack of concern, and secondly, economic growth is given pride of place above all else. But the Olympics challenges national pride and China's pollution is a foreign, as well as domestic, concern.

Naturally, the Government is concerned to create an orderly civil society and environment, but most certainly that can wait a little while longer until all these environmental protection measures are properly affordable. This delay is building into a dangerous catalyst for unrest in the country. There are countryside protests over polluted rivers. Factory effluents have caused workers to smash up plant and machinery. Fish, a major source of protein for many inland town and city folk, are poisoned and dying and the Government has responded with a 'green GDP' campaign initiative, a curiously ineffectual palliative, which papers over the problems by doling out energy efficiency targets – almost all of which it fails to meet. Another old refrain is sounded, '*Shang mian you zheng ce, xia lu you dui ce*', there are policies from above, but ways of dealing with them from below.

This environmental degradation provokes widespread local activism. International groups like the WWF and Greenpeace are also operating in China, but often as registered businesses rather than as NGOs, which heightens local suspicion of further meddling by foreigners. Forceful direct measures taken by activists invariably lead to their being jailed. Courage comes at a heavy price: detention and physical restraint is used to quash dissent. And all the while, that vital balance in the country is poised precariously along the rich/poor divide, buffeted in the struggle between reformers and conservatives in the Party. People are dragged headlong by a belief in the thrust for prosperity at all costs, if China is not to fall back into chronic social instability.

The thrust for prosperity is one which is not going to be met by domestic activity alone. The prospect of continuing environmental degradation whilst serving the global consumer is becoming unacceptable. The cash surplus of China is shifting overseas, regionally into Vietnam and Cambodia and further afield into Africa and South America. The Chinese will import expertise in cleaning up the mess and export purchasing power to pollute somewhere else. Others' backyards are fair game – they have no *guanxi* connections.

Culture and society – a home truth

Over the airwaves comes the headline news from China that the Starbucks coffee shop in the Imperial Palace precinct in Beijing has been ordered closed as an affront to the Chinese national culture of tea-drinking. It had been allowed to open under a compromise agreement whereby no signage was permitted. (A good wine needs no bush?) This was surely another small but significant instance of local culture always being liable to frustrate, trump or even snuff out the best-laid strategy. Or is it again a retaliatory measure against US interests? Probably not: more likely another example of how foreign 'connections' are easily amended.

CHAPTER 12

Harmony and people

> I hear and I forget. I see and I remember. I do and I understand (*Chinese proverb*)

Customs and practice control behavior. You have to do, to understand. It is a feedback process commencing with values through attitudes to behavior and back to customs. Adaptation in behavior feeds through to basic values and *vice versa*. Indeed as one Western anthropologist neatly puts it, 'Whatever else modern anthropology asserts – and it seems to have asserted almost everything at one time or another – it is firm in the conviction that men unmodified by the customs of particular places do not in fact exist, have never existed, and most important, could not in the very nature of the case exist.'. The Chinese are modified by their history. Accepting that Chinese values and behavior are different from the West implies that strategy may adapt but can still retain harmony as a primary custom. The harmonic control in Chinese custom is not a sound wave but a brain wave – a cerebral signpost to good relations. It is a mixture of philosophy and practice, with Confucius the relational preacher.

The collective (peer) pressure to conform from childhood in China makes for careful citizens. Harmony is the chord which is constantly struck within the social group – the family, the school, the company. Any discordance or open disagreement, even debate, is immediately discouraged. This is from fear of crossing or antagonizing others and of making enemies of them. Historically, to be involved in a lawsuit has been to invite shame and opprobrium.

A small vignette of the importance of harmony in everyday life: you are sitting with your (Chinese) family in the park enjoying a picnic. A few yards away (people are rarely more distant than this in China) another family plays a wailing song on a radio, which drowns out your conversation. You get up and in a friendly way (*Mafan ni* ... Would you mind...) ask them to turn it down a little. Your own family remonstrate volubly. It is the height of ill manners. You have jolted that precarious balance which must be maintained if you are to rub along together. Networks, like ships, should pass in the night.

An agreement to agree on detail later

There is little to no contract law enforcement in China. Reputation and face (*mianzi*) are culturally strong. Economic exchange is dealt with in the same manner as in Europe when state contractual enforcement was weak. Relations and standing in the community are extremely important. It is essential to ensure, therefore, that any exchange is relationally secure and that protection from opportunism is available. Such protection is through *guanxi*. Lawyers are unnecessary, except possibly for drafting something suitable for stock market release, unless they are well connected. Yes, lobbying and plea bargaining are global.

A contract for the Chinese is merely a way station on a long journey – more of a Heads of Agreement for them, since it is but a starting point. Initially it was a very basic document reflecting the *pro forma* structure favored by the Ministry of Foreign Economic Relations and Trade. Trying to include Western caveats and provisos whilst updating all the additions and changes necessitated by the updating of Chinese law over the last few years will take longer than the business project itself. The Chinese manager will always agree a basic contract – thus 'hooking' the Westerner into future negotiations.

Thereafter, at the business interface, the obligations and responsibilities of the respective parties will be agreed, not as potential sanctions, but as the mechanism of compromise to redress any imbalances. The Chinese have an aversion to any recourse to law and are certainly not a litigious people. It is preferable to resolve disputes and disagreements through discussion and by reaching an acceptable accommodation. 'My word is my bond' has the same force to bind in China – but in a slightly different sense: the bond here is rather one of relational trust and engagement than an I.O.U.

HRM – one human does not a resource make

Two (and more) humans create a relationship, a foundation for the construction of emotional and economic exchange and for building resources in the game of survival. The evolutionary way forward is by managing human relations. The Chinese use the harmony principle above all else. The individualistic West uses self-help gurus and powers of positive thinking – but relational harmony? No thanks, too much like work.

The Chinese concentrate hard at creating and maintaining relationships. If a flight to Beijing has a return date in one week, then six days will be taken up for relational purposes and the last day will be a disastrous rush. The Westerner must maintain an open mind and an open return. It could be the third or fourth visit before harmony is sufficiently established to warrant any real discussion.

This horrifies the US investor – and the Chinese manager knows it. Waiting until the baggage is checked for the return flight before offering a concession, but a take it or leave it concession, to the visitor is a successful ploy. Establishing a proper relationship from the outset, and that takes time, is essential. Most Western whingers fail to appreciate the subtle techniques of Chinese negotiation.

It is, however, so much simpler to think of humans as resources to be commanded and perhaps even consulted, but not as relationships to be cultivated. In such simplicity lies the downfall of the West. Human resources are treated as commodities. Managers of the West must move on, beyond group dynamics, to relational management and sets of mutual obligations, or the Chinese will retain their increasingly competitive advantages.

Harmony and, in that respect, being trustworthy and dependable provides a solution to a greater number of relational problems than any individual concentration on self-esteem, self-worth or a Myers-Briggs picture parade of psychological subjectivity.

A philosopher, a sage, not a warlord nor a high priest

Confucius lived in the state of Lu (present day Shandong Province) from 551 to 479 BC, and was no prophet but a disappointed counsellor to local rulers. He despaired of constant warfare and civil strife and retired at fifty to devise a means of restoring harmony to Chinese society. His teachings evolved from dialogues with disciples and his wisest sayings are set down in his 'Analects'.

Confucius can come across as an enigmatic snob, going on as he does about 'the superior man' but at his best he is superbly shrewd and wise. He is particularly down on misbehavior in public: 'respectfulness, without civilised behavior, becomes laborious bustle; carefulness, timidity; boldness, insubordination; straightforwardness, rudeness'. Hints of incivility in the West, when interpreted by the Chinese, will thus take on hues of cheek, cowardice, mutiny and bad manners.

Confucianism, however, is not a religion; rather it is a set of moral precepts, an ethical code designed to regulate the affairs of a state. It was not until the Han dynasty (c. 200 BC to AD 200) that his teachings were adopted in practice and temples built in his honor. His main teaching was that human relationships are naturally hierarchical – everyone must meet their obligations in these predetermined or voluntary relationships: ruler/subject; father/son; husband/wife; elder brother/younger brother; friend/friend. Only the last is not immediately hierarchical.

Most interestingly, there is no provision in his teaching for dealing with the stranger. The importance of these relationships is such that they define the position of the individual, the 'self', within Chinese society. The Chinese manager is, therefore, identified through his relationships – defining the allocentric, collectivist self. The foreigner must create a relationship to be identifiable. His or her company is a good starting point – the juridical person will then slowly become the trusted individual.

Confucianism has provided a backbone of family values, respect for elders, civility, personal integrity and personal trustworthiness. The Chinese tendency to deal with familiar foreigners as 'old friends' rather than through contracts is a clear enough consequence of this. It is also responsible for the Chinese inclination towards authoritarianism, denying subjects or subordinates any participation in decision making (such as voting).

A modern promise of prosperity, but with a catch

Another partial conclusion, within China, relates to a potential loss of control by the government. It takes very little for promises to remain unfulfilled. There are some making money, but many, many more in the rural areas who are not. People's expectations are higher than the planned economy can provide. Shanghai old town, for example, is rapidly disappearing under construction boots. Hard hats are so common that the younger engineers wear them, like baseball caps, back-to-front. We're not coolies, they proclaim, we look through theodolites.

Across the river from the historical Bund, the developing financial district in Pudong is more Tokyo than Tianjin, less Mao and more Marunouchi. The shopping mall, with its super brands, is quite magnificent. The office ladies and Shanghai salarymen go there and eat in *sushi* bars and *ramen* restaurants. But when Beijing decides it's time for anti-Japanese rhetoric, those bars and restaurants stay empty – at least for an acceptable number of days. Once the political point is made, the queues reform.

Such mass movement at the crooking of a finger creates a conundrum. What if the economic miracle fails to cascade down to the majority of Chinese? What if political powers call for another sacrifice and are turned down? In overhead signs at Shanghai airport, the authorities made it clear that penal law is being enforced to allow 'the harmonious development of economic prosperity'. Such a balance of commitment allows the great Chinese ship of state to sail with a fair wind – but she is tender, slightly unstable. It is as if the authorities expect a sudden squall to tip the ship.

Beijing airport, for example, warns the local (in Chinese) and the foreigner (in English) of the sections and sub-paragraphs of statutes governing the policing of borders. Ignorance of the law is certainly no defense, but a belief that such red neon notices are required smacks of fear, not fortitude. Does the foreigner, or national citizen, need constant reminding that the law is there to be obeyed?

And that defense will, ultimately, prevent democracy gaining a firm foothold. Trust, outside *guanxi*, is terrifyingly low. When asked to vote between Party members, any normal citizen says no. Who are they? Why should I vote for someone I do not know personally?

Harmony and people

Until a satisfactory opposition can be formed, so that a vote is between policies, not people, democracy will come a long way behind *guanxi*. In fact, most people with a vote are told what to do. Chinese votes are cast in the harmonious development of democracy.

Such traditional leanings slow any form of democratic process in China. Is democracy then an impossible dream? Probably not, but certainly it will be culturally difficult to implement. In the meantime, as a small step in a Westerly direction, flush toilets have been installed for visitors to Master Kung's birthplace. (This is a Chinese joke, in case you thought we were merely being harmonious.)

Chinese culture, however, is not solely derived from Confucius. The feminine *Yin* and masculine *Yang*; Buddhism; Daoism, the fatalist view; *feng shui* – the superstitious matching of the flows, literally relating to 'wind' and 'water'; all serve to set out the singular and quite distinctive characteristics of Chinese cultural controls.

A double of the other gender

If you think *Yin* and *Yang* are a pair of Chinese twins, it is because they are – but about as far removed from being identical as is conceivable within the cosmos. For the Chinese they are the two interlocking forces at the heart of things, perfectly counterpoised and held in check. You see them most graphically depicted making up the sphere at the centre of the South Korean flag with other symbols from the ancient *Yi Ching* (Book of Changes) – which determine good and bad fortune.

The forces of *Yin* and *Yang* have to be in balance, say the Chinese, for the world to turn on its axis. There is much soft astrology and cosmology woven around them (the late US president Ronald Reagan would have loved it), but essentially they derive from ancient divination and represent the opposites of human and material nature – *Yang*, the positive, masculine, the Sun, the soul; and *Yin*, the negative, feminine, the Moon, the body – without any one of which the world is suddenly out of kilter.

They are deemed to affect and regulate intergalactic relations, the state of society and bodily functions. They correspond very roughly to the *primum mobile* in Western cosmology. They are an endlessly fascinating alternative dimension; the fusing of positive and negative forces, the clashing of magnetic polarities as opposites attracted, a circuit completed and centred by an 'earth', without which there are sporadic 'shortings' of current, of the life force itself.

Whether scientific or metaphysical, such study yields extraordinary insight into the Chinese psyche. In everyday speech, the best Western analogy is possibly 'swings and roundabouts' or 'snakes and ladders'. *Yin* and *Yang* ensure that you lose by gaining and you gain by losing. How's that for a tough psyche to crack?

Imported provision for the afterlife

Buddhism was imported from India into China about 2000 years ago. Its introduction is famously chronicled in a great and humorous classic, *Journey to the West*, in which a monk on horseback with a clever pig and a wise monkey for traveling companions, returns with the new teaching to China.

Buddhism was founded by an Indian prince Siddarth Gautama, a contemporary of Confucius, who came to be known as the Buddha, The Enlightened One. Buddhists believe that all living creatures are destined to suffer a cycle of birth, death and rebirth, which can only be broken in humans by meditation, self-denial and the giving up of worldly goods to the poor. Those who have attained enlightenment are the *bodhisattvas* (saints) who await the rest of humankind on the threshold of Nirvana. In this Mahayana form of Buddhism, believers call on *bodhisattvas* like Guanyin (Goddess of Mercy) to intercede for them in achieving enlightenment.

It reached its high point of influence in the Tang dynasty (c. AD 600–900) but, as with the later dissolution of the monasteries in England, it suffered severe persecution by the state, from which it never fully recovered. Today many temples destroyed during the Cultural Revolution have been rebuilt. The parallels with Christianity are, of course, striking – particularly in the aspect of appealing for mercy in weakness. In reality, if you are male, large, bald but fat, you will likely have your belly rubbed for luck by appreciative passers by, since you make a very convenient surrogate Buddha for them.

Harmony and people

Alternative lifestyles

While Confucius deals with human nature, Daoism deals with man's relationship with the Universe around him. According to the Dao, harmony is achieved not by trying to change people's conduct or to tame nature, but by adapting to one's surroundings; the bamboo bends with the wind but stands up again afterwards. It has a great popular appeal in pointing up the paradoxes of life: weakness is strength (water wearing down rock); inaction is often the best action.

Daoism was supposedly founded by one Lao-zi (old Master), another contemporary of Confucius, who left city life to become a hermit in the western mountains. Fortunately, frontier officials got him to write down much of his observations and musings. He craved immortality through meditation and breathing exercises, and was also prey to the great human fantasy of flying – levitation to the clouds features prominently in popular paintings. Daoism explains the Chinese streak of fatalism and long suffering in the face of oppression and bad government.

Popular wisdom has it that all successful people claim to be Confucians. Failures are invariably Daoists because they seek to stand the world on its head. Modern Daoists would join the Greens and campaign as activists for the environment and against the Bomb and new motorways – if they were only allowed to.

How to make work play and play work

That renowned character from the mediaeval morality plays, Five Wits, was compounded of the five essential mental faculties – Memory, Imagination, Fantasy, Estimation and Common Sense. Which faculty is more highly developed in the Westerner and which in the Chinese? More tellingly, which one does each exercise more sharply for true mental recreation and fun? The logical Western mind differs considerably from the Chinese. However, this is not a matter of casting aspersions on each other, but of recognizing our relative strengths, so that we may complement one another.

Because of the very concrete nature of their life, the Chinese seek refreshment in the parallel universe of fantasy – dream and make-believe are their dearest recreation. You have only to watch a Chinese film to appreciate their supreme power of magical realism, evocation and imagery. You have only to watch them gambling. . . you must never in this context speak about risk. Westerners, conversely, seek to throw off the shackles of abstraction by making concrete projections in their mind's eye – this is the power of imagination, as Shakespeare said, to give *'to airy nothings a local habitation and a name'* – hence the spinning jenny, the telephone and the hovercraft. But the Chinese have their fantastic fireworks – so much more escapist and colorful.

Keeping the ill-wind away

The Chinese believe in the importance of the spirit of place in the siting of homes and offices; in the juxtaposition of favorable features in the location they build on and inhabit. The study of *feng shui* shares the same concern as Western geomancy, when it attempts to divine the best lie of the land for building and positioning from a handful of scattered earth. Homes, offices, factories and graves are constructed in such a way that they maintain the close press of mountain, wind, water and dragon spirits in delicate balance.

If you see someone like a local government surveyor wandering around carrying strange instruments – could that be a theodolite/compass/set square/plumb line/spirit-level? – this is the *feng shui* man. He will study the ground, the prevailing wind and water courses and the position of trees to determine the most favorable location. The trick is then to site the building near the head of a dragon or the tail of a tiger – invisible forces which are highly benign, unless disturbed – when they can wreak havoc. Beware the fast-running river by that pleasant sheltered bank – it will race away with your money downstream. The carelessly assembled location plan can spell disaster.

Building or even renting an office without paying due heed to *feng shui* will assuredly affect your staff and bring ill-fortune. The carved Chinese lion statues outside banks, notably the old HSBC head office in Hongkong, guard the vaults from the flowing escalators and elevators and were placed there by *feng shui* advisers. Peace of mind

Harmony and people

can certainly be bought, even for Schindler 'rivers' and Otis 'waterfalls'.

It is this belief in a field of forces which must be kept in constant equilibrium that underpins the practice of *feng shui*, this search for invisible springs and affinities, the mysterious inter-connectedness of things, the relational prime factors.

Chinese man's most important commodity

The Chinese are made up of individuals in a collectivist society. There are restrictions on the individual and on his or her actions. Group harmony, rather than individual needs, is sought. Importantly, the effects of a collectivist culture are such that networks develop and subsume the individual within them: 'self refers to the individual in individualistic societies; among the allocentric majority... in collectivistic societies, the self is generalized to include a network of certain other persons'. The cultural context will control different personalities by promoting characteristic response patterns.

Face, however, is the individual's defensive relation to the network of *guanxi* – the idiocentric counter to a predominantly allocentric culture. It is an important element in *guanxi* transactions and is two-dimensional. Face is dignity, self-respect and prestige but is a mixture of personal behavior and attributed or achieved status. The importance of face is relevant to the maintenance of harmony in the group.

Whilst maintaining harmony, we would all arrange, if we could, to appear in as favorable a light as possible when we put on a public face. We are – with the exception of the extremely unworldly, perhaps – susceptible to some small vanity and flattery. The Chinese are most adept at 'giving face', that is, enhancing the esteem and regard in which seniors, elders and colleagues are meant to be held. They do this through solicitous and deferential attention, questioning and concern, and by making way, giving precedence to other people's needs, actions and opinions.

Praising someone to his managerial superior gives great face. The mishap or minor calamity that the Chinese fear is the suffering of, or causing, a 'loss of face' to others through inattention, carelessness or insensitivity. Real or imagined slights can cause real humiliation if publicly perceived to have been suffered. The agonized refrain can then be heard: 'But where can I put my face? I can't hide it or put it in my pocket.' The exposure has been too naked. Causing someone to lose face is on a par with character assassination as a social sanction. But not in barbarian society – the ease with which one can err in front of a foreigner is a useful learning device for the Chinese.

What might, therefore, constitute libel or slander and grounds for a Western law suit is, in China, as nothing compared with the visible and audible damage inflicted to the reputation and *amour propre* of the person affected, when witnessed at first hand by others. What in the West might be lived down with a self-deprecating laugh, becomes in China a matter for memorably poignant recrimination. Dueling, on a point of honor, would be the closest Western analogy. Any failure to acknowledge the status of senior officials or to consult with a particular authority in seeking approvals will never be forgotten – such is the power of the established order of doing and being.

Opportunism then becomes controllable within the relational network. Fear of loss of face is very real. But at network peripheries there is little mutual obligation and poor facial control. The present Chinese problem of official 'opportunism' can thus be partially explained and is not without Western precedent. Western opportunistic investment and behavioral finance is often thought as the tension between greed and fear. In contrast, as we point out, the Chinese tension is between greed and *guanxi*. If there is no ostracism within one network for actions detrimental to other networks, then greed takes over. The property developer network and local officials may prevent any loss of face by bending or ignoring penal law. Face, within the *guanxi* system, no longer tempers greed in a humane fashion.

Overseas, however, the established order is different. One of our respondents, working in the UK, notes that Western self-deprecation allows her considerable leeway in the learning process: 'well when I talk to the British I don't really care about looking silly (laughing) but... honestly... when in China I am concerned very much about my performance'.

Western trial and error creates a faster search for solutions; face is less of a problem within a protective legal structure.

Linguistic mountain-crossing demands adverbal tensing

There are few distinct tenses in the usage of Chinese verbs. The tense is indicated more by qualifying adverbs than by suffixes. Hence the general sense conveyed is that of living in a kind of historic present. We recognize that the Chinese revere the past and that they go forward looking backwards. This burden of harmony through time is borne by the use of proverbs and parables in speech and pictographs in their written language.

Two issues are important to remember:

- The question of time becomes very subjective. The past, present and future are not immediately part of the grammatical construction. Indeed it is worth considering that time overlaps in Chinese thinking. Western concepts of time are related primarily to equations involving simultaneity. The four dimensions of space–time are needed to specify an event. The Chinese search for harmony (rather than truth) requires language to be less specific (even tending to obfuscation) and space and time are flexible constructs. Western women are not averse to compressing time – such as counting each year after their 21st birthday as composed of 24 months. A Western male emphasizing the number of lunar orbits to an earthly one quickly learns the opposite of harmony.

- Anecdotes are the means of revealing and making meaning clear between Chinese and Western managers when abstract concepts are discussed. Just as Christian parables have served as examples of conceptual thought, so the Chinese manager is able to understand meaning much more easily through practical vignettes (a visual story board) rather than hermeneutic analysis of sentences and descriptions.

When harmony is the overriding principle, rather than the truth, it is essential to be adaptable in discussing space, time and meaning. Just imagine the legal horror of accepting fable rather than fact. Rudyard Kipling, who knew that the East could not be hurried, explains:

when all the world would keep a matter hid,
since Truth is seldom friend to any crowd,
men write in fable as old Aesop did,
jesting at that which none will name aloud.

That sums it up.

Becoming your own alter ego

Increasing harmony and trustworthiness can be partially achieved by the adoption of a solid Chinese name. It helps if the Western name is sufficiently phonetic to be pronounced easily. The adapted effect is designed to create an established, less alien sense of conformity – it is, after all, only an attempt to bring the pronunciation into phonetic Chinese characters. The bearer of a name like Leigh or Lee, for example, will have little problem devising a suitable moniker: William Leigh could become Li Wei. Call in a bilingual lawyer only if your name is Algernon Prendergast. An adapted, subtle translation is needed (rather than a clumsy transliteration).

It is vital that any Western name has a handsome appearance, sound and meaning in Chinese. The pattern of success starts early and sets the note of dependability. Time spent with a lawyer or local business partner in choosing a name to grace your business card is well invested. It is, after all, one of the first steps in successful personal and corporate marketing. The Chinese manage very well themselves. Their names, being phonetic, render easily into English, such as, Li, Wang, Han, Bao. It is with their chosen English first names that they can really stand out. Who can deny that a Wellington Chu, a Peter Pan or a Napoleon Wu demand attention and recognition, whatever their physical and moral stature?

The world's most-spoken secret language – clues to breaking the code

Mandarin Chinese (*Putonghua*) is the *lingua franca* of East and South-East Asia, spoken or understood by over one-fifth of the world's population. It is a four-tone, phonetic, grammatically simple language which sounds business-like, precise and pleasant on the ear – even when spoken by people who are evidently not scholar officials.

Harmony and people

The purest form is spoken in Northern China and the best and most distinctive in Tianjin and Beijing, where the inhabitants roll their tongues around certain words, providing a musical flourish to sentences. Formerly the preserve of missionaries and machinery salesmen among foreigners, Mandarin will soon become the most popular language and medium of instruction throughout Greater China. It is therefore harmonious for the Westerner dealing at a boundary with Chinese organizations to learn some of the more common words and phrases – a task quite easily accomplished even by the more tone-deaf and tongue-tied of communicators.

Reading and writing the language is, of course, somewhat more demanding – but greatly facilitated by the fact that many of the simpler characters are stylised pictures (pictograms) or symbols which clearly depict a person, the crescent moon (a month) or a stream (water), for example. Taking up the art of brush-stroke calligraphy is one way of discovering the beauty and balance of these characters, together with their meaning and their frequent use of metaphor in search of harmony.

Learning a few phrases of greeting and courteous enquiry leads all the more quickly to that bonding of aspiration with trust that tends to cement relationships. Herein lies no reaching for the moon, but a simple earnest statement of intent.

Human aspirations are universal. Robert Browning's

> *Ah, but a man's reach should exceed his grasp*
> *Or what's a heaven for?*

chimes well with the Chinese saying:

> *Yan gao, shou di* – eye high, hand low

in its soulful brevity.

Dui bu qi and *Bu hao yisi*

A very useful expression – after *Ni hao* (Hello), *Zai jian* (Goodbye) and *Xie xie* (Thank you) – is the one that is the most spontaneous and natural. This is *Dui bu qi* (Sorry or Excuse me). When completely lost for words, a foreigner may utter this simple phrase to a Chinese with the total assurance that such prompt fellow-feeling will be felt. It means instant exculpation from unintended physical or verbal offence and is unequivocally conclusive.

Another great leveller is *Bu hao yisi*, which is used as a preface to an awkward request or admission or adverse news and means roughly, 'I am really discomfited/embarrassed'.

It is a tacit acknowledgement of another's face and also demonstrates a cultural awareness of the need for harmonious relations between people, breaking down the barriers of facial expression and spoken language. In short, both expressions are swift dispellers of consternation and can be used to turn someone down without hurting his or her feelings, without letting them lose face.

Pai dui

These are the two most magical little words in the Chinese language. They have the power to persuade without cant, coercion or cajolery. When uttered in any public place where you must queue or wait for a place at a counter or a window at airport immigration, in a railway station, in a post office they have an instantaneous effect. They mean 'Get in line!'. There's no room for droll British or American outrage or irony or Continental cursing here; just a simple appeal to the national conscience in one individual. Just dare them!

Meiyou

This is the word heard most commonly in China. It can mean variously 'No', 'It's off', 'There ain't any', 'No way', 'Not on your life', 'It's more than my job's worth', 'It's not there' or even 'Gone!', 'Empty' or 'You're wrong'.

Meiyou guanxi – 'It doesn't matter' or 'It's of no consequence' – is used as a calming device as often as not to exculpate a foreigner from some crass *faux pas* or indelicacy of speech or behavior. Basically, he's not networked so no worries.

Harmony and people

Meiyou wenti – 'No problem' or 'No trouble' – invariably means that there is a problem, but the Chinese are too polite to point it out at an early stage. When the second syllable of *meiyou* is heard by itself, there is an instinctive feeling that there must be something missing. *You wenti* is a wake-up call, translated as 'Houston, we have a problem'.

The Chinese reckon in millennia

Patience is not a virtue in China; it is a practical necessity. Real patience is nurtured and finally born by a lengthy cultivation of such a strength of spirit that we must fall back on ancient Victorian usage to express it. Fortitude is part of it, forbearance another, but the right word has become so rare that is has fallen into disuse. That word is longanimity. Note that it is one of the last fruits of the spirit, not one of the first sterling qualities of character.

Long-suffering must be endured in the tortuous, but ultimately triumphant quest for the Holy Grail of a contract and a longstanding business relationship. The Chinese character for patience is pronounced *ren*. This should be on the desk of everyone doing business with Chinese organizations. Try intoning its single syllable as a soothing invocation in times of high stress.

San shi liu ji – zou wei shang ji

Finally, when it all gets too much, the Chinese way is to up sticks and walk off. This particular Chinese expression can be expressed rudely or politely – such as 'Just stuff it' or 'Forget it'. It is the ultimate sign of exasperation. 'Just leave it, we've had enough'. Even Chinese perseverance is not inexhaustible.

Such failures in perseverance are now more likely than not. The pressures on the proletariat are increasing. They are not limited to price inflation but also affect the conflict between the developing economy and the environment. Provinces are very protective, with limited information being communicated on common environmental issues. Observers have estimated that 70% of Chinese waterways are polluted, with nearly half a billion people suffering poor quality water. The Party mandate needs massage... in a big way!

Values are the mainspring

Traditional values – honoring of ancestors and striving through education to advance the family's standing – are embedded in a tribal and clan way of life. They have re-emerged vigorously after many decades of suppression. Mao outlawed Confucianism as feudal and the Party line is still that all religion is superstition. There have been cases, for example, of US messianic zeal easily converting overseas Chinese on educational programs in the US to Christianity. Beijing then quickly switched government training courses to the more pagan UK. State atheism is used much as the Nazis used it in Germany to create an ideology of invincibility in war or by the French revolutionaries to overthrow their monarchy and establish an entirely new-made order of absolute equality and justice before the law of man.

It is based on the fear that religion (particularly foreign, imported religions) will weaken and dissipate the Party's authority. The reality is that the theories of Party dogma have become quite detached from the ancient practices of the people, the locomotive of the state uncoupled from the people's van. What this means is that the real power to move people to action and to order the outcome of events is reverting to the village headmen and clan leaders. These are the officials who will settle local disputes through the authority vested in them from control of ancestral temples and shrines.

The Party has progressively cut back taxes as a gesture of appeasement to the people. Thrown back on their own resources, local authorities are developing a spirit of entrepreneurialism to help themselves replace these revenues. Local temple authorities and clan associations are the first lines of recourse for this reformation.

This is the era of integrated religion, which the Party finds convenient not to discourage. The Falun Gong movement and the Christian Church are still held in great suspicion and closely monitored. Their rising number of adherents attests to their growing appeal and the precious oxygen that they supply in a country where people are accustomed not to breathe too deeply for fear of inhaling either toxins or persecution. The fresh air and space created by these forced measures of personal autonomy are at last restoring to the Chinese people their natural rhythms of commercial enterprise and initiative.

CHAPTER 13

Beyond control

> An isolated system shall pass from a state of order, through states of relative disorder, until it reaches the state of maximum chaos (*The Second Law of Thermodynamics*)

China is now less isolated but is still a system in a state of relative disorder. Political control is designed to adjust individual behavior and to implement strategy. Leaders may guide strategy by putting in control systems. Leaders appeal to the people – for votes in a democracy, for obedience in a non-democracy. Leaders use value-based rationality but prefer emotional rhetoric. Promises made to democratic voters are as empty as the promised utopia of totalitarianism. Neither has the higher moral ground – both are strategically specific. Leadership is hierarchical, leaders choose their controls carefully.

The problem for the Chinese leadership is the same as that for the West. Why should foreign ideals cross a national boundary without control? The Chinese people had a civilized way of life whilst the West waddled in the Dark Ages. The Chinese will not adopt Western leadership values. This chapter looks beyond simple controls to complex systems.

Western leaders are trained in the West, but Chinese leaders are also trained in the West

The new generation of Chinese leaders are those who went overseas in the first period of reform from 1978, mainly as students and visiting scholars to Europe and the USA, retaining strong basic human values. There is some similarity between Christian ethics and Confucian moral guidance. The difference between the value systems

– and it is a big difference – is that Western ethics are based on the individual doing what the personal conscience believes is right, while Confucian morality depends upon the individual doing what the group believes is harmonious. Western values are shaped largely by a sense of individual guilt; Chinese values are driven largely by an anxiety to avoid group shame.

Chinese leaders understand this, but the West tends to ignore it. Individual rights are not the same as group rights. They intersect, of course, as rather different notions of honor and integrity. Harmony within a community is important. The Chinese do not enshrine any form of human rights legislation. How can it be enforced? Group behavior is self-correcting and so is group economic behavior – unless the groups are of opposing networks. Chinese controls govern Chinese group behavior.

Much economic theory is based on 'rational man' yet Western individualistic rational man failed in Japan. It will also fail in China. Chinese economic strategies are very long term. The Chinese leadership is turning its economy into a market economy, but this economy is based on collectivist, not communist, nor capitalist, ideals. Chinese economic management must eventually clash with the West's. Chinese economic behavior has not changed under different governmental structures and is 'in some sense a natural outgrowth of Sinitic culture'. Western leaders must survey the topography of Sinitic culture before creating any road maps – or else cliffs and canyons await (witness the Middle East).

The transfer of information – a Chinese intranet

Several decades ago Western best practice resulted in the growth of conglomerates, the massive multinational firms that seemed to know no national boundaries. Subsequent advances in market information started to restrict the benefits of internal corporate knowledge across disparate businesses. Single focus strategies came into vogue. But the restricted and relational nature of information sourcing and analysis in Chinese organizations indicates that the conglomerate is presently the best way to go in China. It is, however, subject to strategic control of an intuitive nature.

The inefficiencies of markets (and the difficulties which Western partners face in the transfer of information) make Chinese conglomerates popular for growth seekers. In particular, the benefits of selling many different Western branded goods through large Chinese organizations does allow greater internal knowledge transfer than through single vertical chains of agencies. Remember that the solution must fit the problem, especially when there are difficulties in transferring and interpreting knowledge. Remember too that the Chinese in the West have access to external knowledge and have privileged access to internal information – quite an advantage for strategic positioning and indicative of an overseas strategy leading to conglomerates by acquisition.

Open plan problem solving

Chinese organizations have Chinese walls and they certainly have Chinese doors. All doors are treated as open. The head of an organization or departmental line manager is expected to know what is going on. 'You are the boss, you should know' is a common refrain in Chinese hierarchies.

Knowledge is gained qualitatively, primarily through the eyes and ears. Strategy is derived from the sixth sense – intuition. A small easily solved problem is often used to commence discussion of the real issues at hand. Indirect communication maintains harmony and only by avoiding the quick solution to the simple problem will the larger problem and its attendant difficulties be discussed and resolved.

A simple minor issue cuts the isolation at the beginning by identifying *common* social contexts, thus allowing a smooth flow through into any difficult and contentious area. The Westerner who only solves the first problem will never get a chance at the bigger one – he or she will believe that the first firm link has been forged in the chain, but it will be the weakest one. The gradual progress to the ultimate prize is not attained by answering simple questions but by setting out the partnership understanding. The Chinese expand control through a form of capillary action, a slow seepage.

Meaning from form

An essential link in the Chinese chain of control is the maintenance of relationships. Letter writing, like gift-giving, is designed to maintain mutual understanding. The letter does not therefore need a strong business structure but should refer to the relationship rather than the object of the relationship. After a general greeting and inquiry as to health and family, it is possible to discuss the business relationship and, in closing, briefly mention any commercial points to ponder. The control is implicit, but also extant.

The greatest exponent of relationship management was the amazing Madame Chiang, fox spirit and firefly light of the life of Generalissimo Chiang Kai Shek. She was a miracle of transvergence. Born as Soong Mei-Ling to a family of fabulous wealth, she was educated at Wellesley College for Women in Macon, Georgia. She made a righteously dutiful marriage of money with power to Chiang, introducing him to the Christian faith, to which he seems to have remained remarkably impervious. But how he played his diamond card! In his country's hour of need for money and *materiel* to keep the Japanese at bay and then fight the Communists, he despatched her to Washington, where she bewitched the Americans into channelling aid to China, giving them to believe that the country was a fledgling democracy.

Still alive at 105, she had issued at strategic intervals oracular writings of such arcane erudition and overwrought syntax that even hardened native speakers of English were sent scuttling to a thesaurus. She had simply entered and spoken to the West from within its own paradigm and rendered it powerless to resist.

Ringing the changes

As in Japan, the virtues of the supreme leadership are not expected to be brought into question. It will take a while yet for the Chinese to get quite accustomed to living without an Emperor. The group is still more important than the individual – the *Danwei* (work unit) used to run everyone's lives – where they worked, lived, traveled and what they consumed.

Even in post-Marxist–Leninist–Maoist China there is still only a very slowly widening freedom of choice in occupation or living quarters, except amongst the most senior cadres or richest entrepreneurs. Chou En Lai, when asked his opinion on the effects of the French Revolution, reportedly said that 'it was too soon to tell'. Chinese change is designed for longanimity.

Individual aptitude simply leads to an assignment elsewhere. It is sometimes enough to make people dream of exile to the country – anywhere. The one exception is, of course, the dispensation made to employees of joint ventures with foreign firms. They enjoy some mobility. Otherwise, most kinds of initiative and innovation are discouraged. Cronyism is rife in the hierarchy of bureaucracy – 'mates' are looked after, but seldom allowed to step out of line. In China, all men are brothers; but they are also their brother's keeper. Natural controls are lateral controls.

Guanxi – not a provincial but a global network

This word – which always looks like a name for one of the provinces of China – is indeed a name for the province of well-placed contacts, influence and decision-makers. We have already discussed how it is changing, but entry to this province remains restricted and can be costly. It is a prerequisite, a necessary routine to making headway and advancing business interests and economic growth. It is a control system and depends upon group logic.

There is much smoke and there are many mirrors in the discussion of *guanxi*. Tapping the term into an Internet search engine provides thousands of references. Many undervalue *guanxi* and others deem it to be overrated. One thing is for certain, it is more misunderstood than any other Asian custom or practice.

There are three basic factors to *guanxi* which are essential to remember in order to understand how Chinese organizations work and managers relate and control:

- *Guanxi* is a dynamic transaction system for the exchange of material resources and of information (knowledge). Transaction cost theory explains the nature of *guanxi* as a governance over opportunism. Resource base theory explains its nature as a control over resources. Real option theory explains when it is worth commencing the initial investment into someone else's network.

- Face (*mianzi*) is transferred through a *guanxi* transaction and reciprocity is created through mutual obligation (*renqing*). Harmony is the purpose. If face is cheap compared to the obligation then a debt may not be repaid. Harmony has a value adjustment in terms of pricing the transfer of *mianzi* against the cost of *renqing*.

- *Guanxi* networks protect the allocentric Chinese individual from penal law (and have done so for many centuries). The networks are therefore retained as relational protection against inadequate contractual law enforcement between businesses. They are also retained within government as a political defense system.

We all have *guanxi* in some form or other. Seeking aid for a problem by entering another network for assistance is not unusual. The Westerner asks accountants, lawyers, even tennis coaches, for help. The relational problem, however, is that the cost of entry to a Chinese network is not immediately covered by credit card or cash. A future real option is created and future manipulation through that option is common.

There are three things necessary for doing business in China – *guanxi*, *guanxi* and *guanxi*. Each of the three is different but explicable. Consider *guanxi* as a dynamic system for controlling Chinese strategy and economic exchange within their social system. Understand it through Western theory and interpret it accordingly. It is not magic. It has a Western mirror image in strategic theories on transaction cost, resource base and real options.

But it can be a tricky matter. The local politicians can see their future options running out when their positions become open for appointment. Gain what you can whilst you can. Peasants know who owns what paddy field from historic *guanxi*. There is a clash when the protection from past penal law is insufficient to protect the family from future appropriation of traditional land holdings. The political network has no obligation to the peasant network – at a local level. Central authority is ensconced elsewhere.

The network boundaries are not part of the *guanxi* process. They are unmeshed gears within a poorly functioning machine. It is only with considerable technical skill at joining together its various components that the machine keeps going. It is this skill which can fail the party leadership, the party politicians. The problem for the West rests with failures between Chinese political and military networks. The supreme command is missing. Imperial edicts and communist diktats can, in modern society, no longer operate on the traditional call to obey or else. The skill is to substitute the economy for the imperial guard. But an open economy is also open to wider relational manipulation – the Chinese machine is oiled by trust, an ephemeral commodity.

The relationship matters

Gift-giving within Chinese culture is very common. The gift, in Western culture, is designed to show appreciation of the giver to the receiver. In Chinese culture, gifts indicate an appreciation of the *relationship* between giver and receiver. It is a process of reciprocity. Subsequent gifts are then exchanged – either in material form or in the form of business favors. Gifts are not bribes, but they do start a trustworthy trend, of giving and receiving, in maintaining, solidifying and controlling a relationship. The levels of the reciprocity will escalate. If in any doubt, be the first to give – the first gift is the cheapest.

Giving or taking a Western-style bribe, for almost all Chinese, is unacceptable. However, it is perfectly in order and indeed sound sense to develop a friendship with people of influence. This is where the confusion arises within the Western mind. Foreigners do not often see a clear distinction between small gifts, given as tokens of esteem ahead of a favorable decision, and an out-and-out inducement paid for services, permits or approvals otherwise probably impossible to obtain.

This distinction is indeed a fine one, but does color and cloud the notion of corruption in China, which does not have quite the rainbow range and hues that it has in the West. The Chinese spectrum is narrower and simpler and pivots on personal relations.

Western corruption is often more insidious; it is the corruption of friendship – and collusion. In the West, where business and friendship tend to be kept apart, there is a well-thumbed rule that mingling them is unwise, if not improper. The Chinese see nothing untoward in marking friendship with small gifts – indeed it is only sensible to do so to keep it in good repair. Why separate friendship from business, how else can business deals be structured?

At the global border, the Chinese will expect to develop and use personal, trusting friendships to advance a joint cause – it is altogether cheaper and more wholesome and ultimately more rewarding in negotiations. Foreign, as well as domestic, controls must recognize this system of organizational and network relationships, and adjust accordingly.

There are no short cuts, but your reputation will precede you

There is no great secret or surprise attached to what makes for a successful outcome in dealing with, and securing business from, the Chinese. A few moments' reflection will acknowledge that the following factors are absolutely fundamental:

- *Previous repute*: This is the single sharpest suit. It is not necessary to be a household name (although it helps), but to be a body known to a third party who can vouch for a trustworthy reputation to any intended client or partner. The network gate opens.

- *Personal rapport*: A good working rapport based on a genuine appreciation of each other's skills. Knowledge and talent is essential. This will take time to establish, but once trust is given, it is sustained through the frustrations of early setbacks to achieve that special strategic alliance. Trust maintains the network control.

- *Patience*: this is not a virtue but a virtual necessity. Trust is not instantaneous, the control retains its initial defenses.

Tenets and beliefs to live and die for

Within a general context, Chinese values can be accepted as: hard work, respect for learning, honesty, openness to new ideas, accountability, self-discipline, and self-reliance. Western values are more individualistic: freedom of expression, personal freedom, self-reliance, individual rights, hard work, personal achievement, thinking for oneself. The problem in the West relates to society providing systems for individual preferences. In Asia, individual preferences are subsumed to societal systems. How else does the world really divide?

The Chinese are a concrete people, where Westerners are more often abstract and idealistic. Suffice it to say that they feel their values viscerally. They live them out with the full force of a fierce, even harsh, love of country and family like no other people, except perhaps the Koreans.

In truth, there are two things, above all others, which make the Chinese feel their values are under assault and which cause them to get immoderately exercised and bent out of shape: the first, any dispute over money – the late meeting of any payment under a debt due; and the second, any questioning of the integrity of the Chinese empire – independence for Tibet, let alone Taiwan, is quite unconscionable. Financial pressures are only acceptable if reciprocal. Territorial pressures can create domestic disruption at the borders, whether Tibet or Taiwan, with future global disruption quite probably emanating from both territories.

MBA (Marketing By Asia)

One immediate area of convergence and potential cross-over fusion in the business area is the MBA Program, which might be more aptly called a Makeover in Business Arts or conversion course in capitalist stratagems for Chinese youth. A main centre of learning in China is the CEIBS – the China–Europe International Business School in Shanghai – where novices are exposed to the esoteric arts of accounting and marketing and the strange new science of management. However, the real value of such a novelty for the Chinese is the extended period of study they may enjoy at business schools in Europe and the United States. In HR Management, or as it used to be called at INSEAD, Man & Organization, the Chinese are second to none.

The chief deficit to be made up by them is in marketing, largely because of the relative lack of branding in their international market (a legacy of subcontracted manufacture for Western brands) and in the poor variety of choice in their domestic market.

The modern Chinese manager has fluency in the language of his or her host country and its commerce, is well trained, educated and highly aware of the global marketplace, its benefits and its shortcomings. Whether representing a state-owned organization or an entrepreneurial enterprise, Chinese managers have a newly acquired sense of spirit tempered only by their seniors' traditional reluctance to make waves beyond a Chinese breakwater. Technological and Internet advances are enabling expatriates to retain their Chinese hierarchy whilst extending their relationships overseas.

National boundaries create disparities – in business operating costs, in the levels of brand investment, of market segmentation, of public relations and advertising, in determining pay scales, promotions and incentives, in the human relations management of recruitment and redundancy, of group versus market tensions, and of population growth and environmental *lebensraum*. For now, the Chinese are spoilt for choice in terms of international partnerships on their domestic turf. The rate of increase in foreign direct investment may be easing, but not its magnitude. The Chinese continue to gain Western knowledge at home and overseas.

CHAPTER 14

Chinese strategy

> He who asks is a fool for five minutes, but he who does not ask remains a fool forever (*Chinese proverb*)

Strategy is dynamic and iterative. It is simply a control system, feeding in past events to theorize a future event. David Hume, the Scottish philosopher, spotted the need for theory centuries ago when he noted that no set of past observations on their own could possibly predict a future one. Using established values and beliefs in creating strategic theory reduces guesswork in dealing with future uncertainty. Strategy links the past and present to the future. It combines the resources of the institution and organization with the retention of future options to decrease uncertainty, and with transactional governance styles in controlling opportunism. Opportunism is probably cultural, strategic and endemic in human nature. How opportunism is controlled and governed differs across the world.

Ultimately, strategy must deal with both uncertainty and the social context – political, industrial and military controls. Leadership, on the other hand, targets the emotional side of the brain when tackling uncertainty. A leader, such as Mao, tries to change a social context to drive home his or her emotional theory. Chinese strategy is traditionally socially driven. Strategy, the predictive theory, draws guidance from a networked system. Decisions are implemented in full cognisance of past historical cultural controls.

But China is changing. The leadership appeals to the emotions of the Chinese. Open the markets! Change our enterprises to become more dynamic! Accept difficulties now for greater gain later! Let the entrepreneur flourish! Make the military mighty again! The past way is not the future way! Overseas experience is being warily tried out domestically and a market logic is now competing with the social and group demands of *guanxi*.

Chinese strategy is, accordingly, slowly moving away from the socially embedded theories of the past and accepting a crafted, market bargaining and learning approach. But beware: this is not an evolutionary perspective – the Chinese markets are not sufficiently effective in creating an 'evolve or die' environment. It is a try it and see approach; an ask and find out approach. Western techniques and practices are being tested for their suitability. Just as the Japanese chose the best and adapted it for improvement, so the Chinese are adjusting Western tools to Chinese standards.

The strategic adjustment is not to the West's advantage. This adaptation of tools does not complement the West's way of doing political or economic business. Until the West takes and adapts socially networked strategies, then the Chinese will have two birds in the bush whilst the Western bird migrates. The social context in the West is now of increasing importance. Certainly the marketing excesses of the West, the hard sell of mortgages and insurances and loans and credit, are now proving to cause those in power some embarrassment. Why bail out the banks when the poor who owe the debt are the ones in need? The pragmatic Chinese managed to integrate their social resources, future options and controls over opportunism some millennia ago. The practice of *guanxi* and the establishment of Chinese values based on relations between people should be copied, not caricatured.

Opportunism is costly to control

To effect economic exchange, a transaction – an exchange of resources – occurs. The potential for opportunism is high. A governance system is required. The Western legal system, however, cannot cope with overly complex contracts. Contracts become unavoidably incomplete. No set of lawyers can possible predict, and cater for, all potential outcomes. Subsequent disputes are resolved after the event and seldom in court – more often in arbitration. The Chinese contractual strategy is to avoid litigation.

Within a *guanxi* network, high levels of situational and character trust depend upon cooperation and reputation. The qualitatively sourced information through the network system also results in limited rationality. The high internal trust levels within *guanxi* networks make 'hearing is believing' a distinct cause of Chinese bounded rationality. In the West, the fear of enforcement of sanctions in contract law serves as a substitute for trust. Westerners happily conduct business with each other without trusting each other. The law protects the buyer from shoddy goods, from bouncing checks and from failures in contractual performance – at least in theory.

In a complex situation, or one operating outside the law – such as tax evasion by tradesmen – the Westerner is more inclined to use a network. Whether from pub or club or Masonic handshake, the new partner in complex transactions, or in transactions involving a grey market, requires a risky level of trust for a satisfactory exchange. Remember *The Third Man* – the black market trades of post-war Europe were very Chinese in character when operating in an untrustworthy environment and a legal vacuum.

Transaction cost theory dictates that trust is warranted when the expected gain from placing oneself at risk to another is positive, but not otherwise. Western strategic theory provides an excellent argument for joining a *guanxi* network when doing business in China. It also explains why trust is low outside a network – where is the gain, what can the outsider bring to the party? At the periphery overseas, the Chinese manager commences with a contract and, once it is signed, accepts a networked relationship ready for future mutual obligations.

How much is an investment worth?

There are increasing levels of uncertainty in global economic exchange. Whether hedging activities, or derivative trading, ease or exacerbate that uncertainty is not the purpose of this argument. Certainly the Western view, that curbs on such activities are unnecessary, does not allay the Asian suspicion that future wealth is being controlled by quantitative computer programs. The market crash and credit crunch in 2007/8 confirm this suspicion.

The past debacle of the US Savings and Loans, and the Long Term Capital Management demise (a most spectacular hedge fund crash), is a stick with which to beat the West. Western indignation about Asian government interference in business is met with disbelief. Did not the Federal Reserve bail out the Western banking system several years ago? Are the reserve banks of the West and Japan not doing it again now? And yet the West continues to suggest that the East should not bail out its own financial and business systems. Blatant hypocrisy!

Recommendations

A focus on strategic decision making at the working level of the individual Chinese has been neglected in the past. Too often management strategy has concentrated on leadership and views from the top. This book subjects the Chinese manager to an holistic overview. In aligning Western economic theory with the Chinese social context, we project a cross-cultural understanding and interpretation of Chinese decision making.

We recommend that Chinese expansionary strategy be now viewed as dependent upon a wider set of governing control criteria, a set containing Western and Eastern characteristics, *en route* to its approximate state of unstable equilibrium. What is unclear is whether any causal relationship exists, or will exist, between social contexts and national strategies, political or economical. We believe that they are intertwined and inseparable. We argue that adaptation to future uncertainty is concurrent with socially different Chinese controls.

The three elements in decision making – uncertainty, context, emotion – create three basic combinations. Strategy (covering future uncertainty and group or social context), national and institutional or corporate controls (covering emotion and social context), and leadership (covering emotion and future uncertainty) must integrate for optimum solutions.

Contrary to popular argument, we do not see leadership as a strategic problem solving element on its own. Without individual emotion for rhetorical arguments, without the social context for the disciples and followers, leadership fails. Leadership is, in our opinion, tactical not strategic. In China, leadership promises prosperity by observing the West, imitating it and then bounding past it. But we must not forget that the leaders of China are engineers first and politicians second. They will concentrate on engineering the future rather than adapting to it. Tactically, they are more likely to imitate than innovate.

Imitations are notoriously prone to errors in the detail, and errors multiply until catastrophic. With lower power distance at managerial levels, leaders must tread carefully to preserve the overall strategy of Chinese economic hegemony. Take emotion out of the equation and objective choices may take a Western path. Greed or *guanxi* becomes a probability judgement: what can I get away with at my own network boundary? Chinese network bias is not the same as Western individual bias.

Unfortunately, the objective strategic choice often fails. The failure of markets to match fundamental pricing has been studied in the West, arguing that strategies are often based on inefficient markets. In other words, inductive reasoning and rules of thumb prevail. The scripting, or framing, of problems often dictates the reply. Is the glass half full or half empty? Errors and bias drive markets away from fundamentals. Communal Chinese conditioning and individual emotion all affect objective market reasoning.

Spanning the boundaries

We may thus conjecture that Chinese transvergence (the change in characteristics towards modern flexibility) is currently closing the following historical gap in business and management practices:

Western	Chinese/Overseas Chinese
Broad ownership (Institutional)	Narrow ownership (State or Family)
Participative management	Patriarchal management
Dispersed decision making (slow)	Centralized decision making (fast)
Initiative encouraged	Initiative discouraged
Promotion on merit	Promotion through *guanxi* connections
Managers work with job description	Managers work as directed
Concentrated areas of activity	Highly diversified operations
Services contracted out	Vertical integration
Accrual accounting	Cash accounting
External financing	Internal financing

However, rather than merely becoming more Western, the Chinese will adapt new tools and practices to maintain their loci of control over operations. The present trends are indicative of several bridges across the divide between West and East: broader ownership (but not control) through flotations and acquisitions, lower hierarchical structures with increasingly dispersed (but speedy) managerial decision making, initiative neutral, promotion on abilities within a group structure, task orientation but under broad guidelines, diversification for knowledge transfer but with a focus for opportunities, contracting out formal legal and accountancy systems whilst retaining internal network cash controls, and a mix of internal and external financing. The hybrid Chinese organization is more adaptive, more aggressive, more focused and more capable of finding solutions to new problems than in the past.

Human obligations or manipulative methods?

The Chinese, without any Greek philosophers to define structural aspects of theory, rely on relational practice to transact and generate resources. Their relational practices have a conceptual structure recommended in the Western literature as a useful form of governance for complex contracts. The corollary implies that for simple obligations between two parties the use of contractual governance is preferable. In transacting with foreigners, reliance on legal principles, rather than Confucian precepts, is affecting obligations at network peripheries and helping to lower manipulative methods.

If a single element in Chinese culturally driven strategy is to be singled out as significant then the potential demise of the *renqing* obligation must be chosen. Present benefit in exchange for a put option, of unspecified size and timing, is a restraint on competitive advantage. Contractual governance for small transactions lessens the likelihood of a *renqing* option being called in an expensive manner in a future unspecified time period. Future unknown obligations, possibly punitive, will become purely optional and not compulsory. Faust would have approved.

Summary and discussion

We can summarize Part II in terms of traditional Chinese values and *guanxi*. Traditionally, China retained its integrity by rejecting barbarian intrusion. The old imperial ways were initially challenged by Dr Sun Yat Sen and then officially swept away by external interference and internal strife. China has suffered remarkably over the past century. The movement from imperial Chinese values through foreign occupation and domestic civil wars to communism and now capitalism would turn the heads of most. Without a strong governing control, a defense against practical, theoretical and ideological change, any nation would have been split asunder. The internal Chinese identity is contained within a group and network control – *guanxi*.

But that control is adapting, altering towards a compromise capable of increased flexibility, continued persistence and patience, decreased levels of manipulative mutual obligation and, when dealing with foreigners, less reliance on face as a control over behavior. There is increasingly less respect for seniority, but increased levels of reciprocity. The perceived authority of the West is insufficient to command anything beyond that demanded by harmonious manners, mutual respect and reciprocity of action. This may sometimes be transformed into mutual distrust and retaliatory action.

Such value alteration is seen in the behavioral changes in *guanxi*. The increasing use of contracts in business – the short-term consideration rather than the long-term obligation – enables a less moderate but more adaptable style of doing things to grow in practice. The need for high trust levels when forming a long-term relationship remains, but the frequency of short-term relationships is increasing. The information and transaction exchange in the *guanxi* network continues, but with more formal analyses and higher 'entrance fees' at the network boundaries.

Summary and discussion

Opportunism is becoming jointly controlled, relationally and contractually, but is thus weakened, with poor relational enforcement and vague legal edicts causing consequent failures in transactional systems. Resources are adjusting to transfers of knowledge of an increasingly formal nature – implying greater numbers of alternative courses of action and less intuitive, more varied solutions to global problems. Future options require high levels of trust in the exchange enforcement, but global trust is not a common commodity outside a cultural network. Unlike the individualistic West, the collectivist Chinese have very low levels of trust beyond their peripheries. A negotiated compromise, an arbitrated level of governance, must ensue. The Chinese will not take the lead; they prefer to follow the *rules* as practised.

But what do the Chinese managers alter when adapting to Western ways? We reviewed a range of queries about the relative importance of external and internal forces to see how the loops in Figure I.1 might alter. The results produced several interesting changes in our inductive approach to any market versus group logics argument:

- Firstly, the Chinese see reciprocity and risk as strategic factors and consider them to be linked to problem solving. You cannot have one without the other.

- Secondly, and perhaps more importantly, the Chinese see holistic decision making as a group strategy. Does that not make more sense? The Chinese seek an integrated, harmonious, group-dominated solution.

- Thirdly, and as a further explanation, the family control, decisions regarding the family, and especially family loyalty, are perhaps directed towards the corporation. Modern Chinese may be turning, dare we say it, Japanese. The family is putting business first.

- We warned that statistical inference can overturn our old ways of thinking but one thing is statistically certain. The Chinese are seeing market forces as significantly more important than traditional collective controls. Increases in the importance of external forces are associated with a decrease in internal group pressures. Conformity is beginning to go. An increase in the use of formal problem solving using Western methods is anticipated.

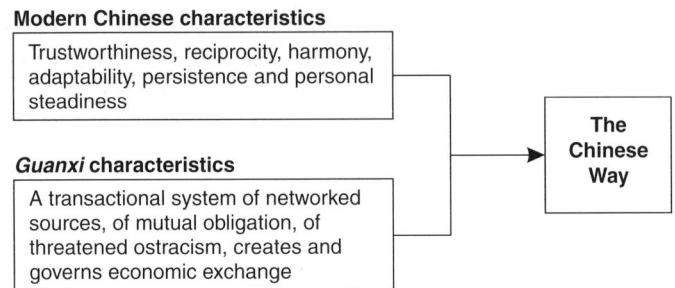

Figure II.1 The Chinese Way.

We should now look again at the implications for strategy and combine, into one set of predictive comments, the knowledge gained so far. See Figure II.1.

The benefits of gaining Western problem solving techniques are held in check by the present strength of domestic control by senior politicians and managers in China. Strategic change contains the caveat that modern Chinese decision making is dependent upon the degrees of freedom delegated from the top. The global Chinese manager, in Europe, Africa or South America, is much less constrained than the domestic operator.

The Chinese can, therefore, maintain their basic ways of doing things in the domestic arena but adjust to global political and economic demands when trading internationally. It is, presently, a partial but aggressive adjustment. Better to take control of the sought-after international resource, either by acquisition or merger or might. Compromise across paradigms is feasible but a new paradigm of partial strategic rules will provide only partial strategies. Partial strategies do not deal fully with uncertainty. Ambiguity in Chinese institutions and organizations is likely to increase in the short term. Deductive *and* inductive problem solving must create successful strategies for adoption into cultural ways of doing things. Then Chinese competitive advantage will be truly challenging.

PART III

Chinese predictive perspectives

> Men of affairs venture sometimes on acts that the common judgement of the world would pronounce absurd; they make their decisions on apparently impulsive and human grounds. (*Joseph Conrad in* Nostromo – *The Silver of the Mine*)

Introduction

In Part I, we provide a theoretical grounding for the divergence in Western and Eastern mentalities and a method of understanding the Chinese (and indeed any culture) by considering the *time*-dependent *rules* in the *space* of a dynamic system. We also emphasize how strategic thinking and problem solving in managers depend upon their views on uncertainty – and their finely calculated approach in the assessment of risk via *guanxi* relationships. Strategic thinking then depends upon balancing resource transactions whilst maintaining future options. In Part II, we provided an explanation of how Chinese perceptions of their place in the world inform their attitudes and we then illustrate, in the Chinese dynamic *space*, the effects of their *time*-dependent *rules*.

First of all, we must accept that the *rules* have changed. Chinese state-owned enterprises were allowed under strict government investment criteria to invest overseas. Since 2003, private companies have been able to do so. The pace of investment overseas is thus changing rapidly due to the institutional alterations at home in China. It is not, therefore, merely the suitability of strategic attraction in the overseas market that has occurred, but the *time* change in the granting of permission from the Chinese authorities.

The accelerated nature of Chinese overseas investment is noted by the United Nations as being dominant in two areas – Africa and Asia-Pacific. In Africa, the advances in Chinese investment place it second only to South Africa; in Asia-Pacific, it is second only to the USA. This diversification can be looked at strategically – as resource control in Africa and border control in Asia-Pacific. In other words, China is taking the opportunity to increase its resource base and to extend its options in both areas.

Out of China

The nature of global economic exchange makes overseas investment not only desirable but also essential to secure competitive advantage. At the present time, the forgotten continent of Africa remains on the periphery of Western vision. The Chinese reciprocal relationship, high context communication and their 'gift giving' predilections make for an automatic match with many African anti-Western governments.

Short-term Chinese opportunism in Africa means immediate assistance to African governments needing commercial essentials – factory output and bills of exchange. Long-term control over commodities essential to Chinese growth is the ultimate aim. In Sudan it is oil; infrastructure in Kenya; minerals, hotels, transport, equipment and more in Zimbabwe, Algeria, Angola etc. (In South America, it is oil, timber and fish. The Amazon rainforest is now being marked Made for China.)

Nothing will be sacred – take the Westernized World Food Program as a further potential gift-giving target. The US control over the aid to the starving ensures good prices for American wheat and for American ships. The total costs of actually delivering a tonne of grain to the Sudanese for example, are estimated at 10–12 times the cost of purchasing the grain on the international commodity markets. If China were to enter the grain markets in a really big way – to feed themselves better – the pricing economics of basic resources feed through the supply chain rapidly. Agricultural prices are taking off, US flag ships are earning high charter rates, and Africa is likely to starve without Chinese help.

China calling

The nature of Chinese reciprocity allows an affinity with the African (helped by no history of Chinese colonialism) to exchange maize for minerals (mainly oil) and rice for mining rights. Cash is exchanged for a present obligation – to be called on later. The extent of Chinese penetration into the global marketplace is underestimated. Economic colonization by China is a product of Western intransigence. Mining resources, and their rise in Western stock and commodity markets, are mirrored in China, but for Chinese oil and mining stocks.

The World Bank positively endorses the lessons of China's transformation policy for Africa. One of their African vice-presidents, Oby Ezekwesili, is reported to have said that Chinese assistance is of a nature which helps African citizens to take advantage of globalization. The incentives offered by China are fundamental, she pointed out, and that 'it does not matter from which part of the world they come from'. Perhaps Orwell's point (see p. 37) is equivalent to the Chinese not being eccentric – and certainly not being new colonials.

The Chinese are, ultimately, bringing African (as well as South American and Middle Eastern) governments into a barter trading pattern, ensuring the long-term future of Chinese factories, fields and population. Present global problems are a result of Western consumerism but future issues will be of Chinese economic demand. Chinese domestic demand will trigger Western inflation and increase, not decrease, friction in global trade. After all, what consumer hardware does the West make that the East actually wants? (Not even airplanes: China is planning to build its own in Tianjin under Airbus guidance.)

Tapping into the Asian source

China is intent on binding relations with the two richest resource hubs on the planet – close to home is Siberia with its largely untapped trove of oil and minerals (with Mongolia, still a vassal state rich in copper and coal, straddling the borderlands) and somewhat further afield is the 'Irabian' Gulf with its abundant oil stream. To the south, Australia and Indonesia are key sources of liquid natural gas. Hydroelectric stations and coal will provide the bulk of home-grown power generation for the present. Coal will continue to be a major industrial fuel for another twenty years until the polluting blight it causes forces its replacement by electricity and nuclear energy. But China's greatest resource by far remains its people – their energy and industry – in the realization of its global aspirations.

The organization responsible for marshalling its most abundant resource for its overseas expansion is FESCO, the government's central casting agency for personnel assigned to work in joint ventures with foreign companies. This organization has designs on becoming a kind of global Manpower, providing Chinese crews and workforces for multifarious infrastructure and construction projects in developing countries worldwide. The difference with Manpower is that the supplier of services can also fund them.

The surplus – silver mountains of the mind

The Chinese trade surplus (on current account) surges and billows bigger by the month, mounting up and drawing the country forward with an awesome impetus. At the present rate, the excess value of China's exports over its imports, its trade surplus, approached $300 billion for the year 2007 (and this is on top of the country's massive foreign exchange reserves). For all the Government's attempts to rein in the boom with taxes, foreign demand for Chinese products has leapt, while imports have fallen in the wake of moves to slow the fevered pace of construction and investment in new materials and equipment from abroad.

China is locked into an upward spiral of processing imported commodities and goods and exporting its value-add into a sizeable mountain. As local firms move up the value chain, this surplus is further compounded. Some partial offset of this excess may be achieved through shifting production overseas via mergers and acquisitions. However, the real resolution of the problem over time will surely come from the Government's boosting industrial and, in particular, consumer spending to reduce the excessive private savings rate. In the short-term, China is unlikely to budge on the revaluation of the *yuan* until it threatens to destabilize the economies of its major trading partners, most notably the United States. It is, however, noted by China that the US sub-prime market in 2007 destabilized the world economy more effectively than any Chinese currency trades. This collapse was more plainly due to crumbling capitalist bricks on Wall Street rather than any protectionist reinforcement of the Great Wall of China.

Nevertheless, the Chinese surplus has to move overseas somehow. Partial offsets of this surplus are the purchase of US Treasury Bonds (about $400 billion held in 2007, with the Japanese holding a little over $600 billion) and diversification of its foreign exchange reserves into currencies other than the US Dollar, such as Sterling and the Euro. China is also moving overseas into a 'sovereign fund' of state investment shareholdings and forays into private equity for exceptional returns via investment firms. However, these are presently small adjustments compared with the real investment lines being laid down in Africa, the Middle East and Latin America.

In Africa, China is establishing special economic zones in Nigeria, Tanzania, Zambia and Mauritius, clusters for Chinese companies with import duties and tax incentives designed to induce these companies to set up permanent bases on the continent. Large amounts are also being poured into infrastructure. At a recent conference with African leaders in Beijing, one African beneficiary claimed that the money came with no strings attached – 'If there are, I can't see them, maybe they're made of nylon'. In Latin America, Chinese direct investment accounts for over one-third of its overall direct investment worldwide – chiefly in Brazil (railways, low-cost housing, communications and satellites), Venezuela (oil production) and Argentina (infrastructure).

The other great Asian giant

India, China's main neighbor to the south, is held at bay by the vast natural buffer of the Himalayas but looms large as an economic rival. It appears to hold a number of aces sufficient to trump China as a serious contender for economic supremacy in the region. These aces include, on the face of it, a more highly skilled workforce and a linguistic, democratic and educational legacy from the British Raj, equipping its citizens with a high standard of legal and commercial understanding. In addition, the government has actively promoted free enterprise and entrepreneurial activities. There is a traditional upper caste of merchants (ranking with priests and warriors) in India and no stigma attached to trade.

Set against these advantages, however, China, unfettered by lower caste mobility ceilings, can offer an undoubtedly greater racial (and non-religious) homogeneity, with higher growth rates and a rather better infrastructure. In addition, the contribution of Overseas Chinese to the national economy is markedly more significant than that of Overseas Indians (unless Mittal Steel, Tata or Cobra beer prove us wrong).

Moreover, it is clear that China's overseas strategy is also to forge strong alliances with potential competitors in the larger emerging economies such as Brazil, Turkey and Central Asia in order to maintain its commercial influence and competitive advantage. The Chinese are also arriving in Eastern Europe and the European Union. Chinese links with Iran and the Sheikdoms of the Middle East are increasing. The West has lost its grip there. Israel is seen as a vassal state of the USA (or is it just democratic reciprocity?). There is an increasing economic and political power base being made available for China – with India as the nearest neighbor.

It is India that threatens China and China that threatens India: the elephant versus the dragon. The USA and Europe are customers but China and India are competitors. The Indian push for global recognition is playing on the Chinese psyche. Recent concerns amongst Chinese businessmen in Beijing are less of the rising yuan and more of the power of the rupee. A race for resources by half the planet's population is a threat to economic and environmental stability. Overseas alliances by China will arise from defensive and offensive strategies. The West may watch and wonder, but the economic hegemony created by Chinese strategic relationships and financial reciprocity will result in a powerful global imperialism. More than grass will be trampled when the two great Asian beasts broadcast their territorial warnings. Harmony may not be enough.

More BRICs in the wall

The way the world increasingly divides is between sources and uses, between suppliers of raw materials and processors of these commodities, between Brazil and Russia on the one hand and India and China on the other (the 'BRIC' countries, or building blocks of a new world order). This division will become more and more apparent as the world approaches the mid-century. China and India will be the chief controllers over finished goods and services, while Brazil and Russia will be their chief suppliers of raw materials for processing.

Demographically, India has the greatest chance to grow over the period, since its working population will probably increase relative to China's in the wake of the one-child policy. Both Brazil and Russia will be overshadowed by India and China by 2050, but of rather more significance, however, are the emerging market strategies of these countries and their relative interdependence. Brazil's great resources of iron ore (for industry) and soya (for foodstuffs) will be highly prized by the other three as essential commodities. Although its growth rate is lower, its prosperity and stability are presently greater than either India's or China's thanks to its globally integrated economy and manufacturing potential.

Russia will continue to trade on its abundant energy resources (chiefly oil and natural gas) which will mask the fall in its working population, its volatile government and its poor infrastructure, while engaging ever more closely with China to dynamize its faltering economy. China has a crucial role to play in curbing Russia's increasingly roguish, bristling and ballistic new regime by drawing off some of its more deadly firepower into more productive pursuits.

India's manufacturing and services capacity, particularly in industrial and consumer goods and especially in IT and programming, will enable it to become a major economic force to be reckoned with as China's major competitor in these areas. China's annual bilateral trade with India has quadrupled over the four years to 2006 to almost $20 billion. Within this vital nexus of interdependence, China's power to galvanize the economies of these other three countries through strategic trade and investment will be paramount.

Over the mid-to-long-term, China is looking to meet domestic demand as a priority. Two-thirds of its people are largely missing out on the benefits of the current boom. Social welfare will have to be a priority if disaffection in the inland and nether provincial regions of the country is not to cause destabilizing social unrest. The levels of medical facilities and social security systems for basic health, welfare and employment will need to be swiftly raised to meet the clamour for equal treatment from many millions who feel marginalized and dispossessed. Larger farming communities will be created and developed into effective economic units and the fall-out of employees from the former state-owned enterprises will need to be taken up in redeployment into jobs in other new industries to be established in Central and Western China, well away from the magnetic coastal conurbations of the Eastern seaboard.

Along with all this, the cost of massive clean-ups of environmental degradation (already a catalyst for widespread organized protests) and of corruption – held in place by officials' threats of mutual whistle-blowing – will need to be urgently addressed as a budgetary priority. Strangely enough the West has a tremendous opportunity to offset its consumer purchases by 'bartering' clean up and waste management expertise. In Taiwan, the influx of foreign expertise in this area during the late 1980s and early 1990s was welcomed. Trading part of China's surplus for a cleaner environment is a safe political step.

China calling

Executive summary

This final part of our book uses the dynamics already identified to create a series of predictive scenarios. We contend that neither the West nor China can afford to rest or continue to act within their present opposing value and belief systems. There is an urgent need to adapt to the use of others' political, economic, societal and technological templates. The advantage to the West is that the Chinese inductive, holistic style of decision making makes them polymaths – capable of understanding and adjusting to different situations and more accepting of other ways of doing things. The disadvantage for the West is that we are very largely monomaths – still mired in single and singular ways of thinking and doing.

15. *National controls* explains the rapid trends in the progress towards internal integration and external adaptation, as Chinese managers' relationships mutate. Gradual shifts are profiled as part of a continual political adjustment.

16. *Strategic controls* illustrates the drivers in the trend towards 'transvergence' (the balanced desire for market forces to accept societal needs) and the behavioral changes which may be confidently anticipated in the Chinese manager.

17. *Modern Chinese management* catches the tide in the movement for a changing society. Relational governance is slowly admitting a more objective style of arbitration rather than state-aided judgements as the endgame.

18. *ChinaTech* shows how a move away from reliance on American hardware and software is gathering pace. A Chinese layer of formatting techniques will produce a unique blend of firewalls – a protection against foreign control.

19. *Qu Xiang He Fang?* is an imaginative projection of the implications of our findings for the new shape of structures, groups and the dynamics of mutual interaction between China and the West. We posit the extension of the Chinese role into the international realm: how global strategies will enable the Chinese to gain vital advantage in political, economic and military power both at home and abroad.

20. *Unpredictable conclusion* – and your guess is as good as ours!

Finally, we summarize our argument and open up a discussion on what might be.

CHAPTER 15

National controls

> Raise your sail one foot and you get ten feet of wind
> (*Chinese proverb*)

To check the wind now blowing through China, Ted Fishman makes an important academic point when he exhorts us all to see 'beyond the amazing stories'. Simple anecdotes are insufficient when trying to understand China. Depth of research and of interpretation is required. Chinese organizations and institutions are changing in response to strong external market stimuli and the urgent need to secure commodity sources and supply. The challenge lies in identifying the time span for change. Military occupation throughout history has altered national ways. Isolation, militarily and economically, is no longer an option. Dominant nations will dominate. It is a question of control. Are Western political systems still dominant or is China on course for a sustained competitive challenge? The stories are out there, and they are explicable.

Let us take 'best practice' as the standard survival mechanism for the *rules* in problem solving. Since geo-political problems are of Western conception, it is Western solutions that are being continually urged on others. By this logic, democracy and civil rights (but with preferential treatment for many) are to be commonly adopted – either as a result of economic sanctions or of military actions. But are Western *rules* truly pre-eminent for international solutions? Is the cure perhaps worse than the disease?

We opened our argument in this book by reflecting on individual rights versus mutual obligations. We also highlighted the Asian tendency towards inductive arguments. From a political perspective where does this lead China? President Putin of Russia allegedly remarked to President Bush of the USA that he would adopt

US democratic *rules* only once he saw them working in Iraq. The Chinese inductive conclusion is that Western democracy only works in the West.

The past is the future China

The Chinese now earnestly desire to close the circle of the last century's misadventures and restore the frayed edges of their Empire – first Hongkong, then Macao and, after that, Taiwan. This last is proving somewhat more intractable in the recovery than the other two, since it has not only frayed but well nigh sheared away from the mainland as well. The pirate haven of old has become a high-tech redoubt, repository and laboratory for China's modernization.

Formosa may yet remain beyond the pale of Imperial reach not in any military sense but in the hearts and minds of Taiwan's people, who are stubbornly true to their own peculiarly Chinese heritage, a mixture of many different regions of the mainland, their customs and cuisines. Democracy has long since sailed past the point of no return on the island and living standards are markedly different from the mainland. Joint accommodation will be achieved only with tough bargaining of the 'one country, two systems' variety. Autonomy for direct trade and investment should replace the trading of territory for negotiated peace.

The single biggest sticking point in relations between Taiwan and China is that neither side will acknowledge the other's position or is willing to compromise. China claims that Taiwan is an integral part of China and brooks no dissent in the matter. Taiwan claims that only the people of Taiwan can decide this. There is in all of this no concept or allowance of choice or democratically taken vote on the issue. It is a zero-sum game and becoming a distinctly perilous one. The results of the 2008 elections in Taiwan dictate its future. The DPP Party raised the stakes alarmingly (and attempted to pre-empt the result) by announcing a referendum on independence for the island. This clearly becomes a dangerous flashpoint, since the military balance has evidently swung in China's favor in recent years.

This is why the Chinese Government is so anxious to maintain the *status quo* – through its initiatives such as reaching out to the Taiwan business community with offers of preferential trade and investment treatment, the United Front strategy. Its natural recourse is to deal with Ma Ying Jeou and the KMT Nationalist Party, the devil it knows best, a potentially friendly devil now moving from opposition into power. The issue is sensitive because it touches on the very legitimacy of the Chinese Communist Party itself as the government of China, because the Party knows that any military action against Taiwan would have horrendous consequences for global stability with China probably losing out. Taiwan knows that they know this, and this critical state of tension will persist until some sort of *détente* can be negotiated. Returning the KMT to power may prove to be the democratic solution for the non-democratic Chinese. This will take the most extreme finesse to handle. The *rules* are complicated.

But after Taiwan? Where will the Empire pull its strings and what overseas connections will be called upon to realize past dreams? The dreams of the mainland masses in their past immiseration are hardly ever about Western baubles. They are about security, freedom from want, a good round meal before sleep and a few half-holidays of happiness. All else is an absurd and lascivious luxury.

Politicians, however, have the luxury to dream, especially of power. Politicians' dreams can be the people's nightmares. What do dreams and nightmares foretell?

The future Asian nightmare

Once known as a tourist playground and raw materials paradise, the countries of South East Asia are using their cheap labor in factories – the plantations of the future. The deft fingers of youth are employed in electronic manufacturing, chipping away at the poverty of their fathers. The inward investment by overseas companies has been immense, but to accompany the hardware production there has been an influx of financial software and expertise turning productive minds to the monetary machinations of the stock market.

The Chinese connections, which linked cash from Taiwan and other overseas Chinese sources, found their way into the great financial game. Emerging market funds, quickly formed by predatory investment houses, channelled cash into stock markets ill-designed for large inflows. Broking houses catered for the housewife as well as the politician and criminal. The housewife sat in the street, restaurant or broking house dealing room, watching the screens, gambling happily in the atheist belief that emerging markets always went up.

The eminent economist John Kenneth Galbraith is better able to sum up the position than we are. He notes that crises are caused simply by debt where, in one way or another, the level of debt 'has become dangerously out of scale in relation to the underlying means of payment'. When the Chinese are selling their granny and her accumulated wealth to speculate in the stock market, we know that a fall is due, especially when the debt is leveraged against granny's farm. Warren Buffet is out – that's a good enough sign for all.

In Taiwan, the senators and sinners had special VIP rooms where they could plot political deals or the ramping of shares. Trading on margin and vast credit from the more unscrupulous broking houses allowed stocks to move in specific directions with particular timing. The overseas fund managers quickly followed 'buy and sell' orders and allowed the VIP rooms to dictate market fortunes. The market makers of emerging markets were not being paid simple salaries – they were collecting from all concerned, all who followed in the hopes of making a fortune.

If Taiwan is a controlled Chinese experiment in financial and democratic freedom, a sample of a larger population and problem, then global *rules* in the Chinese *space* will fail. The Taiwanese financial market in the 1980s sounded sufficient warnings, which were ignored by overseas players. The gambling instincts of the Chinese and their predilection for gossip suits an emerging market. Everyone can take a punt, but more importantly, they can circulate rumours, believe in their inside track, argue furiously over half-baked prospectuses and convince themselves that their mother's second cousin, working as a cleaner at a potential new listing, had discovered the true nature of the company's fortunes in a waste basket. The foreigner obligingly follows, claiming that index correlation within Asian markets reflects economic integration. The foreigner should have visited the VIP rooms. Only now, nearly a generation on, is the Taiwan market back to its late 1980s levels.

National controls

So, when Shanghai sneezed in the spring of 2007, the instability in Western financial markets revealed a poor immune system. A minor market, ramped and rampant, causing global fright? Could the sophistication of Western hedging systems, of computerized arbitrage, of incredibly expensive fund managers, count for so little? Can the West be that vulnerable, dependent upon Chinese fiscal decision making and taxi-driver punts for market direction? Is genius in short financial supply or is it erroneously measured by Wall Street bankers' bonuses?

And when the US sub-prime market causes the Western capitalist *rules* to fail then Western central banks step in. Capitalism's open markets and loosely regulated activities are really examples of Western ways which are not applicable to the opportunistic and secretive Chinese. Can China not remain a global workhouse keeping Western electorates sweet with cheap consumables and low attention spans? The Chinese dream is diverse but it does not include foreigners, their chaotic markets and *post hoc* regulatory controls. Control of China, by China, and for China, is a central policy of Beijing.

Of course, Asia does have its foreigners, its own diversity. There is considerable variety in the characteristics and habits of mind of the East Asian peoples – just as among Europeans, the Germans, Italians and Finns for example, have very different languages and cultural identities. However, the strong thread which binds the political and trading tapestries in East Asia is identifiably Chinese. Local Asian governments know this but may not admit it. Their problems are primarily those of cohesion – keeping the indigenous population under control – and their problems increase in inverse ratio to stock market valuations. Race riots are not the preserve of LA.

As Western and Asian protectionism increases, we believe that China will become embroiled in anti-Chinese sentiment in Asia. The sparks will be North Korea and the Bahasa speakers of muslim Malaysia/Indonesia. Both feel threatened by Chinese influence. Malaysian democratic elections in early 2008 are causing concern to the ruling Bumiputra who see local Chinese (and Indian) votes as challenging. The Japanese may continue to suffer from historical mistrust but they do not make up an important component of overseas populations (except perhaps in Hawaii and Peru). Jealousy of Chinese trading abilities elsewhere in Asia (and Wall Street) will increase with political support for regional expansion – backed by at least the threat of military pressure – emanating from Beijing. Tibet is a first major step on the road to consolidating Chinese power. And yet, strange as it may seem, Japan will prove to be the natural barrier to Chinese expansion. An old and ancient set of volcanic islands have a proud people with a determination to maintain their independence at all costs.

Regionalization, therefore, not globalization, is the primary political challenge for the Party. We must remember that the Chinese government and state-owned enterprises are run, in the main, by engineering graduates. The political approach is very mechanistic and often keeps the old engineer's trick of at least a 10% safety margin in any design. In other words, Chinese diplomacy is not one of smooth words and soft actions. It is often calculated with slide rule precision and if it means brinkmanship then it will be brinkmanship with something up the sleeve. Gnawing slowly away at the problem will ultimately bring the solution. But it will be a solution based on equilibrium. Do not tell the Chinese to do something that you will not do yourself (remember Confucius).

To save energy, the Chinese are holding air conditioning temperatures above 25 °C. How much more cold is it in a New York or Houston office in the summer? What about energy saving and global warming? So do not invade Iraq and tell China to lay off Tibet. Chinese policy is practical and primarily regional.

CHAPTER 16

Strategic controls

> Better the head of a chicken than the tail of an ox
> (*Chinese proverb*)

At the Western interface, in contact with the UK way of doing things, Chinese managers have been observed and questioned. This has enabled us to identify a degree of structural change in Chinese strategic decision making. From a global perspective, there are demands on the Chinese manager to comply with international legal and accounting practices, especially given the recent increase in companies listed on overseas stock exchanges. Conflict is possible where traditional relational control over economic exchange is superseded by legally enforceable contracts and financial reporting standards. But what is it that is creating potential conflict?

In two words: Western consumerism. Consumers create demand and demand makes money for Western governments – why else have taxes on goods and services? China is meeting much of the demand, banking the Wal-Mart shopper. But the debt from the West, the Chinese dollar dues, must be paid. The debt due from the US to China is now large enough to create problems for China. Just as a thousand dollar debt gives the customer a problem, a trillion dollar debt gives the bank a problem.

China's problem is such that there is no Western strategic solution. If there is, then why is the West not resolving it? Telling the East to do it the Western way did not work for Japan, so why should it work for China? Slowly and inexorably, China's traditions will alter to resolve the problem Chinese style. The first step will be to stop buying Western tickets for a Chinese show. Creating its own markets in the *space* with the simplest *rules* is not merely a case of domestic consumer demand. Chinese control in the overseas financial services and commodity markets is an essential Chinese strategy.

Their traditional cultural values are now adapting to make that possible. Values such as conservatism, non-competitiveness and even 'face' (*mianzi*), are all decreasing in their power to control Chinese behavior. The Internet, a low context (not face-to-face) method of communication, is also altering the way many Chinese traditionally interact. The West is more accustomed to written, verbal and low-level body language transfers of information. The Chinese need for relational interaction is not lessening within the younger generation of managers, but personal interaction is now increasingly being substituted by an electronic interflow of information – one which can quickly create misunderstanding.

The most important business changes are in the relationships between parties. The deferential nature of the hierarchies in Confucianism, discussed in Part II, is decreasing. The *guanxi* network of connections and relationships is altering. The human obligations of *renqing* are now of a much more manipulative nature than in the past. It is as though economic forces are prodding away at traditional restraint, causing a warping and a piecemeal application of Chinese relational values.

Local inroads and responsiveness

So far we have concentrated on the relational adjustments necessary for regional reaction to foreign trade with China and for global integration and growth of Chinese operations overseas. Growth is accomplished by modifying overseas Chinese activities to satisfy local institutional requirements, in particular legal, regulatory and trading needs. We have not yet focused on local responsiveness – making inroads locally within the overseas markets.

The simplest method of overseas localization is to concentrate activities within one's own expatriate community. Chinatowns are an excellent example of this. Protection is provided amongst fellow countrymen. Indeed, at the time of writing, it is estimated that there are at least 100,000 illegal immigrants within the UK's Chinese community of perhaps half a million souls. There is sufficient collective protection available to create further growth in legal, and illegal, activities. The triad networks are an excellent example of a cancer within overseas communities. Large Chinese restaurants provide excellent cover, not least for money laundering activities. Overseas Imperial guards can easily be avoided – most foreigners do not speak any Chinese dialect and the Chinese communicate in nothing else.

Real local responsiveness will occur, however, when these activities move into the overseas domestic arena – and we are not talking about locals dining in Chinese restaurants. We mean Chinese trading and service industries expanding into domestic activities. Initial attempts to allow a Chinese interest in an American oil company were rebuffed by the US Government on behalf of Conoco. But the learning process continues apace. The financial controls, banks and investment houses are already bought into. Next could we see a Chinese takeover of a foreign national supermarket chain, an airline, a railway company, a utility provider – who knows? The Western ways of capitalism offer returns to investors, but there are also returns for predators. Should Chinese placements overseas be only for foreigners to invest in China?

At the moment the Chinese are operating two strategies: a domestic socially embedded one and a strategy of slow movement into international, markets. Once the learning process of overseas ways is sufficiently assimilated, then local responsiveness and global integration will become one strategy, a strategy for economic hegemony. Such a strategy is taught in Western MBA courses, and taught to increasing numbers of Chinese students. Middle Eastern students may line up for advanced nuclear physics, but the Chinese are interested in globally applicable strategic management.

It is a change from the traditional, obligatory and demanding relationships of Chinese *guanxi* that is providing greater freedom for the Chinese to act in a more adaptable fashion across international borders. The transnational nature of modern Chinese managerial tendencies suggests that strategic decision making is increasingly varied. Flexibility is the key to the 'way things are going to be done'. There is a transvergence emerging, a conflation of relational networking with market contracts.

Petulance or power

Harmony in Wall Street is not traded in the Western market. When Google decided to go public in the US they eschewed the power brokers of Wall Street. They calculated their own initial public offering price. Unlike in the days of the dotcom boom, Wall Street spat the dummy. The Street's petulant reaction was to talk down Google until fear dropped Google's choice of initial pricing. Shortly thereafter, the market drove Google back to higher (and higher) levels. There is no right and wrong in this story, but there is a lesson for the Chinese. Why let control of your destiny rest with barbarians?

If every overseas Chinese presently working in Wall Street, the City of London and other major financial centres were to clear her desk or pack his wallet and move to a Chinese investment and broking house, the old financial cartels would find imitation painful. Our first prediction is that Chinese relational networks are strong enough to set this strategy in motion – either through acquisition (we must remember that past greed used the capital markets as sources of both income and capital gain, so control is possible) or imitation. Control over one's own destiny is a primary Chinese drive – a protection against external aggression and uncertainty. Better the head of a chicken than the tail of an ox.

A lack of moderation, increased opportunism, decreased mutual dependency, and changes in traditional ways must not be confused with individual destinies. The Chinese traditionally dislike teamwork, it means working across networks and not comfortably within them. Teamwork links individuals and, traditionally, the Chinese links with Westerners are fraught. As middle management gain greater autonomy in flexible, flatter organizational structures, so the need for collective action becomes more important when the middle and lower management network is extended. Foreigners are now part of the extended relationship.

It is, therefore, these simple alterations in Chinese relational networks which reflect the changing nature of Chinese economic strategy. The *guanxi* networks are primarily information and transaction networks. They are behavioral controls. They are supported by common collective values, reflecting the attitudes necessary to govern Chinese behavior. It is the increasingly knowledgeable and increasingly specialized network which will make the first major move overseas. It may not be an organization in the Western sense but it is a company of prime movers in an economic sense. The removals van is heading for the Western financial services industry. First stop, Blackstone; second stop, Barclays; third stop, Bear Stearns; Merrill Lynch; Morgan Stanley; Standard Bank; and then... the rest of the alphabet? The removal van stopped at Bear Stearns, courtesy of the US Federal Reserve, forcing a firesale. The Chinese have now withdrawn their declared interest and watch and await the consequences of the slaughter on Wall Street.

Here comes the judge

We can now produce a further global prediction. Chinese expansion overseas will not be led through the legal or accountancy professions. Historically, the divergence of practices, the different *rules*, has just been too large for any convergence to take place in the short to medium term. The Chinese competitive advantage, however, rests with the contractual nature of the Western professions. Subcontracting of accountancy and legal services is perfectly acceptable in the West. There is no need to imitate, merge or acquire – merely to pay the pipers to play in the counting houses and inns of court.

Imitation within China is, on the other hand, extremely likely. Copying Western legal statutes and accountancy regulations for adaptation in China enables international demands to be met. Enforcement, however, will remain *relational*, but the statutes will be there for external inspection. The most important concession to the West will be for *ex-post* governance of contracts through arbitration. This allows a negotiated outcome between two parties in contractual dispute to be settled – quicker than adversarial legal combat, and cheaper too.

Feeling the stones

We see a continual adaptation in Chinese relational practices. The Chinese are expanding the range of strategic options in response to differences between domestic and global categories of economic exchange. Resolving new global problems provides opportunities for implementing strategies previously not considered in the decision making process. In this way, traditional methods of implementation can be adapted, but not necessarily abandoned, in favor of the new.

For example, the problems emanating from quality control in Chinese manufactures are not merely deemed to be an internal factory specific problem. Cheaper outsourcing copies the West, but when the Western buyer forces Chinese factories down in price, the outsourcing to less expensive, less reliable local suppliers creates an imitation which goes badly wrong – only the price, but not the quality, is outsourced. The Chinese meet this issue with government-led delegations to the West, clearly signalling a relational priority level.

Strategic change in Chinese relational management creates strategies incorporating both Western and Chinese characteristics. Crossing the river, by feeling for stepping stones, makes clear the direction for success, but not the timing of a successful arrival. Patience remains a highly regarded Chinese value.

For example, the larger investments by the Chinese in overseas corporations may be eclipsed by a plethora of stealth vehicles on the OTC or AIM markets. Patience here would allow an ultimate reversal by acquisition into suitable Western organizations when the timing is right, the credentials are established, and the vagaries of the market are understood.

CHAPTER 17

Modern Chinese management

Those friends thou hast, and their adoption tried,
Grapple them to thy soul with hoops of steel
(*Shakespeare* – Hamlet, *Act I, Scene III*)

The debate over whether Chinese ways are converging to Western ways is misleading. It somewhat misses the mark – it is a convergence of *problems*, not national ways of doing things, that is forcing both East and West to change traditional values and *rules* over past best practice. Global economic interaction, the opening of China's borders, and external and internal economic growth – all these create strategic problems different from those previously encountered. The wind is blowing stronger as the sail is raised. A convergence of international problems is resulting in a convergence of strategic controls over decision making. Chinese solutions may even use Japanese past practice as a guide.

System theory argues for balance, allowing for relational control at a complex level and market governance at the simple exchange level. The integration of transaction cost and resource base theories creates additional control and helps guide competitive advantage. Trust lowers transaction costs, but is not often identified as a core resource in an organization – *the Chinese believe it should be*. Trust is a reciprocated attribute for safely governed economic exchange. Real option theory brings investment criteria into play – thus creating integrated governing controls over strategic problem solving in a complex period of uncertainty.

The management resources, domestic and global, governing transactional 'deals' are explicable in a simple reference to the dimensions produced in Tables I.1–I.3. The relational network of Chinese economic exchange is maintained whilst the legal concept of the firm as a contracting partner is processing to Western ways. We can summarize the modern Chinese international manager's behavior in three simple facets:

- Adopting a relational, people approach and governance for complex contextual issues, but a contractual, task approach and market governance for simpler, specific issues. There is a decrease in power distance with increased heterogeneity of problem solving characteristics and a loosening in the traditional constraints of face and *renqing* obligations. In terms of resources, this implies a non-social commitment; run the African strip mine efficiently and then move on.

- Resolving ambiguity in business through the acceptance of different time frames for sequential or fluid transactions. The Chinese will choose between either structured Western styles or fluid Chinese styles subject to the complexity and requirements of the task. In terms of financial investment, they put the cash into a deal using Western market principles, but then create shareholder control on a relational basis. This can be seen in terms of Chinese attitude to risk – they do not do full, formal financial calculations but base their risk assessment on the relational obligation for future renegotiation. The Chinese will operate where the City banker would be frightened of mud on his or her Gucci shoes. Risk management attitudes in Wall Street will alter.

- Combining a factual based approach with an expressive style, depending upon the complexity at issue. Formality is subject to governance issues, given that communication requiring high levels of trust (for example, within a network) will remain informal and high context, but with peripheral, formal 'contractual' trust increasing. In political and diplomatic discussions, the Chinese will talk first and talk again, seldom ever taking the lead, but will go with the flow of the group. North Korea and Iran are good examples of resolving Western confrontation.

Reaching the extremes of these dimensions should create either a compromise in values or a 'pick and mix' approach to orientation, task, communication and presentation style. A control system interpretation allows the inputs and outputs of the problem solving process to be understood. It also allows the global manager, Western and Chinese, to note the most suitable strategy for the particular context. Learning to howl with the wolves depends upon finding your place in the pack, your new peer group.

It is a leaner, meaner pack of international experts that the Chinese are creating. On the domestic front, the level of managerial expertise is much lower in proportion to the demands of the economy. That level is now rising, with feedback from Chinese expatriates creating a dynamic of traditional swift, intuitive decision making, unencumbered by Western stakeholder round robins, but accompanied by formal, problem solving methods to produce a Chinese strategic hybrid.

Stakeholders

This hybrid, it must be noted, does not recognize stakeholders. Traditional imperialist ways continue to consider workers as paid servants – part of the household but not of its decision making. Shareholders have bought shares and are free to sell them. What long-term benefits beyond initial capital restructuring do shareholders bring? (The Chinese may have a point here, even Western regulators are concerned about hedge fund buying on margin for short-term shareholder ploys.) A jail term imposed on a Chinese executive in Singapore, for false financial statements on the trading of jet fuel, was a preventative measure designed to reassure other shareholders. The executive, however, did no wrong in the eyes of the company stakeholder – the Chinese government. And it will happen again when Chinese state funds are at risk overseas.

It is here that the West is worried. The large state-owned investment entities have been accepted as wise investors – Kuwaitis, Norwegians and others have used sovereign wealth funds to recycle petrodollars. But China, through China Investment Corporation, plays by different *rules*. It is recycling imported dollars in a non-transparent way and possibly in a speculative manner. Again, Western hypocrisy comes to the fore. Opaque hedge funds are acceptable, whereas opaque Chinese sovereign funds are not. Despite assurances from the Chinese Prime Minister that any investment into UK companies from their $200 billion sovereign wealth fund would meet transparency and corporate governance requirements, uneasiness remains about the potential extent of such incursions. In fact, the sum available for such investment is not nearly as great as it first appears, since much of the fund, nearly $70 billion, is likely to be spent in China itself on very necessary and urgent reform of commercial banks.

Two points of principle must be made to explain the fear. Firstly, the retention of relational controls in a Chinese company with a hierarchical reporting and response structure does not comply with Western legal governance for corporate responsibility. Secondly, market reliance on shareholding as a financial investment (buy low and sell high) does not create true stakeholders. In large Chinese listed companies, the state is the only controlling stakeholder (think Bank of China and its tax rebates, its waivers on bad loan provisions). In any entrepreneurial publicly listed companies, the controlling family is the stakeholder (think Li Ka-Shing, or the Australian-American-Asian Rupert Murdoch).

When dealing with Chinese companies, the acceptance of mutually beneficial reciprocity may prevail long term or may prove to be only a useful partial accommodation. Neither national nor strategic controls are stable at a boundary. Controls govern systems designed, within economic *space* and *time* constraints, to theorize successful *rules* over business transactions. Or to put it simply, Chinese *rules* control a trial and error approach for ways to do business better than before, creating purely Chinese strategies for the survival of the fittest – a Chinese strategic evolution.

Mutation in major national characteristics

Macro-economic wanderings need now to give way to micro-management simplification. There are six major 'view-finders' that we may focus directly on the Chinese as they attempt to clarify future global uncertainty. The first is a change in traditional values, retention of which could become a hindrance to economic growth. The second is the extent to which a Chinese individual may be affected within a changing collectivist society. Thirdly, the autocratic, hierarchical dependence structure in China engenders a less than forthright ability to discuss and resolve problems. Fourthly, the human-hearted characteristic (a feminine trait) profoundly affects the harmony of relationships. Fifthly, a tendency to take a long-term view can affect strategic decisions taken in particular circumstances and contexts. Finally, the relational and transactional nature of *guanxi* creates an inevitable emotional conflict with objective strategies.

The following descriptions of expansionary Chinese can now be made with confidence:

- Traditional values are gradually waning and are not observed to be much hindrance to economic growth. In particular, there is a significant anticipation that general wellbeing and contentedness, will rise, acting as a spur to economic and entrepreneurial activity with a concentration on material benefits.

- Increased individualism is not yet evident, but some change in the collective nature of the Chinese individual is likely The one child policy, for example, is creating a 'me' generation which is altering relational transactions to allow increased focus and task commitment for individual gain.

- A significant levelling is expected in the autocratic, hierarchical structure of Chinese relationships. A Chinese value, moderation (or the middle way) – associated with decreases in power distance – is now significantly lower in importance, indicating a continuing (and uncompromising) demand for economic growth and personal benefit.

- Relationships within Chinese society remain important but an increase in masculine, aggressive attitudes, within a trusting network, is possible. Outside that network, as Chinese internationalize, a more assertive attitude will prevail. The Chinese, for example, prefer to watch the antics of other players before making their move. This impassivity is a prelude to, not a substitute for, swift action. Proof of recent and modern aggression rests with the Sinosteel hostile bid for the Autralian miner, Midwest.

- The strategic decision making of the Chinese manager should retain its traditional long-term orientation, but shorter term 'opportunistic' strategies will be deployed. This can be observed in the way Chinese funds are flowing overseas through the China Development Bank, the targeted acquisition often surprised by their speed. A good example is the swift acquisition in early 2008, by the Chinese, of 9% in Rio Tinto Zinc in an attempt to prevent oligopolistic controls by mine owners.

- A major change in the characteristics of *guanxi* is anticipated. The *guanxi* structure of the expatriate Chinese has already altered substantially. The primary change is in the reduction of any onerous ongoing *renqing* obligations. The traditional control of 'losing face' is decreasing in importance. The modern *guanxi* structure is anticipated to be one of increased adaptability, thus confirming in many respects the processual nature of strategy. Reciprocity is anticipated to maintain its prime importance and significance in creating and sustaining mutually beneficial transactions. There is, however, a need for compromise with Western contractual ways, but not as a stakeholder.

What we reveal can now be interpreted with the strategic theories discussed in Part I. Respect for seniority in overseas expatriate Chinese is now way down the pecking order of relative importance, implying that hierarchical control over opportunism is being replaced with another transaction cost – the paid up 'contract' rather than 'face' or a future obligation. The overseas Chinese is less prudent, uncontrolled by moderation and less concerned with Chinese tradition. Trustworthiness, reciprocity and harmony remain important to both the domestic and global manager, along with high levels of adaptability, persistence and personal steadiness – a set of valuable Chinese resources when meeting the vacillating West.

The meeting of the waters

If we now compare Chinese core values with Western values we can observe the primary differences between them.

Western constitutions and legal systems enshrine and safeguard the rights of the individual. The key provisions made have evolved from the principles of morality, justice, equity (or fairness) and pluralism, which form the basis of the common law. Notions like equality before the law and *habeas corpus* – which requires anyone detained or arrested to have a legal hearing before further detention or imprisonment – have their UK roots in the Magna Carta of 1215 and are the bedrock of values, legal precedent and case law governing the behaviour of individuals in society.

Although democracy is based on the rule of law and allows a government to govern only with the consent of the people, abuses of power are quite common, precisely because the existence of a power is a matter of law, not of fact. Thus, the corruption of friendship may subvert the system, since public office-holders have natural emotional controls as well as social legal personalities. Individuals need recourse not just to legal redress – which may take some time and be expensive – but, more urgently and importantly, to a very present help in times of trouble, which the *guanxi* culture provides.

Effectively, *guanxi* means practical recourse through particular people to a possible solution to a problem – in the English sense of 'using connections'. But in its binding power of obligation, it has the socially institutional force of law. Its use is never simply based upon an altruistic granting or exchange of favours. It is always based upon anticipated reciprocation in roughly equal measure or value on some unspecified future occasion.

Literally, *guan* means a door – a door which is open to you but shut to others; and *xi* means to cement and further relationships. Taken together the terms convey exactly Shakespeare's exhortation from Polonius to Laertes in *Hamlet* that such valuable relationships should be bound with '*hoops of steel*'.

However, there are certain key elements in the basis of this relationship which set it apart as an individual social connection of ongoing reciprocal obligation. These are the various areas of common ground which form the basis of the *guanxi* relationship:

- Locality – native home town or province or dialect spoken
- Kinship (actual or claimed) – Clan membership (often based only on a common surname)
- Workplace – long years of association with colleagues facilitate new private business start-ups and financing
- Trade associations/social clubs – functions similar to Lions or Rotary Clubs in the West

- Friendship (as opposed to kinship) – the affection, credibility and trust it affords

The principles governing *guanxi* are somewhat more subtle. A *guanxi* relationship (as opposed to friendship) is:

- Transferable – it can and often does result from a third-party referral
- Reciprocal – exchanges of favors are obligatory
- Intangible – the exchange of favors is open-ended
- Utilitarian – based on mutual gain/advantage
- Context-specific – there is more art than science in exercising sensitivity to the danger of *guanxi* approaches being misconstrued as either instrumental or manipulative
- Strictly personal in nature – it has no group validity

In short, as Yadong Luo says, 'Confucian social theory is concerned with the question of how to establish a harmonious secular order in a man-centred world'.

Two features stand out from this conceptual framework of these core value systems:

1. The essential practicality of the Chinese approach versus the more abstract and theoretical construct of the West;

and

2. The 'bottom-up' thrust of applied Chinese values versus the 'top-down' drive of enforced Western law.

Figure III.1 encapsulates these features and also illustrates the basis for transvergence, which is not only possible but quite likely to occur, as authoritarianism gradually recedes and individual people in China gain greater scope for self-determination in a wider world. The Chinese element of *renqing wei*, human-heartedness or the milk of human kindness, is the key to bridging the gap in understanding. It is the primary drive and wellspring of mutual support in small communities which feel oppressed and beleaguered all over the world, a visceral response to external threats. This spontaneous

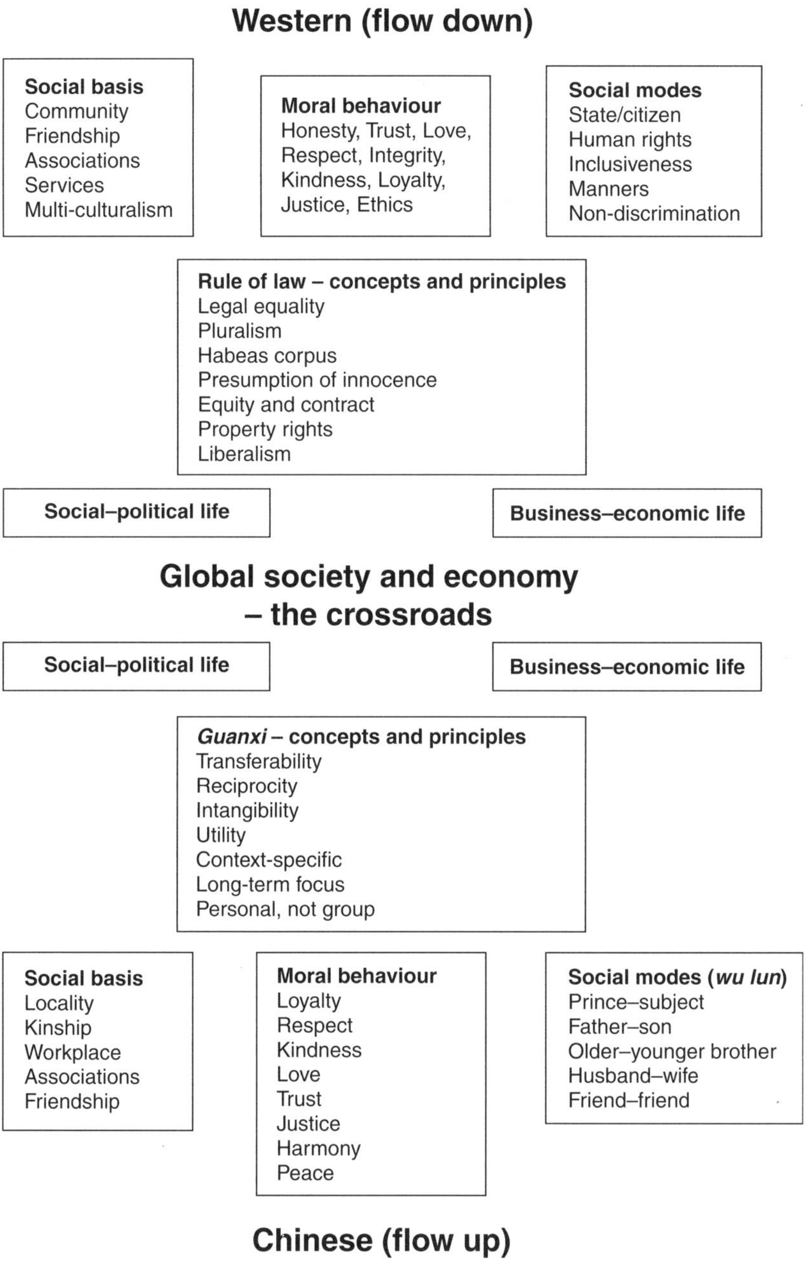

Western (flow down)

Social basis
Community
Friendship
Associations
Services
Multi-culturalism

Moral behaviour
Honesty, Trust, Love,
Respect, Integrity,
Kindness, Loyalty,
Justice, Ethics

Social modes
State/citizen
Human rights
Inclusiveness
Manners
Non-discrimination

Rule of law – concepts and principles
Legal equality
Pluralism
Habeas corpus
Presumption of innocence
Equity and contract
Property rights
Liberalism

Social–political life

Business–economic life

Global society and economy – the crossroads

Social–political life

Business–economic life

Guanxi – concepts and principles
Transferability
Reciprocity
Intangibility
Utility
Context-specific
Long-term focus
Personal, not group

Social basis
Locality
Kinship
Workplace
Associations
Friendship

Moral behaviour
Loyalty
Respect
Kindness
Love
Trust
Justice
Harmony
Peace

Social modes (*wu lun*)
Prince–subject
Father–son
Older–younger brother
Husband–wife
Friend–friend

Chinese (flow up)

Figure III.1 A conceptual framework of core value systems.

gesture of humanity freely offered without calculated expectation of any reciprocation or return of favour is like a grafting made to replace a failing human limb or faculty of mind or body. It is never just a sticking plaster, much more an annealing spirit, a solidarity of the soul.

The shift from personal trust (verbal agreements) towards institutional trust (legal agreements) will thus be a very gradual process as the context changes to encompass the global expansion of the Chinese. With diversification in ownership, partnership, managerial competence and productivity, recourse to *guanxi* connections will become an optional alternative rather than a pressing necessity. *Guanxi* relationships also inhibit the appointment and promotion of individuals on merit. With foreign involvement, Chinese operational culture and relational policy are likely to undergo significant modification to meet the demands of economic networks for local compliance.

Ring out the changes

We have pointed to a drop in the importance of traditional values. Theoretically, we would expect them to wane, given present Chinese economic growth. All traditional values are falling inversely to stock market valuations except, our research found, for *contentedness*. Those Chinese gaining overseas experience but not actually expatriated have an overall greater retention of traditional values, but expatriates are just as driven by the desire for stability and contentment.

The 20th century, it must be remembered opened, closed, and reopened China's gates. It brought the dissolution of the Imperial edict and its civil service under Sun Yat Sen, the Greater Co-Prosperity Sphere of the Japanese occupation brought more external oppression, the civil war laid bare both nationalist and communist ideologies, and the Age of Reform is now swiftly eroding tradition. We cannot blame the Chinese for craving more contentedness through globalization.

This is, we believe, a reflection of both a desire for greater wellbeing and a result of appreciating the benefits of Chinese success. The traditional Confucian emphasis on 'keeping face' may be succumbing to that desire for success. The Chinese are modernizing but they see the modernization as making the old idea of being happy with one's lot as more important than before.

Perhaps five and certainly ten years ago, a focus on wealth engineered a drive against poverty. The desire for a secure income stream, a place to call your own, and an element of stability in a rapidly changing environment are altering and reshaping national dimensions. Two statistically significant changes are occurring. Firstly, there is a decrease in hierarchical structured obligations, which allows for greater autonomy of action and decision making. Secondly, there is an increase in male dominating behavior, which makes for a more aggressive approach.

We are seeing the values of the Chinese becoming considerably more adaptable. This adjustment is networked and institutional rather than organizational in its importance. Increased network flexibility and greater managerial adaptability are a consequence of globalization and the attendant different ways of doing business. The implications are, thereafter, for individuals attuned to a non-hierarchical structure to assert themselves forcefully at a time of economic expansion. And we mean forcefully.

As far as Chinese values are concerned, let us consider in brief detail the personal values composing power distance (the *kowtow*, the tugging of the forelock). They are no longer in tremble mode. Important values are changing with a significant increase in the importance of *adaptability*. An increase in the overall level of *personal desires*, coupled with a decrease in *moderation* and with lesser importance attached to *prudent behavior*, all paint, at first sight, a rather alarming picture of Chinese aggression.

Even at second sight, the thought of imprudent, immoderate, avaricious, but adaptable Chinese managers creating a competitive advantage over Western counterparts should rattle Wall Street and the City. This is not a land of cheap labor but a country of commercially astute businessmen. On reflection, of course, we recognize the recent changes as being merely imitative. But it is a powerful imitation that is occurring.

Implications for organizational structures

In a dynamic economic interaction there are three major elements: problem solving techniques, institutional and group forces, and market and organizational forces. Economic theory explains the tension and equilibrium – the new balance sheet of cultural controls – between the forces. Chinese organizations will continue to maintain the duality.

It is, in many respects, a logical recommendation to join the dynamics of national decision making with the dynamics of Chinese institutional and corporate tensions. The differences within Chinese domestic management may be attributable to societal group forces prevailing in the entrepreneurial sector but external market forces prevailing in the state-owned sector.

Or is it vice versa? Is restructuring closing the gaps in management methods? Change in strategic orientation is best measured through problem solving styles. The politician, the financier and the organizational manager are, after all, employed for problem solving and decision making purposes. The overseas expert returning to China will make different decisions from his domestic colleagues. He or she will seek profitability by minimizing wasteful resource usage. Formal techniques will include investment based upon returns on capital, corruption will be frowned upon but not eliminated, and the environment, education and the family's future will drive economic demands. Contentedness is not merely a color television.

Strategic implementation – political implications

The adaptation and reconfiguration of Chinese values and characteristics have strong practical implications. We have noted that a desire for competitive advantage sparks increased heterogeneity in problem solving. This, in turn, creates internal network restructuring. Institutional structures may mirror the traditional hierarchical Chinese organization, but bit by bit there is a process of realignment to reflect a joint interface between domestic and global strategies, focused on the customer.

The systemic, relational controls shift to combine low and high context 'bandwidths' in communication. This allows processual adaptation to Western managerial and organizational patterns. Synergistic learning is being harnessed to heightened strategic effect. But it is not convergence – it is a Chinese hybrid and must be recognized as such.

The problem with processual strategies is that they are of a bargaining and learning nature. Deals will be struck which may be mutually beneficial to the parties concerned, or they may be detrimental. Normally the economic exchange would not be damaging to third parties but, from an environmental perspective, it is essential that a switch to Chinese global strategies retains some systemic control. The effects of a trial and error process on global warming may be too late, on the Amazon rainforest too much, on energy savings too little. There is nothing in this adaptation which would limit Chinese exploitation of global resources.

Neither, of course, is there any apparent curtailing of Western consumerism. The Chinese produce what the West buys, the Chinese then buy global raw materials and emission credits to produce even more. The Chinese produce, the West buys, the Chinese then buy… Goodbye Maldives.

Pressure brought to bear on Chinese political controls by the West must be offset by an accommodation of traditional ways, of seeking mutual reciprocity. Present demands for China to agree internationally accepted accountancy regulations are being muted by the acknowledgement that Chinese organizational controls and cross-subsidies between institutions are more flexible in China than in other Western countries. An acceptance of other 'ways of doing things' reflects an understanding of group controls balancing market governance to achieve integrated solutions to global problems.

The individual but collectivist Chinese manager

It is unsurprising, given the considerable current interest in China, the rapidly changing economic environment and the pressure for organizational and institutional reform, that the vast majority of Asian economic research has concentrated on Chinese domestic issues and Chinese influences in the Far East. At the centre of the structure, the Chinese individual has not been sought out for detailed formal examination. Conditioned to a Confucian hierarchical control, he or she may have been seen but not heard. About one another we remain remarkably uninformed.

Yet the individual Chinese is surely little different from his or her global counterpart in the desire for self-improvement, hope for a future of greater wellbeing and a genuine interest in achieving harmonious relationships based on mutual respect. Their personal values create a compromise at the interface of East and West.

Successful Chinese networks will alter their structure, not only in tackling Western influences but also in controlling the balance sheet of managerial resources. The relational interface, the boundary of information and economic exchange, will either match up compatible networks or not. Some translation, by both parties at the interface, is necessary. A mutually beneficial relationship should arise at a global interface.

Globalization has, however, brought a shift in micro-economic behavior. The national influence of *guanxi* as an extension of the village collective can result in tension between familial networks and managerial networks – the former personal and the latter organizational. Global and domestic strategies are beginning to merge into a more aggressive fiery dragon with wings.

A blinding flash of the obvious? Arguing the obvious is a minor advantage of the statistical method. The major benefit of statistics, however, is in demonstrating the not so obvious or, even better, demonstrating that the intuitively obvious is deductively not at all obvious. (Who said statistics had no philosophical roots, beyond damned lies?)

There is an intuitive feeling among many Western observers that Chinese change should be reflected in greater individualism. Becoming more like us than not. Somewhat disappointingly for theocrats, we did not find true cultural or biblical affinities. We did, however, find institutional and network hybrids, allowing individuals to shine in a much more flexible structure.

International adaptation and interpretation

A recap of the position may be useful as we begin to close. The Chinese have group (relational uncertainty) issues and market (economic uncertainty) pressures to resolve. Uncertainty can be interpreted with Western economic theory. Change in the social and market contexts can be measured and any personal views on risk investigated. Adjustment to economic uncertainty can be emotionally driven, but social controls exert a powerful constraining influence, especially within the collectivist Chinese culture.

The use of Western economic theory helps prefigure the nature of national controls across a Chinese managerial boundary. It follows from this that Western theory on transaction costs implies that the Chinese will maintain relational (*guanxi*) governance for complex or longer- term exchange, but will accept simple, short- term market governance, where enforceable.

The high context (face-to-face) personal communication of Chinese culture accelerates the exchange of complex information, with the group network controlling the transfer of knowledge as a resource. The cost of entry to the relational network, however, is high for simple transactions. Gaining trust at the network periphery is not free – hence the economic benefits in restructuring for enforceable governance. Trust as a resource becomes increasingly valuable.

Real option theory, in analyzing investment criteria, provides clear indications of a decrease in the traditional ongoing, but uncertain, future obligations of *guanxi* practices. The increasing use of the Internet, a low context, channelled and indirect information flow, should ease the route to contractual governance.

The crossing of these routes from different strategic positions will make up for the historical lack of guidance on relationships at a foreign interface. Tensions between group and market forces add to traditional solutions by generating trial and error strategies. A responsive and integrated strategy equips the Chinese manager with a larger set of ways in which business can be done. He or she is more likely to take chances and circumvent Western best practice. There is no best practice for Africa. China cannot be blamed for tackling it their way.

The bubble that tries hard not to burst

The Chinese stock market has raced through all previous levels and risen vertiginously high over the past two years. 'It was still going gangbusters', said the China correspondent of an international news agency. He reckoned that the severe Shanghai correction of February 2007 had a sudden, jarring effect on the New York and London exchanges, but that the later Chinese fall in May 2007 – which followed the effect of dampening stamp duties imposed by the government against overheating – had a barely perceptible impact on foreign markets. 'It has to be remembered that the market is entirely policy-driven. Nowhere is investment in it based on fundamentals'.

The Chinese have very few tools for assessing opportunities and limited exposure to foreign markets. The sole concern of Government is that market performance should not affect social stability. It continues to spur feeding frenzies and to fire speculators' lust for a swift profit. The banks pay a very low rate of interest on savings accounts, so it is little wonder that their natural bent is to open a broking account to play the stock market. The sudden 'discovery' of the joys of Western capitalism and public companies is exacerbated by the lack of alternative saving, joys now tempered by the knowledge that markets go down as well as up.

Japan faced similar issues in the 1980s and did not fare well. The Japanese corporations played their part – encouraging Japanese mafia *yakuza* to disrupt shareholders meetings, to 'persuade' reluctant homeowners to sell property and aid large construction projects, and to protect poor balance sheets with hidden loan accounts. Somehow, it does not seem dissimilar to modern China.

So why will China not follow the same deflationary course as Japan? One answer is the lack of democracy – buying votes through overstimulation of the economy is unnecessary. Another answer is the strong family value system in China, so that a *kowtow* to the corporation is unlikely. But the overseas expansion will ease the domestic heat. The government's engineers love infrastructure projects. Have theodolite, will travel. Have heaps of cash, will travel far.

The country is awash with funds from every side. This accumulation of capital is unprecedented in the history of any national economy. A small fraction of this enormous superfluity, some $3 billion, is

Modern Chinese management

invested with Blackstone of the US, an international private equity company, for exceptional future returns. Barclays Bank, for its unsuccessful foray into Dutch banking territory, received funding support from China Development Bank and Singapore's Temasek. Due to its unsuccessful foray into the US sub-prime derivatives market, it received credit funding from the Bank of England. In a couple of steps, the Chinese are thus linked to the Bank of England!

However, from the midst of wonder and amazement at the vaulting scale of Chinese financial muscle, faint shapes and shadows of crocodiles can be made out under the surface of the apparently boundless lake of liquidity. Boosted by new market listings and staggering new supply contracts with Africa, Chinese banks are now valued at levels rivalling the world's largest – one was recently valued at $250 billion, second only to Citigroup. These valuations are swollen by the sheer mass of the influx of foreign investment funds and subscriptions to new issues of listed companies. From being public service institutions as lenders to state-owned enterprises, the banks have become conduits for the delivery of commercial lending and risk management, ostensibly to internationally acceptable accounting and reporting standards.

The greatest concern is for the quality of the assets on their balance sheets and the greatest fear is that these assets are over-inflated by cross-valued investments in other listed Chinese companies. On the liabilities side the true extent of bad or unrecoverable loans is masked or baldly understated. All these signs point to an inevitable contraction and consolidation of the Chinese banking sector, if it is not to default under the pressures of any eventual downturn in the economy. The core business performance of many companies may be mediocre, but this is routinely compensated by successful stock market investment. The banks lend to the state as before, but now also to home buyers, a considerable customer base with property ownership now relieved from communal control. These same loans are disappearing in the maw of the market with potentially perilous consequences for China and the world.

Yet it is the global nature of the Chinese expansion that both challenges it and protects it. A slowdown in external demand for manufactured goods is exposing Chinese overcapacity and reliance on cheap labour (with Vietnam, Laos and Cambodia competing on low value products). Chinese growth is in its banking sector and surviving foreign banks will buy into Chinese banks once Chinese money arrives in the USA and Europe to ease the credit squeeze. Almost by osmosis the technological transfer of accounting and financial expertise is happening. One senior Chinese academic commented to us that he used to earn money translating Warren Buffet's newsletters into Chinese, and selling them as 'good trading' practice for the local punter. Then the foreigner arrived with fund management and cash. The foreigner, however, is tied to the foot soldiers of the Chinese market. The wall of money from mattresses is altering the structure of the market. There are no fundamentals by Western standards. The Hongkong Government bought into the market in 1997 to save it. The belief that the market is underwritten by the Party is persuasive. The belief that the US, Japanese and European markets are at least partly underwritten by their central banks is no less persuasive. If China is different in terms of process, but not in terms of policy, then it makes a fair trading base for inward overseas funds and for outward Chinese investment.

Brain gain rather than brain drain

Official estimates show that some two-thirds of Chinese who have studied abroad since the 1980s have elected not to return to work in China. Jobs at graduate level had not been easy to find. The Chinese diaspora worldwide has reached some 35 million in 150 countries. This tide is turning now with new growth in China, but domestic demand will continue for Westerners and other Asians. Foreigners make up the skills deficit in areas of expertise which have simply not been developed to the more exacting requirements of international trade, manufacturing and investment.

There will thus be a need to recruit an increasing number of qualified foreigners over the short-to-medium term to lift the level of core competencies across the board – initially in areas such as banking, insurance, investment management, broking, accounting, actuarial practice, management consulting, manufacturing and engineering quality control, sales, product branding and marketing, and business planning. As the main urban conurbations become more crowded and polluted, there will be an equally pressing demand for experts in environmental protection, town planning and surveying, transport and communications, disease control and treatment, and the regulatory control of markets.

These skill gaps, according to the Asian Counsel of an international mining company, have resulted chiefly from the Chinese education system of rote learning which discourages questioning of teachers and thus the development of enquiring minds. It is the capacity to think critically which is most keenly needed, the ability to form and present an independent view, to make a case for a certain course of action, strategy or point of view. This is particularly important in the transvergence of all cultural aspects of, for example, a successful technology transfer. A cadre of middle management needs to be created and developed in Chinese companies and joint ventures to ensure the effective communication and implementation of production, quality control, distribution and marketing plans and processes.

The teething troubles of such companies as Volkswagen in China with quality control issues, and in the acrimonious joint venture between Danone and Wahaha, can be traced to poor levels of middle management. Risk management is another key area, where foreign banks like RBS, HSBC, Santander, UBS and Goldman Sachs are now playing an essential role in establishing a sound basis for extending commercial credit to Chinese at home and overseas. Domestic Chinese have hitherto been accustomed to receiving and spending working capital and loans from State banks without proper accountability. The Western opacity of the slice, dice and splice debt packages should hold no fear for the Chinese.

Unlike Western Europe or the USA, China is keen to transfer management thinking by encouraging overseas learning by students. Chinese universities are now producing too many graduates who are complaining of the lack of opportunity. The card up the sleeve remains the overseas student. Jobs are scarce and many students are taking Master's courses in English speaking universities (and France and Germany). A satisfactory English assessment test (or foreign language pass) gains them entry to an overseas university. Single child family parents find the cash for their only offspring. The future Chinese Master will be in corporate management and financial engineering not kung fu.

The graduates are heading overseas on Master's programs but are also complaining of a lack of practical application. The Chinese demand for overseas experience of a non-theoretical nature will not result from Western educational systems but from Western organizations and institutions. The overseas Chinese postgraduate may be welcomed home but prefers to remain overseas. Practical overseas experience will increase the opportunities for Chinese networks to expand on a global basis.

The experience increases through practice in an atmosphere of experiment. Technical advances require testing. For mobile phone and chip/pin technology, New Zealand was the sealed laboratory of the R&D departments of big Western organisations. If a few Kiwis complained about quality or capability, the world was deaf – but not the technocrat. The products were tested and developed in the antipodes before launching in Europe, North America and Asia.

The Chinese are doing the same overseas. Their civil engineers are being trained in Africa for the infrastructure and civil engineering projects required in China. Returning after a year or so, they can set about rebuilding China having served their overseas apprenticeships. Financial and marketing abilities are being honed in New York and London. Democracy, we have already argued, is an observable experiment in Taiwan. China knows that technology transfer is nothing to inward skills transfer.

And modern skills are more often led by overseas Chinese. Taiwan and mainland China presently trade more than $100 billion across the straits. Over a million Taiwanese are estimated to be working in (or should it be on) mainland China. Inward skills are in manufacturing, electronics, and contractual techniques with foreign buyers. But with the Chinese product price index heading into double figures, those skills are also transferable to South East Asia, the new recipient of Chinese cheap labour *largesse*.

ChinaTech

> People everywhere love Windows
> (*attributed to Bill Gates*)

China's technological advance is extending into software but not to a love of Windows. The challenge to the Microsoft Corporation is primarily governmental. The European Union has taken steps to prevent continuing dominance of the software industry by curtailing Microsoft's marketing and supplier practices. Google challenges the Internet search, email and chatroom powers of any large internet service providers. The Apple Corporation retains its hardware and software distinctiveness. But they are American.

The Chinese have no desire to assert global domination in the software market, but neither do they wish to be subservient to calculating American power. China recognizes that there are opportunities in adaptation. Linux is open software, supported by experts who are tired of seeing the dominance of Microsoft. Linux is also much less liable to hacking attacks. Its development, from a small beginning in Sweden, comes through layer upon layer of additions and refinements by software experts and addicts.

The Chinese government has decided that Linux can be Sinographed or turned into a domestic software system. This adaptation, by creating specifically Chinese programming, will allow a China-only version of Linux to be deployed across Chinese governmental (civil and military) establishments, followed by businesses as the Customs and Revenue services begin to demand its use for filing purposes. American dominance in hardware development and manufacture will lose out to the Asian entrepreneur. Soon the software systems in Asia will be Asian competitive, but also Asian compatible; not a bamboo curtain but a bamboo firewall.

In the meantime, the power of the Internet is not being released in China. The prevention of full Internet search access by companies such as Google and Yahoo is a trade-off. A compromise of integrity by providing censorship? In return for what? Advertising rights, market penetration, a stay of execution? The Chinese reliance on reciprocal arrangements means that there must be a deal in China which allows foreign firms to stand up in the storm that blows from the anti-censor quarters of the globe. The Internet is partially controllable; its software and hardware is partially controllable. The new Chinese search engine is in hand and could be backed by Google for an Asia-only market. Just be patient.

The thrust of technology and innovation – overtaking the West or replacing the Soviets?

China already has the capacity to produce much lower-cost innovations in areas like energy, transport and communications. This is clearly a great threat and competitive challenge to industries worldwide. It will become a magnet for research and development activities by multinational firms, who will bring the necessary cultural software for China's hardware for innovation. To boost its naval power, for example, new aircraft carriers are in hand. In spite of taking out one of its own space satellites in 2007 as target practice for its new range of ballistic missiles, the Chinese government vehemently discounts any intention to engage in an arms race in space (and vigorously denies any thoughts of knocking out US spy satellites, yet fancies a man on the Moon by 2020). China has demonstrated that its navy is now a real threat, above and below the sea.

Their ability to fire an oblique warning shot across the bows of the US Sixth Fleet in the Pacific shows clearly enough that they have no desire to be at the mercy of US forces. It seems that the real ghost in the machinery of the Chinese economy is neither the Party nor the Army, but quite simply protectionism. China still reserves unto itself the following key industries: armaments; power generation and distribution; oil and petrochemicals; telecommunications; coal; aviation; and shipping. In addition, machinery and car manufacture, IT, construction, iron and steel, and non-ferrous metals will remain under the beady eye of the state-owned enterprises. Banking licences are on a preferential basis.

This military and economic protectionism is entrenched nationalization on a grand, macro, scale. It allows very limited room for manoeuvre by the private sector – let alone foreign investors – in the development of technological innovation in the economy, except in areas like textiles, fashion, retail and tourism. However, the potential for China to produce world-class research is likely to be realized within the next ten years. Its universities and research centres are very well endowed and release a rising stream of engineers and scientists intellectually equipped to build innovation and technology. This will be acquired as often as it is developed in-house.

Witness the leapfrogging effect of a purchase of a British automotive technical centre as a springboard for the export of a new range of cars from China. To make this happen the Chinese government initially encourages competition – Nanjing versus Shanghai, the former having knocked down, transported and rebuilt the British Rover plant whilst the latter uses the technical and intellectual rights to create its own version of a world-beating car. Then the government supports consolidation; one industry, one organization.

To steal a march on the West, China will develop rapidly its capacity to originate, innovate and invest in technologies for new product development. Key high-tech areas are fibre-optics, semiconductors and chips for the electronics and communication and security/surveillance industries. Major advances have already been made in mobile-TV chips and digital recognition scanners (for reading facial bone structures). Innofidel claims a capacity to transform mobile handsets into micro-TVs and their scanners set in front doors enable people to do away with house keys. But these are still minor breakthroughs in an era of highly sophisticated disruptive technologies which threaten the continuity of many international product lines.

The global knowledge and expertise gained by the overseas Chinese counter the US and other major Western countries' protection of their high-tech proprietary rights. There is a real fear of its being copied and reproduced by China to undercut Western sales, markets and military uses. Short of stealing or gaining foreign proprietary knowledge by industrial espionage, China has to produce its own home-grown innovation in order to compete in world markets. The scientists and engineers, graduating every year from its universities and colleges of technology, are beginning to catch up on the levels of knowledge and teaching achieved at MIT or Imperial College, London. But the much more likely route to attaining any kind of parity with the West is via acquisition. Guided by the Chinese government, Lenovo's buyout of IBM's PC business and Shanghai Automotive's purchase of Rover are prime examples of this trend. Others are following.

By their brands ye shall know them

At home, however, the security of the domestic market share of major brands such as Lenovo, Haier and Hwa Wei in computers, white goods and telecommunications, limits the need to spend on advertising and branding. Why worry about foreigners' intellectual property – if they don't want it used then don't make it available? The overseas ability for Lenovo to pick up IBM personal computers dictates a policy of buying a brand but also of recognizing the worth of that as an asset. When more politically sensitive assets and resources are needed we could see Sino-Africa buying out Anglo-American. The Chinese have made it to outer space, now for inner space.

It is likely to take a generation to build up Chinese brands into solid by-words for quality and reliability. They will slowly move up the production value chain, innovating through joint venture and acquisition into a more acceptable quality and design. Haier is already set to test manufacturing and sales in overseas markets by building a new refrigerator pilot plant in Carolina in the US. These companies currently have little or no brand recognition, which is hardly surprising when the history of Coca-Cola, Toyota and Microsoft is examined. They also have to shake off China's image as counterfeiter, faker and infringer of intellectual property rights.

The accusations of shoddy goods, a thinly disguised protectionism, are as much an indictment of Western buyers' and consumers' greed as of poor quality control. The ease and impunity with which so many products can be faked or 'knocked off' in China actually has the effect of discouraging and disincentivizing invention and innovation. Why invent and patent a new product or technology if someone is going to steal and copy your idea? But outsourcing because of a squeeze by buyers – well that is just imitative.

Ultimately anything and everything is negotiable. It is here that the ongoing process of trial and error will allow the justification of experiment and the adaptation of present values and beliefs. Globalization is not a Western standardization of hamburger, cola and fries. It is a unique stage in world economic progress (colonialism was not globalization) and it is one which will be categorized by heterogeneity not homogeneity. Giving and receiving of face, creating mutual obligations, demonstrating goodwill, trustworthiness and a commitment to long-term relationships – all of these mark out the modern Chinese manager. The Chinese connection or the Western contract? Globalization of economic exchange is letting you choose.

CHAPTER 19

Qu xiang he fang?

> Be not afraid of going slowly, be afraid only of standing still (*Chinese proverb*)

Where is it all going? Our deductive investigations confirm the inductive belief that an expansion across global dimensions is preferable for competitive advantage. Understanding another point of view is useful – but to what end? Regenerating traditional governing controls over problem solving requires a dynamic interaction with the environment. The Chinese *guanxi* networking practice provides that dynamism, an increasingly frenetic dynamism.

Western economic and strategic theory, relying perhaps on academic reductionist and deterministic ideas, is now redressing a past omission. There has been a failure to recognize the dynamic, practical nature of an integrated approach to strategy. The most significant demonstration of Chinese adaptability is a non-Confucian strategy for flexibility. The flexibility is designed to meet the foreigner in domestic and global exchange.

The traditional practice of *guanxi* will not recede – its conceptual structure is recommended as a useful form of governance for complex contracts. The corollary implies that for simple obligations between two parties the use of contractual governance is less costly. There is, therefore, some directional convergence to Anglo-Saxon ways. In transactions with foreigners, greater reliance on legal principles rather than on purely Confucian precepts has been in evidence.

The Chinese are not yet unrecognizable from the past but are, without doubt, undergoing surgical enhancement. The strategic 'nip and tuck' remains unique to Chinese practice but its attributes are also argued to be beneficial to Western multinationals. Reducing uncertainty in a related series of economic transactions is an essential global strategy.

Westward Ho!

China's forward offensive into many areas of the wider world is like a reprise of the fabled Star Raft adventure of Admiral Cheng Ho to Africa in the 15th century. This time, however, there are advance bases and plentiful supply lines in place. Government agencies are arranging and providing premises and warehouses as bridgeheads into overseas markets, a permanent support network of diplomatic, banking, customs, tax and insurance assistance to Chinese investors in overseas industries. This is designed to expedite trade engagement, market access and entry and intelligence gathering worldwide.

In South-East Asia, China is hungry for acquisitions to satisfy its voracious appetite for oil, gas and timber. This hunt is state-driven and Chinese companies are not always sensitive to local anti-Chinese sentiment in the societies of Indonesia, Malaysia, Singapore and Vietnam, where they may be regarded as *nouveaux riches* interlopers with little understanding of local history and culture. The potential for environmental damage is very high in these regions and dangerous flashpoints may be brewing unless China becomes much more aware of these antipathies.

In Central Asia, China is buying up oilfields in Uzbekistan, Kazakhstan and Turkmenistan to secure its energy needs. It has forged a close alliance with Iran for further supply of oil, chiefly for military purposes. This incursion into the former Soviet sphere of influence has naturally disquieted and angered the Russians. But it has also forged military alliances and cooperative exercises with the old Soviet vassal states, allowing Russia and China to maintain a wary strategic relationship.

Russia, China's nearest neighbor and former mentor, is engaging in a volume of bilateral trade which increases at a rate of nearly 40% a year. The two countries are bound by the import–export of machinery, high-tech products and construction materials, and have agreed to collaborate on technological innovation in energy, transport, biotech and infrastructure development.

In Europe, China is following the route taken by Japan and Korea, building factories and providing jobs. Made in Europe has a better brand ring than Made in China, but does mean that a future Made in Europe can also be classified as Owned in China. It is globally expanding by the acquisition of local companies, buying up plant and technology with the added advantage of shipping facilities operations to China, if they are no longer profitable overseas. This type of asset strip is a fine capitalist ploy, learned and adapted by the Chinese.

In Africa, China is driven ever more keenly by the need to suck up all available oil (from Nigeria and Sudan), copper (from Namibia), metals (from Zambia), iron ore (from Mozambique), diamonds (from South Africa), timber (from Cameroon) and even cinnamon (from the Seychelles). It has played fast and loose with local leaders, dictators and warlords providing wholesale financial and technical assistance in exchange for these vital commodities. It has, however, fallen foul of some regimes, where its arrival has brought no 'trickle down' benefit to the local economy. Its own laborers are typically flown in to complete projects, causing great resentment among the locals. In Ethiopia, Chinese workers have been shot by rebels and at a copper mine in Zambia, where local workers went on strike, Chinese foremen have been known to fire on them. All these incidents act as lightning rods for international opinion, but also serve to sensitize Chinese to the tensions and difficulties of operating across cultural boundaries. China derives around 25% of its energy needs from Africa at present and its direct investment in the continent has risen from $5 million in 1991 to $50 billion in 2006.

In the Middle East, China already has a well-established presence through CHINAMEX (China Machinery and Electronics Products Exhibition Centre), based in Dubai. This serves as a major trade platform for Chinese incursions into the Gulf States and the surrounding countries in North Africa and Eastern Europe. These markets have a growing appetite for Chinese products, chiefly light industrial, agricultural and food machinery and equipment, petroleum and natural gas equipment, textiles, refrigeration and medical equipment and hi-fi and video equipment. The 'Dragon Mart' in Dubai, at over one kilometer in length, is the largest permanent international showcase for Chinese merchandise. One small step for China, one great leap for the Chinese.

In the US, we have already seen Chinese approaches to acquire oil companies like Unocal rebuffed – a prime example of American protectionism and fear of ceding control of energy resources to China. Sinopec, the State oil behemoth, and CNOOC, the offshore exploration company, will not give up easily and will continue to press their claims to tap into existing conduits for energy, as demand rises at a rate of over 10% a year.

South America is probably the most resource-rich continent and another prime target for China's insatiable hunger for commodities to power its growth – copper from Chile, oil from Venezuela, soya from Brazil. President Chavez of Venezuela is clearly accommodating to China and has received $700 million in credits from China, while Cuba is working with Sinopec on offshore oil exploration. Latin America is to receive at least $200 billion in Chinese investment over the next decade. This is the pattern of Chinese political power emerging everywhere, as a champion of the developing world and of Third World solidarity. Money for nothing and your checks for free.

Perhaps with its 20% share now purchased in Africa's biggest bank, Standard Bank, China will need to guard against a growing perception that its initiatives of investing in many poorer Third World countries are simply a new form of colonialism. Its policy of studied non-engagement with local matters (in a long tradition of self-sufficiency and self-regulation) will run the risk of being compromised unless some of these matters – like employment and environmental concerns – are not squarely addressed. By using their relational techniques, rather than contractual, the Chinese are presently able to cloud the issues and to hide the extent of their control. For Africa, and particularly for Sudan, it is now the West, colonial epaulettes replaced by chips on the shoulder, which dares to accuse China of a failure to exert control in Africa, washing its hands in a bowl of Chinese alms.

The plan to advance Chinese interests on a broad front overseas, according to an informed China-watcher at a European industry association, has three main planks. Firstly, they are setting up a network of branches of the 'Confucius Institute' (a centre for Chinese language teaching and sponsorship of cultural events), attached for the most part to universities, as a catalyst to further mutual understanding. He points out that there are more Chinese studying English in China than there are native English speakers in the world. Maybe a little reciprocity from the West in the Mandarin department could do wonders in easing China's transition onto the world stage. Secondly, he says, the Chinese plan a major friendship initiative through sport and sporting exchanges in the wake of the 2008 Olympics. China has only recently embraced competitive sport in several disciplines like soccer, rugby and athletics, where it previously had no experience or tradition beyond acrobatics, gymnastics, table tennis and badminton. Thirdly, the associations of returned students from the US and Europe will serve to maintain and strengthen links with their *alma maters* and facilitate access and collaboration with foreign and Chinese research institutions. Knowledge becomes a relational commodity.

The action and spirit of these initiatives are well encapsulated in China's perception of its own soft power in the world. The country sees the main concern in international relations shifting from military and territorial issues to economic and trading issues. It recognizes that the rate and impact of interdependence in the international economy is increasing and believes that in making these strategic moves it will substantially reduce the apparent threat it poses to less powerful nations.

In the aftermath of the 2008 Olympics in Beijing and the run-up to the Expo in Shanghai in 2010, China presents a smiling, accommodating face. It will now begin to assert itself forcefully through its relational power with a hardening of its negotiating stance on trade and human rights issues. Fewer concessions can be expected by the US and the EU in any extensive revaluation of the *Renminbi* (at least once the *yuan* absorbs the Hongkong dollar, fixed by the British, a quarter of a century ago, at 7.8 to the US$), liberalization of financial markets, trade quotas and market access and entry by foreign firms. Protectionism in the West reinforces China's global stand: protectionist *rules* are equitable to all! It may be simply a question of who blinks first.

But China will still have a point. The Triennial Central Bank Survey for 2007 indicates that the *daily* turnover in global foreign exchange markets is in excess of US$ 3 trillion. There is no way that such daily turnover is related to trade in anything beyond currencies themselves. Indeed, the Central Bank figures show that spot trades are much less than forward swaps and derivatives, with the latter making up more than half of the daily turnover. How easily will China give up its currency to hedge funds' forward positions? The Asian currency crisis of 1997 was not so long ago, still rankles and suspicion is reinforced by the 2008 Wall Street debacle. The Chinese currency will not strengthen under speculative forces but we predict that, after the Olympics, the Chinese Government will engineer a short, sharp and substantial increase in the Yuan versus the US dollar.

China had a bad experience of the West in the 19th and 20th centuries and there remains a deep-seated feeling that reparations are in order to redress the damage done. Public opinion in the country will remain squarely behind the Government's efforts to defend national interests and uphold national pride at any price. The country is now unashamedly mercantilist in its trade ambitions – this strategy is designed to benefit itself, not its trading partners. Its currency exchange rate gives it a massive advantage, underpinning production exports and jobs. It is looking mostly to engage with foreign companies which will bring it innovative processes to advance its technology swiftly, enhance its export-driven industries and provide jobs, particularly in rural and inland areas. If the foreign companies do not buy into China, then China will buy into them.

There is scant likelihood that China will move in the direction of Korean or Taiwan-style democratization in the short-to-medium term. Because of tough thought-control in the media and with continuing restricted Internet access, the vast majority of Chinese are quite ill-informed about the true nature and state of affairs outside China. Thus they lack a sufficient basis of comparison or bandwidth to determine the merits and advantages of any alternative form of government. Even with free choice, who can defend the prostitution of Western political parties to big business, to spin and vote buying, to lobby groups? Trading votes for money is illegal, but buying political clout is only a matter of interpretation. Perhaps it is Western style democracy not Chinese style communism that is the true illusion.

CHAPTER 20

Unpredictable conclusion

> Explain things as simply as possible, but no simpler
> (*attributed to Albert Einstein*)

Will the West ever understand the East? We can come to a partial conclusion – partial in terms of part of the way along a global route. The Confucian 'way of doing things' is certainly adapting to an interface with foreigners – an interface known from past experience to be very different and probably still dangerous. A hybrid form of global governance is more likely than a simple acceptance of Western *rules*.

Demands for China to improve its legal system, for example, are demands to play by Western economic rules. The Chinese penal system is well established, its relational governance for transactional obligations is well ordered. The Chinese can integrate the Western low context *rules* together with Chinese high context but complex *rules*. In doing so, only the obligatory nature of Chinese networking, the *renqing* demands in *guanxi*, is weakening. But it depends, as we know, on the economy. Growth is a necessary but insufficient condition for stability.

And with growth comes a paradox. It was Jonathan Swift, the English satirist and author of *Gulliver's Travels*, who probably pointed out that legal systems were like spiders' webs, catching small flies and insects but letting large wasps and hornets through. In other words, legal systems have their own *guanxi* and, as the system grows, so the connections become more powerful. China understands this well. What else is a US Presidential pardon for, if not for those who are well connected?

Going global – spurred by WTO entry in 2001

China's strategic overseas investment policy has several key drivers. Chief amongst them are access to energy and raw materials, acquisition of technology, brands and know-how, escaping excess competition in their domestic market and switching production to host countries to cut production costs. Another major spur is their desire to break free of the constraints of foreign direct investment-style manufacture, working domestically to produce exclusively for foreign brands.

There are three main planks to its strategy:

- Manufacturers are encouraged to invest globally in developed countries to piggyback on higher productivity and technology, creating much greater overall benefits than lower labor costs alone.

- Mergers and acquisitions and foreign share investment are being used for the purchase of financial controls and trophy brands, providing an immediate and ready-made set of products, marketing and distribution channels and trained personnel. Major intermediaries in these transactions will be the foreign banks with cross-shareholdings in China.

- Strategic alliances are being set up, aimed at gaining market access, sales outlets and research and development facilities and resources at major corporations and universities.

Types of new planned investment will vary as follows:

- Start-ups in greenfield sectors and areas abroad, chiefly in electronics, electrical appliances and textiles. Firms like Haier, TCL and Gree have all performed a pioneering trail in setting up production lines overseas.

Mergers and acquisitions will continue in five main areas:

- Financial control through, for example, banking in Africa (Stanbank), Europe (RBS and Barclays), US investment (Blackstone, Merrill Lynch *et al.*).

- Oil exploration with CNOOC the biggest offshore oil producer in Indonesia and increasingly active in Latin America, chiefly in Venezuela and Cuba.

- Extension of production and marketing facilities via tie-ups like Shanghai GM with GM Daewoo and TCL's buying into a leading German electronics company at auction.

- Reversed contracted processing, such as that achieved by Wanxiang Group automotive parts producer, in buying over the American UAI Company, reducing its costs dramatically and supplying $25 million worth of brakes to UAI a year.

- Acquisition of technologies, tapping into state-of-the art technology by buying companies that own it.

Investment in R&D:

- Development of independent intellectual property rights and registering patents and trademarks overseas. The high-tech communications name brand Hwa Wei has already established eight regional R&D centres and 32 branches overseas.

Strategic integration:

- Chinese companies will be positioned in alliances with major multinationals to achieve a synergistic strength in foreign markets. The TCL Group has merged with Thomson in France to increase its market share in the color TV and DVD business by using Thomson and RCA brands and marketing networks and a manufacturing network throughout Asia, Europe and the USA. Indeed, the movement overseas is accelerating through acquisitions – if the state-controlled funds are being given a tough time acquiring investments overseas then let the quoted banks and insurance companies be the new juggernauts.

Overseas investment (approximate figures courtesy Deutsche Bank Research) is shown in Table III.1.

Table III.1 Chinese overseas direct investment.

Asia (chiefly Hongkong, Thailand, Singapore, Indonesia, Cambodia)	60%
Latin America (chiefly Brazil, Venezuela, Cuba, Argentina)	16.3%
Africa (chiefly Sudan, Algeria, Nigeria and South Africa)	6.9%
North America	6.7%
Europe (chiefly Russia, Germany, UK)	6.3%

Unpredictable conclusion 199

In 2006, Deutsche Bank's report indicated that the leading companies, such as Sinopec, Petrochina, Haier, Baosteel, CNOCC, Lenovo and others were increasing their overseas acquisitions with annual outflows in excess of US$7 billion. But the big move in 2007 is into the financial sector with China's banking investments approach $20 billion and overall M&A investments nearly $30 billion. Not bad as opening tactics in a global strategy.

The Olympic effect – brake or booster?

'This is a bride getting dressed for her wedding', said our guide for the day, a long-term resident foreign banker, indicating the broad, new, four-lane boulevards which have opened up in the last few years and the proud perpendicularity of the CBD or Central Business District, continuously sprouting buildings like gigantic toadstools. The rising stumps of the China Television headquarters look for all the world like the base of the Eiffel Tower in 1880s Paris. 'You see the one on the left. It's been constructed with a ten degree tilt from the vertical – an instant Leaning Tower of Pisa.' The Bird's Nest Olympic stadium is a surreal sculpture of tangled wrought iron. Grandiose plans had been laid down to carry the Olympic torch to the summit of Mount Everest to emphasize China's staking of its claim to Tibet.

A senior Chinese economist boldly asserted that the country will not suffer a slowdown, but that neither will it become a developed nation after the Olympics – as Japan and South Korea have done after their Games. He has claimed that these Games will not significantly boost the economy. He even suggested that growth will plateau after the Games, particularly in Beijing. All this he claimed in the face of a 20% increase in fixed asset investment to hasten industrialization and modernization and the clear record of China's being the world's fourth largest economy in 2007 and firmly set to become the second largest, supplanting Japan, in the years after 2008.

The process of beautifying the city continues apace with planting of floral banks and painting of the more decrepit façades of *hutongs* or back lanes and alley ways in a standard swash of grey, which renders them curiously invisible, like unobtrusive stage flats. One *hutong* house has a notice taped to its door: 'Please do not bother us. These are ordinary living quarters'. Such is the concern for the preservation of these single-storey, semi-slum dwellings with their secluded inner courtyards that visitors take an almost prurient interest in prying into them to make sure that they are still intact.

In the city's parks, squads of very young laborers planted fresh shrubs and water grass seedlings to grow into healthy greensward by the summer and autumn of 2008. Factories were shut down for months before the Games to allow all the construction dust to settle and the miasma of hydrocarbons and industrial effluent to dissipate. The city enjoyed a brief respite from its heavy air pollution and the constant pall of haze which hangs over it. Dogs are not allowed out in public in the inner zones on pain of hefty fines for owners, fearing the fouling of the footpaths (a salutary warning to Brussels, should it ever dream of hosting an Olympiad).

Property values have been driven to ridiculous heights by 2008 hoopla and they are riding for a fall afterwards; but there is also intensive new investment culminating in a huge, new airport terminal and new subway lines. This is but the cool, moist tip of the desert storm of China Rising. The real challenge for the Government to meet is slowly to slake the ravenous hunger and thirst for jobs and knowledge of the 700 million *Lao Bai Xing* – the 'Old Hundred Names' peasant farmers in the countryside. If they fail to hasten progress there, they will surely not prevail.

In conclusion?

Now take away the figures and the rhetoric and remember that the Chinese government, since the Reform, has emphasized the concepts of *fa zhi* (rule by law) and *ren zhi* (rule by people) within China. These concepts will, of course, be slow to process through the bureaucratic machinery, but they are being engineered and fine tuned at the moment. The interim stage means that *guanxi* continues as the time-honored way of getting things done. Even when a lawyer is paid with a handsome fee, the Chinese would still feel that they have a future obligation to a successful advocate. It's in the nature of the network.

Unpredictable conclusion

Just as *guanxi* has three major facets, so Chinese behavioral choices are governed by *qing*, *li*, and *fa*. Human feelings, *renqing*, are explained earlier in the book and imply relational obligation. The *wu li* are the five (*wu*) ordered relationships in Figure III.1 showing the rationale of the relationships. The rules or laws or principles are denoted by *fa*. In China these three choices of behavior are in a strict order. That suggests that whatever happens in China, *qing* is the first option that one should take. The ordering of those feelings is dictated by *li*. Government and national (as opposed to communally networked) rules or *fa* fall last in line. The conscientious objector would follow *qing* well before enforced *fa*.

One of the biggest barriers to predicting where China is going is the Western belief in an order to things – not so much a belief in the paradigmatic continuation of physical laws, but a belief that society must be ordered by imposing societal law. The Chinese don't think in that way. The concept that laws are for the guidance of wise men but the obedience of fools is an excuse for disobedience mirrored in the Chinese *nan de hu tu* (hard to translate, but basically meaning that wisdom and foolishness can be interchangeable).

The Chinese believe that chaos and ignorance can sometimes protect them, as they then have options to stay silent or escape. This ability is called *da zhihui* (superb wise). A society with complex laws allows the interpretation of the meaning to be ambivalent – wise or foolish then depends on the outcome. Even the rigorous one child policy is failing with increasing wealth and understanding – get rich, calculate the fine, pay it, and have another kid!

China has gone though continuous upheaval over the last 100 years. Past guarantees are gone. The US Constitution has had fewer amendments in 250 years than China has had in half a century. A desire for contentment through *qing* is probably more important now than ever. The West certainly retains much ambivalence and, if the 2007 global warming meeting in Bali is anything to go by, the USA is a greater threat to clear international *fa* than a horde of Chinese *qings*.

Who can say how the future of global interchange will work without relationships? One respondent told us of the Chinese illegal immigrant on a British train. He spent 90 days traveling, partly in hiding, *en route* to the UK, and then worked 12 hours per day, 365 days over the last year in a Chinese restaurant. He talked about Chinese dead bodies on the Russian mountains during his trek to the West, but disassociated himself from them. He was happy, he had made it, the others had not. He took the gamble and had won. That's life.

It is not possible therefore to make a predictable conclusion from a value system that depends on hardship for happiness, on chaos for opportunity, on complexity for protection. The more that is known about the Chinese, the less that is understood. But be assured that hardship, chaos and complexity fit better with *qing*, than with *fa*.

Summary and discussion

A snapshot of the country towards the end of the first decade of the 21st century looks something like this: the centre ground is held by the President in his charmed circle of nominal power, within which he is expected to orchestrate the direction of the economy. In fact, he has extremely limited room for manoeuver within this designated *space* without somehow widening the scope of his mandate to draw to himself some real power and authority to act from civil society. Against him is ranged the army like a huge potential landslip. They rely on his patronage, as do Party cadres, to maintain their wealth, property and business activities.

This bizarre balance of totalitarian socialism with *laissez-faire* capitalism is highly precarious and the major cause of chronic tension and uncertainty within the current regime. The Old Guard of retired general and Party members, as well as the young princelings, the rising heirs of Party cadres and thus of natural privilege, are mired in the machinations and plottings of an almost mediæval statecraft.

The real Grand Question which is now posed is this: how on earth is this poisonous tension and uncertainty to be eased without some gradual systemic shift towards legitimizing the dissent and opposition of the dispossessed and disenfranchised in China – which will otherwise fester and ferment into even more uncontainable revolt and further rebellion? The answer, of course, lies in the area of greatest paradox: how to reconcile the burning patriotism every Chinese feels with the murderous feelings of hatred provoked by the impasse of fear, fear of losing control over personal destiny. In short, how can China create and enfranchise a loyal opposition and stop treating dissenters as enemies of the State?

This will require the most extraordinary moral courage from Chinese intellectuals – whose fear is still a palpable obstacle to progress in this direction. Intellectuals, from Socrates and Galileo to Luther and Solzhenitsyn, so many of them latterly supine over Katyn Wood and the Cambodian killing fields, cowed, compliant or heroic in the McCarthy and Maoist purges, have been brave sporadically but mostly cowardly. Human nature is human nature – fear will cause the face to fall below the parapet. But it is not just the Chinese fear of systemic chaos that is so present and alarming. It is its *spatial* predecessor, a messing up of the old order, a *mélange* of half baked *rules* and confusing *time* spans that mixes old systems with new dynamics, that has already arrived.

Superpower?

We have shown how the hidden levers of power in China have been subjected to such unprecedented stresses and strains in recent years that traditional *guanxi* mechanisms have warped and been forced to adapt in accommodating new pressures from below. The groundswell and sway of public opinion, the see-saw of influence, is tilting in favour of those who are being left behind, chiefly the inland rural poor whose near destitution in the wake of the great surges in coastal prosperity is already the focus of continuous, unresolved unrest. The Party is now very much alive to the gaping disparity in the distribution of new wealth.

Party officials define *guanxi* in terms of their own supposedly hierarchical rights and percentages of entitlement, while the rural peasantry use it to describe the bonds of extended family and ancestral land roots and usage. Whose is the more just and rightful claim? Here lies the rub and the dilemma. The sop of partial dispensation from paying local taxes is hardly sufficient compensation for loss of ancient title to land, when housing, transport and education costs make the unequal burden of living almost unsupportable. Once the economy is marketized, then the price of this land bubbles way beyond the meagre means of landed peasants to repossess it as their own: their sense of dispossession grows mordantly keen.

The proverbial Emperor came perilously close to being shown up as wearing no new clothes in 2006, when Ernst & Young pointed out that China's massive foreign exchange reserves could be said to have been eclipsed by the total volume of its bad bank loans, amounting to roughly the same figure. The Chinese were moved beyond mere indignation to outrage by this aberrant assertion, claiming that since cash was a circulating medium it should be channelled wherever it could best lubricate the economy. This demonstrated yet again, in a peculiarly forthright way, how measure and degree are largely relative matters in China ('foreign moon more round' again).

A probable conclusion

Economists discount discontinuities. They are unexpected and unpredictable and they are factored out of most calculations. Oil shocks, Gulf wars, Suez closures, Harbin pollution, Archduke assassinations – history is full of the unexpected. Following the bombings in London on 7 July 2005, mobile phones were pretty useless; landlines worked, but the mobile networks were allocated to security and safety officers. In modern China the use of mobile phones is extensive and increasing. A small panic, normally contained in recent years, could now allow a breakdown in communication. That would be quite disastrous. Chinese rumours spread quickly and that squall threatening the great ship of state will whip up over the horizon before the authorities can act.

Our final prediction is that an accident, probably of an environmental nature, will create that panic. The pell-mell drive for economic prosperity is a drive designed to keep the population under control. Energy and infrastructure failures will frustrate many. Inflation in foodstuffs is approximately 25% a year and President Hu is determined to control this, scaring those bankers with credit problems. The old Emperor's mandate allowed the population to overturn the Emperor if he failed them. No need for spoiling ballot papers, no need to vote them out nicely; for the Chinese have a stronger, traditional hold on the politicians' empty promises of 'a chicken in every pot'. They're entitled to another revolution. We read an unsavoury global one in the dynamic runes.

Organizational competitive advantage

Our book is mainly about modern Chinese managers tackling the global economy, but it also touches on their organizational structures. Our interpretation is of contrasts and changes in the Chinese social context – hence our emphasis on Chinese relationships and reciprocity. Any resulting improvement in competitive advantage, for Chinese domestic and global economic exchange, is a benefit of their great success in imitating and adapting.

International problems from increased globalization in the industrial, service and trading sectors can be of greater commonality at the boundaries of trade than of greater disparity between domestic issues of nations. Transnational strategies, locally responsive but globally integrative, are in demand. A compromise in ways of doing business is called for. Such a compromise is feeding back into China through overseas expatriate networks.

Calls for open market, open government, open judicial action, enforcement and openness in network relationships are being heard at senior party levels. Economic growth is not an excuse for environmental degradation. High-tech initiatives and more objective problem solving will balance rural production of food and water with urban expansion and consumption. The robbing of peasant to pay politician will cease. For North America and Europe, however, it will require a behavioural change to match China's move, from global factory for the patrician to economic proxy for the plebeian. The last bastion of communism may yet use capitalism to benefit the developing nations of the world – subject to a mutual relationship, of course.

Can we provide a summarized set of tips for the international man and woman when the Chinese come calling? What do you need to know and do in order to prepare? The following points highlight the most important aspects:

- Understand that the Chinese are of a less moderate but more adaptable disposition in an international context. The variegation in their controls over decision making is making them *less* not more easy to understand. The Western (default) defence is to accept Chinese relationships and the adoption of mutual obligations in order to match Chinese long-term strategies. Diplomatic problem solving should focus on increased reciprocity beyond any initial agreement.

- The integrated findings of our study into modern Chinese cultural characteristics – of manipulative *guanxi* and of greed competing

Summary and discussion

with 'face' in a period of intense economic growth – are concerning. They call for a strategy of incorporating modern *guanxi* relational governance with the contractual governance of the West. An acceptance of group and market controls, and their ultimate effect on global strategy, requires an adjustment, not through more market openness, but through greater social fusion.

- Chinese global characteristics map dynamically with Western economic theory to explain Chinese economic and strategic practice. The need to apply integrated, not piecemeal, Western theory must be met when devising strategies to deal with Chinese practices, both domestic and global. Flexibility through holistic, non-confrontational strategies is the only solution. Threatening the Chinese with sanctions or tariffs simply signals that any mutual relationship is off limits. It is Western consumerism that made the Chinese powerful; it is the West that opened the Asian door. Reciprocity is the key to a two-way flow.

- A sequential interpretation of Chinese behavior is necessary: think in terms of control systems. Changes in the systemic perspectives are changes in the governing criteria over strategic problem solving. Avoid simple comparisons of *rules* across business paradigms. Concentrate on the contexts and specifications governing the *rules* of Chinese strategy. Try to adapt or change the context, not the *rule*, because the *rules* for the Chinese always follow the context.

A final discussion

Western interpretation is essential to our argument. China is faced with a dilemma. How does a society, firmly entrenched in the communal family move into a market economy? The trial and error market strategy is in conflict with the tried and tested societal relationship. The schema in Figure III.2 synthesizes our arguments.

Chinese strategy can be interpreted as balancing the tension between domestic societal ties and needs with the global integration necessary for crafting and applying global economic and military expansion. Change and adaptation will mainly be achieved through an imitative problem solving ability. Such transvergence is governed

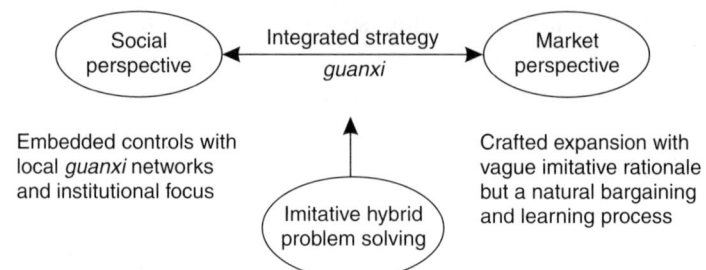

Figure III.2 Dynamic conflict.

by the dynamics of social versus economic forces. In some respects, China has recognized what the West has not: the need for a balance between societal and market forces. The British National Health Service is a prime example of a need for some equilibrium, where the argument runs that there is a correlation between MRSA bacteria (with the spread of infection in hospitals) and the marketization of cleaning contracts to outside agencies: societal control losing out to market focus.

The schema in Figure III.2 does, therefore, offer a solution to problems raised in any discussion on national characteristics and organizations. Minor discrepancies in the initial control conditions (even insignificant differences in national controls) produce large differences in actual strategic outcomes. The problem solving technique is driven by tension between the social context and market uncertainty. Where the West can be imitated then the solution is simpler for the Chinese. The major problem therefore is the West's attitude of 'do not do what I do, do what I say'. Rightly or wrongly, the Chinese will imitate the capitalist, military and environmental practices of the West – and reciprocate in a tit-for-tat fashion.

The dynamic conflict will not be in stable equilibrium. The control adjustment at the cusp (the broad arrow) can adapt to new problems with increased knowledge. Niche-driven growth, with that knowledge, is now following Western expansion and taking overseas opportunities. Cheap labour is no longer a Chinese defensive strategy.

In some respects labour is no longer cheap. When Beijing was building for the Olympics, workers were seen atop old cement-clad, metre diameter pipes. Armed with sledgehammers, they broke up the cladding to recover the steel reinforcing rings of the pipes. At the same time, China had excess steelmaking capacity to the tune of 120 million tonnes. There are clear micro-management versus macro-economic issues. Mismatched labour and capital is an expensive waste of resources.

But so is the problem of jobless masses. Whilst moving agricultural processes into modern farming methods (running like a Deere rather than a Dao) is positive, what will the farmers' families do with mechanization? There are not enough colleges for the future mechanics, engineers and agricultural specialists. There are only jobs on building sites.

Increasingly, this 'new problem' for China uncovers the dynamic forces which open borders can stimulate. Bounded rationality, profit maximization and competitive advantage apply as spurs to the institutional activities of the Chinese. Controls over opportunism, resources and investments are altering from traditional governance. But they are not aligned and struggle to balance demand, supply and direction.

Stripping Earth's resources merely to serve present market demand is not a long-term solution. Problem solving using Chinese systemic controls will help to check Western consumer sprees. In Chinese tradition, if it ain't broke by all means adapt it – but don't replace it. The West, in a mirror image and reflective mode, must emphasize relational and reciprocal structures when globalizing. The West should reduce the clamour for open market economies and look for societal, group solutions.

Integration of Chinese practices is, however, still leaving something to be desired. Adjustments designed to improve political and economic governance and to decrease future uncertainty must be complementary. Individualism may yet follow the dynamics of global problem solving but it will take some time. So will any form of democracy.

China's definition of democracy is this: 'The Chinese Communist party governing on behalf of the people... while upholding and perfecting the people's democratic dictatorship'. It is, of course, a splendid piece of nonsense, an exquisite oxymoron – almost as good as 'the dictatorship of the proletariat' itself. China is shadow boxing with its demons – oxymorons creating the harmonious choice of referee. Perhaps the Chinese definition of democracy is no less valid than Alan Coren's rather more accurate and concise argument: 'Democracy consists of choosing your dictators, after they've told you what it is you want to hear'.

The notion of dictatorship being somehow perfectible is particularly aberrant, since by definition it is rule by the will of the one individual, not the many. It is a *reductio ad absurdum* of the concept of concord or harmony, this imposition of a collective cast of mind on the thinking and behaviour of an entire people. The supreme irony is that the Greek philosopher, Plato, was no champion of democracy, regarding it as corrupt and inefficient. He thought that the best government was by a Philosopher King with a court of wisest advisers – roughly what the current Chinese leadership apparently aspires to.

Their problem is that, having done away with their Emperor (and possibly with Confucius as well), they are made up of technocrats – engineers, scientists and economists – who are visionary on infrastructure but somewhat short of the spirit of free enquiry and debate. This is why they fear democracy, because it could produce another *da luan*, a great chaos with people claiming that they know what is better for them: autonomy, argument and choice – something beyond the passing contentedness brought on by shopping for consumer goods.

In his speech to the 17th Party Congress in October 2007, President Hu mentioned 'democracy' no fewer than sixty times. It has become a weasel word, a kind of decoy or shield and buckler against criticism in the tortuous process of the Party's political evolution and internal reform towards allowing a very gradual participation so far denied even to lower-ranking members, not to mention the people. As in ancient Greece, fully three-quarters (and more) of the people remain excluded from participatory government. The party elite are the only true 'citizens'; the rest of the people remain effectively, as in Athens of old, the disenfranchised 'slaves'. Until freedom of speech and assembly and movement, popular sovereignty (i.e. the vote), and political and religious freedoms with economic and educational opportunities, are all extended, the country remains in an intractable bind of mutual suspicion, fear and anger between government and governed.

Summary and discussion

The good news is that there is a certain historical inevitability about the outcome of the current storm which is brewing. The economics of survival dictate that the exchange rate question be addressed, not least to curb inflation and redress trade imbalances, but mainly to unlock the true potential of the private sector in China and its legions of budding entrepreneurs, ready and willing to create employment opportunities. Taiwan is the controlled experiment and it seems to be working.

In China, most of the old (SOE or State) warhorses are knackered beyond hope of recovery and still put an almighty strain on China's manpower and banking resources. The transition to viable economic management and income redistribution in the country can only be built upon the four-wall framework of a sound business economy:

- A banking system – which does not misallocate its resources
- An accounting system – which accepts international reporting standards
- A legal system – which truly regulates business, allowing for failures and bankruptcy
- A professional management cadre – which is the master, not the servant, of technology

If these four institutional walls can be built upon firm foundations, then China will indeed become an industrial giant to rival all other powers and to lead the world as an engine of growth and regeneration for its new dominions and dependencies overseas. Subject, of course, to Western reciprocity!

In closing

Our arguments throughout this book have been based on principles laid out in Part I, on the anecdotal and empirical evidence of Part II, and the predictive jumps in Part III. We do not acknowledge a flat earth. Although we would not argue against such imaginative projections, our arguments are simpler. Collaboration and connection can only be achieved by working *across* relational networks, not purely within them. The need for increasing the use of strategies designed for success at reciprocal interfaces – across boundaries – will ensure competitive advantage. Reliance on purely Western ways of doing business will not.

A final contrasting picture of China at a crossroads is exemplified in the retention of harmony against the odds. On yet another piece of brownfield, a city site demolished by courtesy of Caterpillar and Komatsu, the Chinese watchman's hut is the last building left standing. The construction workers have not yet flooded in to float another office block. Outside the hut, in late Autumn sunshine, a table is covered in bright, green baize and four elderly family members play *mahjong*. Although battle may be joined, this isle of tranquillity in the dust and rubble defines the moment – peace in their time!

In sum, then, humans enjoy problem solving and play this game whenever they can. The scientific community makes its major advances through paradigm change. Problems, difficult within one view of reality, become solvable through another. Heavenly mechanics are simpler with the Sun, not the Earth, at the centre of the planetary system. Unfortunately, heresy, when challenging past practice and peer groups, is still a common accusation. It is a brave scientist who solves a problem, the unit of scientific achievement, through paradigm change.

But the units of political, economic and societal achievement should be no less. Advances in financial techniques, in operations and methods, in the knowledge that increased production can have a psychological as well as mechanical dynamic, in the understanding of group and network forces; all of these create paradigm shifts and more opportunities for evolutionary survival, benchmarked as a better 'way of doing things'. Our major predictions may fail, but if we have helped cross the paradigm border between West and East, and their domestically exclusive strategies, then we will have achieved a measure of minor success.

The Greeks and Romans may have conquered their known world but the Chinese rested secure in theirs. Ancient Mediterranean philosophy and language dictated Western ways – neither better nor worse than ancient Chinese philosophy and language. Both cultures have survived; past strategies have succeeded. But Western ways are not Asian ways. The *rules* of the strategic system are being redrawn.

Summary and discussion

West and East can no longer rest within their own faiths. Their political and economic paradigms for successful survival are quite different and must adapt at their respective boundaries. The pressures for modern survival will alter the Western ways of doing things as surely as the Chinese are changing theirs. The problem is that they have commenced their change and are happy to leapfrog from the past, over the present, and into the future. The West is wishing and hoping that its past will sustain its future.

The Chinese are adding Western ways to their national and rational systems. For Western systems, global imitation of Chinese harmonious ways is called for. This should mean more mahjong and less poker. It will also mean playing in a global team. This coming era will be one of Eastern impact and Western response. Our fathers rode off into the sunset to discover the West; our children must ride East, into the sunrise.

Postscript

Hindsight is wonderful. This book, however, was not written from hindsight but from theoretical argument and practical experience. The recent Chinese overseas economic expansion in 2007 and 2008 bore out several of our main predictions. We anticipated their making a play for a large mining company, perhaps Anglo-American or an Africa-based entity, but not their taking a share in RTZ, nor their making a hostile bid for Midwest in Australia; yet such actions follow directly from our predicted aggressive strategies and are consistent with strategic expansion in controlling resources and borders.

Tibet and Taiwan remain intractable borders of control for China. The US sees Tibet as a chance to attack China whilst China points out US hypocrisy on torture and human rights. A future stand-off between the two great nations is quite likely. China will only talk to those who recognize their borders and territories as integral parts of their country. Potential conflict with Taiwan is now averted by the KMT's victory in the March 2008 election. KMT policy is to establish direct links with the mainland, building closer relations and a 'common market' to help revive Taiwan's faltering economy. It also seeks a formal peace treaty, paving the way for Taiwan's accommodation as a quite different Special Administrative Region.

Meanwhile, the recent credit crunch is allowing those with Chinese or Middle Eastern cash to use their liquidity at a frightening speed. We did not foresee this (we were looking East, not West). Western central banks moved slowly to ease the credit situation and the Chinese have done enough to bail out a weakening Wall Street. Chinese overseas expansion is clearly accelerating. The global door is held open not only by hordes of swift feet but also by hoards of credit and cash!

References

Our references are sectioned by Part and by Chapter. Where we have taken ideas or concepts from other authors for argument or discussion, then their book, journal or newspaper article is referenced. Where direct quotations are used, these are specified against page number of book, journal etc. Where we have read interesting articles which gave us food for thought, we have put them into the general reference list as they may prove interesting to others. Where we have written from our own experience or from anecdotes heard over the years, we have either preserved the anonymity of our sources or have written from memories of the events themselves. For business and management practitioners, the intelligence and experience gathered from lengthy discussion into the night are often remembered not for their intensity, but for their consequences. We are publishing the more useful results.

Part I

Introduction

We make a simple start but should anyone wish to have a stronger background to the study of management in China we would suggest Tang and Ward (2003).

1. Convergence and divergence

Winder (2004) provides an argument for measuring differences across nations. Floyd (1999) points out that only minor differences partially converge. Ralston *et al.* (1997) argue that convergence may be caused by ideological change, a crossvergence. Child and Rodrigues (2004) note the power of trust within networks. For expatriates, Lincoln *et al.* (1978) were one of the earlier research groups to spot how adaptation to a host country's values could occur. The quote on being locally responsive and globally integrative is from Bartholomew and Adler (1996, p. 11).

2. Decision making and problem solving

The concept of restless capitalism comes from Cook (2004) with dynamics as a subject for management study updated by Gummesson (2006). Natale *et al.* (1995) classify ten steps in problem solving updated by Harrison and Pelletier (2000). Mackinnon (2008) presents the steps in Figure I.1. Haley and Tan (1999) provide evidence of five Asian problem solving styles and Engardio (1991) notes their wheeling and dealing prowess. Freakonomics is a popular book by Levitt and Dubner (2006). Adler (1997, p. 16) links behavior and values to culture in an interative, circular process. Popper (2001) looks at the logic in preventing infinite regress. The dynamic system of *space*, *rules* and *time* is clarified mathematically by Casti (2000).

3. Imitation and innovation

Much of this chapter is more intricately analyzed in the seminal work completed by Nelson and Winter (1982). North (1997) provides information on the historical changes in Europe. There is considerable research available on changes to Chinese organizations and Cooke (2005) is certainly worth reading from a management perspective. The concept of paradigm shift (Kuhn, 1962) is introduced.

4. Paradigms and worldviews

This chapter relies very much on Kuhn (1962, 1970). Getting the basics right is important and Kuhn (1962, pp. 156–7) provides the

References   **217**

arguments for the quote on 'faith' as a foundation for any paradigm. 'Paradigm' no longer holds the terror for the authors it once did. Latin masters used the term to cover the recital from memory of the complete conjugation in all its tenses of a Latin verb – a very holistic, even Chinese, discipline!

5. Strategic shock

Simon (1960, 1976, 1987) is the acknowledged expert for the arguments in this chapter. The quote on solving problems and reconciling dilemmas, however, comes from Trompenaars and Hampden-Turner (1998, p. 6). That the Chinese way of doing business (Nelson and Winter (1982) called this a 'way of doing things' or a routine) is irrational and chaotic is an unfair piece of abuse often mentioned when Western values are challenged. As Rutgers (1999) argues, rationality and values are intertwined. Spinney (2004) explains the dynamics of uncertainty, social context and emotion. Saunders (1980) discusses the mathematical ease with which cusp catastrophe happens in a dynamic system. The rest of the argument is for your consideration.

6. National strategies

Mintzberg (2000) and Mintzberg *et al.* (1998) provide further information for advanced discussion of the arguments in this chapter. Deal and Kennedy (1982) describe different corporate styles of management and Sun Tzu is a good historical comparison. Lewis (1992, 2005) is, we believe, an important observer of human nature (see Table I.1). As a business practitioner he categorizes in a useful manner the whys and wherefores of different national behaviour. Hofstede (1997) and the Chinese Culture Connection (1987) provide links into Table I.2. Batonda and Perry (2003) provide greater detail than we discuss in this chapter. Marx (1999) creates three dimensions clarifying business behavior across nations (see Table I.3).

7. Chinese practice and Western theory

Perhaps we forget that Orwell (1986, p. 122) could be argumentative and politically incorrect for his time, but he has a point with globalization, an unusual concept in old Burma. This chapter, however, belongs to Williamson (1996) for transaction costs and opportunism, to Barney (2001) for resource-base theory and competitive advantage, to Pitelis and Pseiridis (1999) for arguing the integration of transactions and resources, but in the main to Leiblein (2003) for introducing real option theory to the integration. The links with *guanxi* are from both personal experience and the general literature. In particular, the dredging of *guanxi* is a concept introduced by Wood et al. (2002, p. 267). Two peer-reviewed conference papers (O'Regan et al., 2006a,b) also provide information for this chapter's arguments. Woolman and Lake (2001) and Luo (2007) generate a legal contrast with our *guanxi* knowledge to help create Table I.4.

Part II

Introduction

This lengthy introduction opens with John Stuttard (2000, p. 32), who interviewed leading expatriate chief executives in China and thus explains many of the business problems being faced by the Westerner in China. Needham is also in the introduction as he places the complexity of China's history into context. Chen (1991) and Fan (2003) provide the basis of a partial Chinese explanation for the country's 'delayed' evolution. Much of Part II, however, is from our own experience or from the anecdotes of colleagues. Part I abounds with theory, but Part II is, as the medical profession might put it, based on clinical practice.

8. Transvergence

Chong (2000) provides evidence on the audit problems in China. The RBS purchase of the investment in Bank of China was widely

References   219

reported in the media and at the boardroom and dining tables of business. The *Financial Times* in August 2005 and Treanor of the *Guardian* (2005) are interesting sources. Leung and Wong (2001) calculated the cost of doing *guanxi*. Mackinnon (2008) relates several of the qualitative comments and introduces the concept of transvergence within a peer-reviewed journal.

9. Induction or deduction

Allinson (1991, p. 10) argues that the Chinese mind is practical rather than theoretical. Losee (2001) provides the raven paradox. Nisbett *et al.* (2001) highlight the holistic rather than analytical cognitive tendencies of the Chinese.

10. Adaptation

We have already introduced Popper (2001) and demonstrated that his Western logic trial and error model is common in Asia (see Figure I.1). Popper's emphasis on problem solving aligns with ours. The historical perspective we give on China is very personal and should be judged alongside more authoritative works. Andre Malraux's *La Condition Humaine* (*Man's Estate* in English translation) is an epic dramatization of the struggles of the early 20th century. The media have commented on many occasions on the Asian Crisis in 1997, but the most enlightening article is by the IMF (1998). Orwell's *1984* is well known but, as we argue, occasionally misunderstood.

11. Chinese reality

Bertrand Russell is famous for his philosophy and Churchill for his rhetoric. Two colleagues related the airline story during a conference (see Liu and Hua, 2004). Chen (2001) describes the Confucian and family nature of *guanxi* in a simple to understand fashion.

12. Harmony and people

Geertz (1975, p. 35) is a beautiful writer (the anthropology quote) but was challenged directly and indirectly by the positivist academic establishment who claimed that the essay was replacing the scientific article (Denzin and Lincoln, 1998, p. 19). Talk about a paradigm problem! The Chinese legal void is well discussed by Allen *et al.* (2005). To understand how the individual is subsumed into a network the work by Schaubroek *et al.* (2000, pp. 514–15) is of assistance – they provide the quote on self referring to the individual or generalized to the network. Kipling is a highly regarded student of the East, although, when talking about truth, he was referring to soldiery. Comparing Browning to a Chinese proverb is a bit of a stretch, but we believe that the contrast is apt.

13. Beyond control

There are many versions of the Second Law of Thermodynamics, but this one, from vague memories of past studies, appeals to us. The quotation about Sinitic culture is from Francis Fukuyama (1995, p. 71). Having personally attended a speech given by Madame Chiang, we can attest to the erudition and syntax. *Guanxi* tends to be oversimplified or overcomplicated. Our references abound with titles involving *guanxi*, but our threefold basic simplification comes from experience. The reader is welcome to challenge us.

14. Chinese strategy

Whittington (2001) provides a solid introduction to this chapter. Reference to Part I will also assist the understanding. For those who think that imitation is safe we would suggest they remember, or 'Google', the Russian Konkordski, a copy of Concorde, which sadly crashed at a Paris airshow in 1973. Our Western to Chinese comparison of corporate and management practices was developed by Backman (1998).

Part III

Introduction

Joseph Conrad (1972, p. 74) was a perceptive observer of human nature. The introductory details for Part III are well reported in the Western and Asian media. It would be remiss to mention one article rather than another but to reference all would be foolish. May we suggest that the voracious researcher starts with LexisNexis and types in as many keywords as he or she feels necessary. The comments on the cost of the World Food Programme came from a cargo superintendent in East Africa. We cannot verify the pricing but given the high cost of chartering US ships (75% of US grain for the poor must go by US flag carrier) they may even be too low. Mrs Ezekwesili of the World Bank is quoted in *China Daily*, Business section, p. 17, of 6 March 2008.

15. National controls

Fishman (2005) provides an interesting update on China. The quotation on the level of debt can be found in Galbraith (1993, p. 20). The contrast between engineers and bureaucrats is well documented by Li (2000).

16. Strategic controls

This chapter uses the information in Parts I and II to create predictive comments. It may be possible to test those predictions once this book is in press.

17. Modern Chinese management

Shakespeare's *hoops of steel* are in Act 1, Scene iii, lines 62-3, of Hamlet. The jet fuel discussion is commented upon by Guerrera (2004). Mackinnon (2008) also comments on elements in this chapter. Figure III.1 is developed from work by Luo (2007) and his permission to use his work in this fashion is gratefully acknowledged. Luo (2007) also provides the Confucian quotation. Redfern (2002) provides information on traditional Chinese values.

18. ChinaTech

Information on Linux and Chinese involvement is available on the Internet, but the Chinese government developments are from a respondent working in the overseas IT sector. Lenovo background is documented by Dickie and Lau (2004).

19. *Qu xiang he fang?*

Again we direct the reader/researcher to LexisNexis for public information in this chapter. The Triennial Bank Survey (2007) is available on the Internet (see http://www.bis.org/).

20. Unpredictable conclusion

Deutsche Bank (2006) provides financial background to this chapter. Sources of trade and investment figures: Heritage Foundation (http://www.heritage.org/); Foreign Policy in Focus (http://www.fpif.org/); Council on Foreign Relations (http://www.cfr.org/).

References

Glossary

We have not put in place a keyword index as we use executive style summaries at the beginning of each part of the book. We believe that this is preferable for the business reader. From an academic perspective, the structure of the book is holistic, with the word *guanxi* constantly cross-referencing with other concepts, thus making any index overly long and very complicated.

We do, however, present a brief introduction to Chinese pronunciation and several important and useful concepts in this glossary. The glossary provides a brief explanation of concepts discussed in the text. You may note that we use Hongkong rather than the western Hong Kong. Chinese words tend to have two characters (e.g. Beijing – north capital; Shanghai – upper harbour; Hongkong – fragrant harbour) and we have opted for consistency, when we remember!

To aid the reader, we should explain that Chinese pronunciation is linked to the Roman spelling more directly than English spelling (think cough and bough) – *q* is a ch sound (chicken), *x* is a sh sound (shame) and the vowels form the tongue and mouth movements (*xiao* equals shyaow). Vowels are more French sounding than English (*u* is ooh rather than you). Tones are very important – *mai* with rising and then falling vowels means to buy, *mai* with a distinct falling tone is to sell. We do not go into detail but merely warn the reader to be careful lest the transaction goes the wrong way.

Term	Meaning
Andre Malraux	20th century French writer and statesman.
Audit	Scrutiny of financial accounts.
Bao	The implicit expectation of mutual obligation and reciprocity in business and social dealings.
Bu xiao	Non-fulfilment of filial obligation.
CEIBS	The China-Europe International Business School in Shanghai.
Chiang Kai Shek	President of China from 1928 to 1931 and from 1943 to 1949. Leader of the *Kuomintang*, the Chinese Nationalist Party. Retreated to Taiwan in 1949 after defeat by

	the Chinese Communists to set up a separate Nationalist Chinese state.
Commodore Perry	American naval commander entrusted with forcefully opening up trade relations with Japan in 1853.
Confucianism	The practical, worldly moral precepts and philosophy of *Kongfuzi* (c. 500 BC), determining the norms of behaviour in Chinese society.
Contractual	Descriptive of a binding obligation, enforceable in law.
Crossvergence	The effects of interpenetration of different national cultures and influences.
Cultural Revolution	A period of extreme social unrest and political upheaval, most intense from 1966–68, resulting in the persecution of intellectuals and bourgeois elements, purges in Party posts and a Mao Zedong personality cult.
Daoism	The alternative, unworldly philosophy founded by Laozi in the 6th century BC, focusing on inner contemplation and mystical union with nature.
Darwin	Charles Darwin, naturalist and geologist, proponent of the theory of evolution and author of *On the Origin of Species* (1859).
David Hume	Scottish moral philosopher, historian and economist (1711–1776), whose legacy has most influenced 20th century empiricist philosophers.
Deng Xiaoping	Chinese Communist leader and prime mover of economic reform and opening up of relations with the West from the late 1970s.
Fa	Rules, laws and strict principles.
Feng shui	Chinese geomancy, the art of siting buildings auspiciously.
Guanxi	Literally 'relationship', but used to mean 'connections' or the network of relationships

References

	formed and used by Chinese individuals to achieve their ends, based on mutual obligation and communal understanding.
Han Dynasty	The period of rule by the dominant (*Han*) ethnic group (206 BC to 220 AD), which later dynasties took as a model for the ordering of society.
Hou men	The 'back door' route, to be taken if the 'front door' is closed to a request or application.
INSEAD	The European Institute of Business Administration in Fontainebleau, France.
KMT	*Kuomintang*, the Chinese Nationalist Party, led by General Chiang Kai Shek (*qv*).
Kowtow	The old Chinese ritual of touching the ground with the forehead in submission to the Emperor and high officials.
Legal	Required or permitted within the jurisdiction of a country's law.
Li	The conduct of relationships.
Lin Yutang	Chinese 20th century writer of popular works like *My Country and My People*, who did much to explain and interpret the East to the West.
Lu Xun	Best-known Chinese writer of the early 20th century, something of a Chinese Kipling in his capture of the spirit of the times in the demotic language of the new Republic.
Luan, Da Luan	Literally 'great chaos', much feared if as a result of a breakdown of civil society.
Mao Zedong	Chinese Communist leader and Chairman of the Chinese Communist Party of the People's Republic of China from 1949 to 1976.
Marco Polo	Italian adventurer who travelled from Venice to China (between 1271 and 1275) and was received by the court of Kublai Khan. His

	account of his travels awakened European interest in trade with the East.
Mianzi	Literally 'face', but used to mean the individual's sense of self-image and worth and the respect shown to others in word and deed.
Ming	Chinese dynasty from 1368 to 1644, overthrown by the Manchus (Qing Dynasty).
Nanyang	Literally 'South Ocean', but used to mean the whole South-East Asian area of Chinese migration.
Needham's Puzzle	Joseph Needham, author of *Science and Civilisation in China*, was confounded by China's failure to develop into a major power by the 19th century, given that it had the world's largest economy in the 18th century.
Opium War	War between Britain and China (1839–1842) following China's attempts to stop importation of opium from British India, which resulted in the ceding of Hongkong to Britain.
Paradigm	A communally accepted pattern or theory setting a worldview.
PLA	The People's Liberation Army.
Putonghua	The most common and widely spoken of Chinese dialects (mandarin is the old name).
Qian Long	Late 18th century Qing dynasty Emperor.
Qing	Expression of feeling through appropriate response.
Qing Dynasty	Chinese dynasty founded by the Manchus, lasting from 1644 to 1912, when it was overthrown by Dr Sun Yat Sen and his supporters to end imperial rule.
Qu Xiang He Fang?	Where is this all heading?
Real Options	Theory that argues for not missing an opportunity to create claims on future

	opportunities resulting from present transactions.
Relational	Descriptive of an obligation based on trust and mutual reciprocity (rather than legal enforcement).
Renqing	Human feeling and sense of personal obligation expressed as an appropriate response.
Resource base	Theory arguing that an organisation is composed of resources which are difficult to imitate yet provide an economic advantage over others.
Rudyard Kipling	The first British writer to be awarded the Nobel Prize for literature (1865–1936), who gave most expression to the spirit of British colonialism.
Sha qin	Literally 'kill or prey on relatives' first for money or favours.
SOE	State owned enterprise.
Sun Yat Sen, Dr	Chinese revolutionary leader who became the first President of the new Republic of China in 1912. Father of the modern Chinese state.
Sun Zu	Chinese general and military strategist (lived c. 4000 BC).
Tang Dynasty	The dynasty that ruled China from 618 to 907 AD, enlarging the country's territory and producing a golden age of painting, poetry and pottery.
Transaction Costs	Theory arguing that the least expensive controls over opportunism in economic exchange should be identified.
Wealth of Nations	Abbreviation of *Inquiry into the Nature and Causes of the Wealth of Nations* by Adam Smith (1723–1790), Scottish economist and philosopher.

Xinjiang	Westernmost province of China with a vociferous Muslim population.
Yi Ching	The Book of Changes, one of the five classical Confucian texts, which interprets the principles of *yin* and *yang*.
Yin and *Yang*	The active and passive principles and prime movers of the universe. *Yin* is the passive principle – female, sustaining, of the earth, dark and cold. *Yang* is the active principle – male, creative, of heaven, heat and light.
Zhi zu chang le	Simple contentment brings happiness.
Zhou Enlai	Chinese Communist Prime Minister from 1949 to 1976. His moderating influence with Mao Zedong brought the Cultural Revolution to an end and paved the way for *détente* with the United States.

References

General references

Adler, N. (1997) *International Dimensions of Organizational Behaviour*, 3rd edn. South Western College Publishing, Ohio.

Allen, F., Qian, J. and Qian, M. (2005) Law, finance and economic growth in China. *Journal of Financial Economics*, **77**, 57–116.

Allinson, R. E. (1991) *Understanding the Chinese Mind – the Philosophical Roots*. Oxford University Press, Oxford.

Backman, M. (1998) *Asia's Overseas Chinese Entrepreneurs and the Asian Financial Crisis*. 5. *Corporate Behaviour, 10–12*. BP 1998/03 – European Institute for Asian Studies.

Barney, J. B. (2001) *Gaining and Sustaining Competitive Advantage*, 2nd edn. Prentice Hall, New Jersey.

Bartholomew, S. and Adler, N. (1996) Building networks and crossing borders: the dynamics of knowledge generation in a transnational world. In: *Managing Across Cultures: Issues and Perspectives* (eds. P. Joynt and M. Warner), pp. 7–32. International Thomson Business Press, London.

Batonda, G. and Perry, C. (2003) Influence of culture on relationship development processes in overseas Chinese/Australian networks. *European Journal of Marketing*, **37**(11/12), 1548–74.

Berrell, M., Wrathall, J. and Wright, P. (2001) A model for Chinese management education: adapting the case study method to transfer management knowledge. *Cross Cultural Management*, **8**(1), 28–44.

Boisot, M. and Child, J. (1996) From fiefs to clans and network capitalism: explaining Chinese emerging economic order. *Administrative Science Quarterly*, **41**, 600–28.

Bruton, G. D., Ahlstrom, D. and Wan, J. C. C. (2003) Turnaround in East Asian firms: evidence from ethnic overseas Chinese communities. *Strategic Management Journal*, **24**, 519–40.

Casti, J. L. (2000) *Five More Golden Rules: Knots Codes, Chaos and other great theories of 20th Century Mathematics*. John Wiley, New York.

Chen, M. (1995) *Asian Management Systems: Chinese, Japanese and Korean Styles of Business*. International Thompson Business Press, London.

Chen, M. (2001) *Inside Chinese Business – a Guide for Managers Worldwide*. Harvard Business School Press, Boston.

Chen, P. (1991) Needham's Question and China's evolution – cases of non-equilibrium social transition. In: *Time, Rhythms and Chaos in the New Dialogue with Nature* (ed, G. P. Scott). University of Iowa Press.

Child, J. and Rodrigues, S. B. (2004) Repairing the breach of trust in corporate governance. *Corporate Governance: An International Review*, **12**(2), 143–53.

Chinese Culture Connection (1987) Chinese values and the search for culture-free dimensions of culture. *Journal of Cross-Cultural Psychology*, **18**, 143–64.

Chong, G. (2000) *Comparisons of Audit Framework in the People's Republic of China and the International Auditing Guidelines*. Paper delivered at the Chinese Economic Association Annual Conference, London.

Cook, P. (2004) *Leading Issues in Competition, Regulation and Development*. Edward Elgar, Cheltenham.

Cooke, F. L. (2005) *HRM, Work and Employment in China*. Routledge, Abingdon.

Conrad, J. (1972) *Nostromo*. Penguin, London.

Deal, T. E. and Kennedy, A. A. (1982) *Corporate Cultures: the Rites and Rituals of Corporate Life*. Penguin, London.

Denzin, N. K. and Lincoln, Y. S. (1998) *Strategies of Qualitative Inquiry*. Sage, California.

Deutsche Bank (2006) *Global Champions in Waiting: Perspectives on China's Overseas Direct Investment*. http://www.dbresearch.com/; accessed December 2007.)

Detert, J. R., Schroeder, R. G. and Mauriel, J. J. (2000) A framework for linking culture and improvement initiatives in organisations. *Academy of Management Review*, **25**(4), 850.

Dickie, M. and Lau, J. (2004) IBM brand loyalty holds key for Lenovo. *Financial Times*, 9 December, p. 26.

Drucker, P. (1969) *The Age of Discontinuity*. Harper & Row, New York.

Engardio, P. (1991) The Chinese dealmakers of Southeast Asia. *Business Week*, 11 November, pp. 60–2.

Evans, P. and Lorange, P. (1989) The two logics behind human resource management. In *International Firms: Change, Globalisation, Innovation* (eds. P. Evans, Y. Doz and A. Laurent), pp. 144–61. Macmillan Press, London.

Fan, K. (2003) Teaching Needham's Puzzle – fostering historical thinking. *Academic Exchange Quarterly*, Fall. City University of Hong Kong.

Financial Times (2004) Textiles revolution (editorial). 26 July, p. 1.

Financial Times (2005) China gold rush hides different strategies (leader). 22 August, p. 14.

Fishman, T. C. (2005) *China Inc: How the Rise of the Next Superpower Challenges America and the World*. Simon & Schuster, New York.

Floyd, D. (1999) Eastern and Western management practices: myth or reality? *Management Decision*, **37**(8), 628–32.

Fukuyama, F. (1995) *Trust – The Social Virtues and the Creation of Prosperity*. Hamish Hamilton, London.

Furnham, A. and Bochner, S. (1986) *Culture Shock: Psychological Reactions to Unfamiliar Environments*. Methuen, London.

Galbraith, J. K. (1993) *A Short History of Financial Euphoria*. Penguin, London.

Geertz, C. (1975) *The Interpretation of Cultures*. Hutchinson, London.

Gratton, L. (2000) *Living Strategy: Putting People At the Heart of Corporate Purpose*. Pearson Education, Edinburgh.

Guerrera, F. (2004) Stake in Asian jet fuel company sold 'to cover mounting derivative losses'. *Financial Times*, 3 December, p. 1.

Gummesson, E. (2006) Qualitative research in management: addressing complexity, context and persona. *Management Decision*, **44**(2), 167–79.

Haley, G. T. and Tan, C.-T. (1999) East vs West: strategic marketing management meets the Asian networks. *Journal of Business & Industrial Marketing*, **14**(2), 91–101.

Hall, E. T. and Hall, M. R. (1990) *Understanding Cultural Differences*. Intercultural Press, Yarmouth, Maine.

Harris, S. G. S. and Chapman, M. K. (2000) *Managers' Strategy Paradigms: Exploring the Influence of National Values*. Paper delivered at annual British Academy of Management Conference, London.

Harrison, E. F. and Pelletier, M. A. (2000) The Essence of Management Decision. *Management Decision*, **38**(7), 462–70.

Hitt, M. A., Franklin, V. and Zhu, H. (2006) Culture, institutions and international strategy. *Journal of International Management*, **12**(2), 222–34.

Hitt, M. A., Ireland, R. D. and Hoskisson, R. E. (2005) *Strategic Management*, 6th edn). Thomson SouthWestern, Ohio.

Hofstede, G. (1997) *Cultures and Organizations: Software of the Mind*, rev. edn). McGraw-Hill, New York.

Huang, G.-G. (1989) On the modernisation of Chinese family business. In: *Ancient Management Practices* (eds. Yi-wei Jiang and Jian-shu Min), pp. 121–34. Economic Management Press, Beijing.

IMF Staff (1998) The Asian crisis: causes and cures. *Finance and Development*, **35**(2).

Jaw, B., Ling, Y., Wang, C. Y. and Chang, W. (2007) The impact of culture on Chinese employees' work values. *Personnel Review*, **36**(1), 128–44.

Kuhn, T. S. (1962) *The Structure of Scientific Revolutions*. University of Chicago Press.

Kuhn, T. S. (1970) Reflections on my critics. In: *Criticism and the Growth of Knowledge* (eds. I. Lakatos and A. Musgrave), pp. 231–78. Cambridge University Press, Cambridge.

Lee, D.-J., Pae, J. H. and Wong, Y. H. (2001) A model of close business relationships in China (guanxi). *European Journal of Marketing*, **35**(1/2), 51–69.

Leiblein, M. J. (2003) The choice of organizational governance form and performance: predictions from transaction cost, resource-based, and real options theories. *Journal of Management*, **29**(6), 937–61.

Leung, T. K. P. and Wong, Y. H. (2001) The ethics and positioning of guanxi in China. *Marketing Intelligence and Planning*, **19**(1), 55–64.

Levitt, S. D. and Dubner, S. J. (2006) *Freakonomics: A Rogue Economist Explores the Hidden Side of Everything*. Penguin, London.

Lewis, R. D. (1992) *Finland: Cultural Lone Wolf – Consequences in International Business*. Richard Lewis Communications, Helsinki.

Lewis, R. D. (2005) *When Cultures Collide*. Nicholas Brearley, London.

Li, C. 2000. 'Credentialism' versus 'Entrepreneurism': interplay and tension between technocrats and entrepreneurs in the reform era. In *Chinese Business Networks. State, Economy and Culture* (ed. K. B. Chan), pp. 86–111. Prentice Hall, Singapore.

Li, J., Khatri, N. and Lam, K. (1999) Changing strategic postures of overseas Chinese firms in emerging Asian markets. *Management Decision*, **37**(5), 445–56.

Lin, X. and Germain, R. (2003) Organizational structure, context, customer orientation and performance: lessons from Chinese State-owned enterprises. *Strategic Management Journal*, **24**(11), 1131–51.

Lincoln, J. R., Olsen, J. and Haneda, M. (1978) Cultural effects on organizational structure: the case of Japanese firms in the United States. *American Sociological Review*, **43**, 829–47.

Liu, Y. (1994) The origin and early development of Chinese law: towards a comprehensive analysis of the period of creativity, with particular reference to penal law. *D.Phil Thesis*, University of Oxford.

Liu, J. and Hua, F. J. (2004) *Leadership Styles: the Chinese Perspective*. Paper delivered at Chinese Economic Association Annual Conference, London.

Liu, J. and Mackinnon, A. (2002) Comparative management practices and training: China and Europe. *Journal of Management Development*, **21**(2), 118–32.

Losee, J. (2001) *A Historical Introduction to the Philosophy of Science*, 4th edn. Oxford University Press, Oxford.

Luo, Y. (2003) Industrial dynamics and managerial networking in an emerging market: the case of China. *Strategic Management Journal*, **24**, 1315–27.

Luo, Y. (2006) Opportunism in inter-firm exchanges in emerging markets. *Management and Organization Review*, **2**(1), 121–47.

Luo, Y. (2007) Definition, principles and philosophy of guanxi. In *Guanxi and Business* (Asia-Pacific Business Series, Vol. 5). World Scientific, Singapore.

Luo, Y., Shenkar, O. and Nyaw, M.-K. (2002) Overcoming the liability of foreignness: offensive and defensive approaches. *Journal of International Management*, **8**(3), 311–31.

Mackinnon, A. (1998) The feast that will damage your wealth. *The Scotsman Business Daily*, 29 January, p. 29.

Mackinnon, A. (2004) *Chinese Management Strategy and Western Economic Theory: an Interpretation*. Presented at Chinese Economic Association Annual Conference, London.

Mackinnon, A. (2008) Chinese strategy – is it crossverging, converging or transverging to Western systems? *Management Decision*, **46**(2), 173–86.

Marx, E. (1999) *Breaking Through Culture Shock: What You Need to Succeed in International Business*. Nicholas Brearley, London.

McGregor, R. (2003) China's economic showcase is developing fast. *Financial Times*, 29 April, Yangtze Delta Supplement, p. I.

Mintzberg, H. (2000) Crosstalk: Strategy and Management. *European Management Journal*, **18**(4), 357–66.

Mintzberg, H., Ahlstrand, B. and Lampel, J. (1998) *Strategy Safari*. Prentice Hall Europe, Hemel Hempstead.

Morden, A. R. (1999) Models of national culture – a management review. *Cross Cultural Management*, **6**(1), 19–44.

Natale, S. M., Libertella, A. F. and Rothschild, B. M. (1995) Decision-making process: the key to quality decisions. *American Journal of Management Development*, **1**(4), 5–8.

Needham, J. (1954–1995) *Science and Civilisation in China*. Cambridge University Press, Cambridge.

Nelson, R. R. and Winter, S. G. (1982) *An Evolutionary Theory of Economic Change*. Harvard University Press, Cambridge, MA.

Nisbett, R., Peng, K., Choi, I. and Norenzayan, A. (2001) Culture and systems of thought: holistic versus analytic cognition. *Psychological Review*, **108**(2), 291–310.

Noorderhaven, N. G. (1996) Opportunism and trust in transaction cost economics. In *Transaction Cost Economics and Beyond* (ed. J. Groenewegen), pp. 105–28. Kluwer Academic, Dordrecht.

North, D. C. (1997) Transaction costs through time. In *Transaction Cost Economics: Recent Developments* (ed. C. Menard), pp. 149–60. Edward Elgar, Cheltenham.

O'Regan, N., Mackinnon, A. and Liu, J. (2006a) *Internationalizing Chinese Business*. Presented at the Academy of Management Annual Conference in Atlanta, Georgia.

O'Regan, N., Mackinnon, A. and Liu, J. (2006b) *Internationalizing Chinese Management*. Presented at the Strategic Management Society Annual Conference in Vienna, Austria.

Orwell, G. (1986) *Burmese Days*. Random House, New York.

Park, S. H. and Luo, Y. (2001) Guanxi and organisational dynamics: organisational networking in Chinese firms. *Strategic Management Journal*, **22**, 455–77.

Peng, M. W. (2002) Towards an institution-based view of business strategy. *Asia Pacific Journal of Management*, **19**(2/3), 251–68.

Pitelis, C. N. and Pseiridis, A. N. (1999) Transaction costs versus resource value? *Journal of Economic Studies*, **26**(3), 221–40.

Popper, K. R. (2001) *All Life is Problem Solving*. Routledge, London.

Ralston, D. A., Holt, D. H., Terpstra, R. H. and Yu, K.-C. (1997) The impact of national culture and economic ideology on managerial work values: a study of the United States, Russia, Japan, and China. *Journal of International Business Studies*, 1st quarter, 177–207.

Ramasamy, B., Goh, K. W. and Yeung, C. H. (2006) Is Guanxi (relationship) a bridge to knowledge transfer? *Journal of Business Research*, **59**(1), 130–9.

Redfern, K. (2002) *Industrialisation and the Evolution of Managerial Values Across Three Regions in the People's Republic of China*. Paper delivered at annual British Academy of Management Conference, London.

Rutgers, M. R. (1999) Be rational! But what does it mean? A history of the idea of rationality and its relation to management thought. *Journal of Management History*, **5**(1), 17–35.

Saunders, P. T. (1980) *An Introduction to Catastrophe Theory*. Cambridge University Press, Cambridge.

Schaubroeck, J., Lam, S. K. and Xie, J. L. (2000) Collective efficacy versus self-efficacy in coping responses to stressors and control: a cross – cultural study. *Journal of Applied Psychology*, **85**(4), 512–25.

Schein, E. H. (1985) *Organisational Culture and Leadership*. Jossey Bass, San Francisco.

Schlevogt, K.-A. (1999) Inside Chinese organisations – an empirical study of business practices in China. *PhD Thesis*, University of Oxford.

Schneider, S. C. and Barsoux, J.-L. (1997) *Managing Across Cultures*. Prentice Hall Europe, Hemel Hempstead.

Segalla, M., Fischer, L. and Sandner, K. (2000) Making cross-cultural research relevant to european corporate integration: old problem – new approach. *European Management Journal*, **18**(1), 38–51.

Simon, H. A. (1960) *The New Science of Management Decision*. Harper & Row, New York. (Cited in Harrison and Pelletier, 2000).

Simon, H. A. (1976) *Administrative Behaviour: A Study of Decision-making Processes in Administrative Organisation*, 3rd edn. Free Press, New York.

Simon, H. A. (1987) Satisficing. In: *The New Palgrave: A Dictionary of Economics* (eds. J. Eatwell, M. Millgate and P. Newman), **4**, pp. 243–5. Stockton Press, New York.

Spinney, L. (2004) Why we do what we do. *New Scientist*, **183**(2458), 32–5.

Spraakman, G. (1997) Transaction cost economics: a theory for internal audit? *Managerial Auditing Journal*, **12**(7), 323–30.

Stuttard, J. (2000) *The New Silk Road: Secrets of Business Success in China Today*. John Wiley & Sons, New York.

Sun, J. (2000) Organization development and change in Chinese state-owned enterprises: a human resource perspective. *Leadership and Organization Development Journal*, **21**(8).

Tang, J. and Ward, A. (2003) *The Changing Face of Chinese Management*. Routledge, London.

Townsend, R. (1971) *Up the Organization*. Hodder and Stoughton, London.

Treanor, J. (2005) RBS closer to China deal. *Guardian*, 28 July, p. 19.

Trompenaars, F. and Hampden-Turner, C. (1998) *Riding the Waves of Culture; Understanding Cultural Diversity in Business*, 2nd edn. Nicholas Brearley, London.

Vanhonacker, W.R. (2004) When good guanxi turns bad. *Harvard Business Review*, April. Product Number: F0404A.

Warner, M. (2002) The future of Chinese management. *Asia Pacific Business Review*, **9**(2), 205–23.

Warwick-Ching, L. (2005) RBS considers China purchase. *Financial Times*, 11 April, p. 24.

Wee, C. H. and Lan, L. L. (1998) *The 36 Strategies of the Chinese: Adapting Ancient Wisdom to the Business World*. Addison Wesley Longman, Singapore.

Whittington, R. (2001) *What is strategy – and does it matter?*, 2nd edn. Thompson Learning, London.

Williamson, O. E. (1996) *The Mechanisms of Governance*. Oxford University Press, Oxford.

Winder, R. (2004) *Bloody Foreigners*. Little, Brown, London.

Winter, S. G. (2000) The satisficing principle in capability learning. *Strategic Management Journal*, **21**, 981–96.

Wood, E., Whiteley, A. and Zhang, S. (2002) The cross model of *guanxi* usage in Chinese leadership. *Journal of Management Development*, **21**(4), 263–71.

Woolman, S. and Lake, J. (2001) *Contract*, 3rd edn. Green & Son, Edinburgh.

Zhu, C. J., Cooper, B., de Cieri, H. and Dowling, P. J. (2005) A problematic transition to a strategic role: human resource management in industrial enterprises in China. *International Journal of Human Resource Management*, **16**(4), 513–31.

Zhu, Y. and Warner, M. (2004) Changing patterns of human resource management in contemporary China: WTO accession and enterprise response. *Industrial Relations Journal*, **35**(4), 311–28.